PUBLISHED WITH SUPPORT FROM **THE GEORGE LUCAS EDUCATIONAL FOUNDATION**

POWERFUL LEARNING

WHAT WE KNOW ABOUT TEACHING FOR UNDERSTANDING

FOREWORD BY MILTON CHEN

LINDA DARLING-HAMMOND

BRIGID BARRON • P. DAVID PEARSON

ALAN H. SCHOENFELD • ELIZABETH K. STAGE

TIMOTHY D. ZIMMERMAN • GINA N. CERVETTI

JENNIFER L. TILSON

JOSSEY-BASS
A Wiley Imprint
www.josseybass.com

Published by Jossey-Bass
A Wiley Imprint
989 Market Street, San Francisco, CA 94103-1741 www.josseybass.com

Readers should be aware that Internet Web sites offered as citations and/or sources for further information may have changed or disappeared between the time this was written and when it is read.

Jossey-Bass books and products are available through most bookstores. To contact Jossey-Bass directly call our Customer Care Department within the U.S. at 800-956-7739, outside the U.S. at 317-572-3986, or fax 317-572-4002.

Jossey-Bass also publishes its books in a variety of electronic formats. Some content that appears in print may not be available in electronic books.

Credits appear on page 275

Library of Congress Cataloging-in-Publication Data

    Powerful learning : what we know about teaching for understanding / foreword by Milton Chen ; Linda Darling-Hammond . . . [et al.]. – 1st ed.
      p. cm.
    Includes bibliographical references and index.
    ISBN 978-0-470-27667-9 (alk. paper)
      1. Learning. 2. Effective teaching–United States. I. Darling-Hammond, Linda, 1951-
LB1060P6796 2008
371.102–dc22

                                                   2008009921

Printed in the United States of America
FIRST EDITION
PB Printing 10 9 8 7 6 5 4 3 2 1

CONTENTS

FOREWORD

Our Foundation began in 1991 with an ambitious mission: to demonstrate how innovative learning environments in classrooms, supported by powerful new technologies, could revolutionize learning. As an organization founded by George Lucas, we believed that the same benefits of technology that were transforming business, health care, entertainment, and manufacturing could be applied in education. Industrial assembly-line models based on the productivity of individual workers were giving way to more collaborative ways of organizing work in teams. Information was being shared more readily and rote tasks were being automated. And this was in the days before the Internet.

In two decades, the world has moved ahead dramatically, but our schools remain caught in a web of educational thinking and systems that originated a century ago—or, some would say, even earlier. The instructional model of the teacher and the textbook as the primary sources of knowledge, conveyed through lecturing, discussion, and reading, has proven astonishingly persistent. Even the traditional form of classroom seating, with students arrayed in rows—a configuration that prevents group work and conversation—is still common. In my boyhood classroom of the sixties, changing the classroom layout might have been impossible, because the chairs and desks were bolted to the floor. Today, with furniture that is movable, there's no excuse. It's clear we first need to unbolt our thinking.

Fortunately, this "dominant paradigm" is showing signs of wear. In our own work of finding and telling the stories of innovative learning in and out of schools, we see many more examples of individual teachers and principals, as well as some districts and even states, implementing new forms of project-based curricula and performance-based assessment. In these classrooms, students are organized in teams, where they must address such open-ended and complex questions as "What is the air and water quality in your community?" "How would you design a school of the future? or a hybrid car?" For these projects, students gather and sift information from many sources, analyze data, and produce products of their investigation for presentation to their peers, families, and communities, in person and on the Web.

These classrooms also benefit from new pipelines for teacher development, starting in schools of education, so that teachers can embrace their new role as learning coach and manager, rather than solely as direct instructor. As in the modern workplace, these classrooms function as a digital environment, where technology enables access to a much wider world of information and students are able to express their multiple intelligences and build on their strengths and interests as learners.

As a Foundation, we have understood the critical importance of developing a research basis for these innovations. We have spent more than a decade documenting examples of project-based learning and cooperative learning in classrooms, as well as in informal and after-school settings; and publishing documentary films, *Edutopia* magazine, and a multimedia Web site (www .edutopia.org). Yet, for these many individual examples to take root in more places, their effectiveness must be demonstrated in educational research. Importantly, policymakers investing funds in the curriculum, instruction, and assessment required to bring these innovations to scale have to base their policies on documented results. These beliefs led to our support for this volume.

With it, Linda Darling-Hammond and her colleagues at Stanford University; the University of California, Berkeley; and the Lawrence Hall of Science have taken an important step forward for the field. Their review of the literature on teaching practices such as project-based learning; cooperative learning; and specific instructional strategies in literacy, mathematics, and science summarizes what is known and what new research is needed. Their analyses take advantage of important new developments in cognitive research in the past decade, such as the landmark volume *How People Learn*, published by the National Academy of Sciences in 1999. Although they point to studies of the effectiveness of these strategies, they also temper the results with an important caveat: effectiveness relies heavily on the quality of the teachers implementing them.

I hope this book will lead to greater shared understanding of the research record on innovative classroom practices. At the same time, it should lead to efforts to invest in the new forms of research designs and measures needed to study these practices and their ways of organizing students and their learning. Perhaps ironically, the types of meaningful learning experiences described here return us to a much earlier time, when learning was more connected to daily life and where young people learned in the company of their elders as well as with each other.

On behalf of our Foundation, I express our appreciation to the authors for their contributions to this important book: Linda Darling-Hammond and Brigid Barron, at Stanford University; David Pearson, Alan Schoenfeld, Timothy Zimmerman, and Gina Cervetti, at the University of California, Berkeley; and Elizabeth Stage and Jennifer Tilson, at the Lawrence Hall of Science. They have brought their acknowledged wisdom as thoughtful and creative leaders in the field of education and educational research to this work. *Powerful Learning* should provoke new thinking about the kinds of "powerful research" needed to support creation of many more twenty-first-century schools and school systems.

Milton Chen
Executive Director
George Lucas Educational Foundation

The George Lucas Educational Foundation **(GLEF)** is a nonprofit foundation that gathers and disseminates the most innovative models of K–12 teaching and learning in the digital age. The foundation serves its mission through a variety of media—a magazine, videos, books, e-newsletters, DVDs, and a Web site: www.edutopia.org.

Online discussion questions for *Powerful Learning* are available at: www.josseybass.com/go/powerfullearning

ABOUT THE AUTHORS

Linda Darling-Hammond is Charles E. Ducommon Professor of Education at Stanford University, where she serves as co-director of the School Redesign Network and the Stanford Educational Leadership Institute. Her research, teaching, and policy work focus on teaching quality, school reform, and educational equity. She is co-founder of a charter high school in East Palo Alto that seeks to offer powerful teaching and learning opportunities to students who are historically under-served in American schools. Among her nearly 300 publications are the award-winning books *The Right to Learn, Teaching as the Learning Profession*, and *Preparing Teachers for a Changing World*.

Brigid Barron is an Associate Professor of Education at Stanford University. She studies collaborative learning in and out of school. Her work appears in books and journals including *Journal of Educational Psychology, Journal of Experimental Child Psychology, Human Development, Journal of the Learning Sciences,* and *Communications of the Association for Computing Machinery, International Journal of Technology and Design*. She has co-edited a book on the use of video as data in learning sciences research. She co-leads the LIFE center (Learning in Informal and Formal Environments), funded by the National Science Foundation in 2005. Barron is PI for a new grant funded by the MacArthur Foundation that will follow students longitudinally as they participate in programs designed to develop their technological fluency through activities such as game design, robotics, and digital movie making.

Gina N. Cervetti is a Literacy Curriculum and Research Specialist at the University of California, Berkeley's Lawrence Hall of Science. She is a literacy specialist, program director, and researcher for the NSF-funded Seeds of Science/Roots of Reading project. Her current research agenda concerns the role of text in learning science and the potential of science-literacy integration to support students' development of academic literacy.

P. David Pearson is Dean of the Graduate School of Education, and a professor in the area of Language and Literacy. He conducts research and teaches graduate courses in the area of reading processes, pedagogy, and assessment with the hope of creating greater access and opportunity for our nation's poorest children. Pearson has written and co-edited several books about research and practice, most notable being the *Handbook of Reading Research*, now in its third volume (with a fourth in development) and an edited volume on *Effective Schools and Accomplished Teachers*.

Alan H. Schoenfeld is the Elizabeth and Edward Conner Professor of Education at the University of California, Berkeley. A mathematician by training, he studies mathematical thinking, teaching, and learning. His major goal is to help create learning environments that open up the riches of mathematics for *all* students. Among the books he has written and edited are his classic volume *Mathematical Problem Solving*, The National Council of Teachers of Mathematics' *Principles and Standards for School Mathematics,* and *Assessing Mathematical Proficiency.*

Elizabeth K. Stage is the director of the Lawrence Hall of Science, the University of California, Berkeley's public science center. The Hall conducts research, develops curriculum materials, and works with teachers and other educators to accomplish its mission of inspiring and fostering the learning of science and mathematics for all, especially those with limited access. Her work in standards and assessment, professional development, and promoting quality science experiences in after-school settings reflect her focus on that mission.

Jennifer L. Tilson is a literacy curriculum developer and researcher for the NSF-funded Seeds of Science/Roots of Reading project at the University of California, Berkeley's Lawrence Hall of Science. Her work focuses on developing effective practices for embedding literacy instruction in the rich context of science, and on methods for teaching scientific language to increase access to academic discourse for all students.

Timothy D. Zimmerman is an academic researcher at the University of California, Berkeley's Lawrence Hall of Science. Trained as a marine biologist and learning sciences researcher, he studies ocean sciences teaching and learning in both formal (classrooms) and informal (aquariums, museums, field trips, etc.) contexts, often incorporating educational technology. His work advances the teaching of ocean sciences concepts, often omitted from K–12 curricula, and promotes a scientifically literate society capable of making environmentally-sound decisions.

INTRODUCTION

TEACHING AND LEARNING FOR UNDERSTANDING

Linda Darling-Hammond

Since *A Nation at Risk* (1983) was published a quarter century ago, mountains of reports have been written about the need for more powerful learning focused on the demands of life and work in the twenty-first century. Whereas 95 percent of jobs in 1900 were low-skilled and required just the ability to follow basic procedures designed by others, today such jobs make up only about 10 percent of the U.S. economy. Most of today's jobs require specialized knowledge and skills, including the capacity to design and manage one's own work; communicate effectively and collaborate with others; research ideas; collect, synthesize, and analyze information; develop new products; and apply many bodies of knowledge to novel problems that arise (Drucker, 1994).

Furthermore, the nature of work will continue to change, and ever more rapidly. Whereas during much of the twentieth century, most workers held two or three jobs during their lifetime, the U.S. Department of Labor (2006) estimates that today's average worker holds more than ten jobs before the age of forty. The top ten in-demand jobs projected for 2010 did not exist in 2004 (Gunderson, Jones, & Scanland, 2004). Thus we are currently preparing students for jobs that do not yet exist, to use technologies that have not yet been invented, and to solve problems that we don't even know are problems yet.

Meanwhile, knowledge is expanding at a breathtaking pace. It is estimated that five exabytes of new information (5,000,000,000,000,000,000 bytes, or 500,000 times the volume of the Library of Congress print collection) was generated in 2002, more than three times as much as in 1999. Indeed, in the four years from 1999 to 2002 the amount of new information produced approximately equaled the amount produced in the entire history of the world previously (Varian & Lyman, 2003). The amount of new technical information is doubling every two years, and it is predicted to double every seventy-two hours by 2010 (Jukes & McCain, 2002). As a consequence, effective education can no longer be focused on transmission of pieces of information that, once memorized, constitute a stable storehouse of knowledge. Education must help students learn how to learn in powerful ways, so that they can manage the demands of changing information, technologies, jobs, and social conditions.

These new demands cannot be met through passive, rote-oriented learning focused on basic skills and memorization of disconnected facts. Higher-order goals demand what some analysts have called "meaningful learning" (Good & Brophy, 1986)—that is, learning that enables critical thinking, flexible problem solving, and transfer of skills and use of knowledge in new situations. Nations around the world are reforming their school systems to meet these new demands, revising curriculum, instruction, and assessment to support the more complex knowledge and skills needed in the twenty-first century, skills needed for framing problems, seeking and organizing information and resources, and working strategically with others to manage and address dilemmas and create new products.

What do we know about the kind of teaching that produces more powerful learning? Based on research on learning and teaching conducted over the last fifty years, this book summarizes much of what is known about effective teaching and learning strategies in three major subject areas—reading and literacy, mathematics, and science—as well as selected strategies that are used across domains and in interdisciplinary contexts, including project-based learning, performance-based assessment, and cooperative learning. We also look at the factors and conditions that can influence the effectiveness of these strategies. Finally, we examine the quality of the research base in these areas, and we identify gaps that exist in our knowledge base and how future research might address them.

INTENDED AUDIENCE

This book is intended for the policymakers whose decisions shape our educational systems, and the teachers, administrators, and other educators who determine what happens in schools and classrooms. Researchers concerned with effective education will also find this book useful for their studies. It gives evidence about the outcomes of successful educational strategies, examples of what they look like in practice, and insights about how they can become the norm, rather than the exception, in our schools.

PRINCIPLES OF LEARNING FOR EFFECTIVE TEACHING

Any discussion of teaching needs to start with what we know about learning, especially the kind of intellectually ambitious learning demanded in today's knowledge-based society. As the National Academy of Sciences summary of how students learn (Donovan & Bransford, 2005) notes, there are at least three fundamental and well-established principles of learning that are particularly important for teaching:

> I. *Students come to the classroom with prior knowledge that must be addressed if teaching is to be effective.* If what they know and believe is not engaged, learners may fail to grasp the new concepts and information that are taught, or they may learn them for purposes of a test but not be able to apply them elsewhere, reverting to their preconceptions outside the classroom. This means that teachers must understand what students

are thinking and how to connect with their prior knowledge if they are to ensure real learning. When students from a variety of cultural contexts and language backgrounds come to school with their own experiences, they present distinct preconceptions and knowledge bases that teachers must learn about and take into account in designing instruction. Teachers who are successful with all learners must be able to address their many ways of learning, prior experiences and knowledge, and cultural and linguistic capital.

2. *Students need to organize and use knowledge conceptually if they are to apply it beyond the classroom.* To develop competence in an area of inquiry, students must not only acquire a deep foundation of factual knowledge but also understand facts and ideas in the context of a conceptual framework, and organize knowledge in ways that facilitate retrieval and application. This means teachers must be able to structure the material to be learned so as to help students fit it into a conceptual map and teach it in ways that allow application and transfer to new situations. The teaching strategies that allow students to do this integrate carefully designed direct instruction with hands-on inquiries that engage students actively in using the material, incorporate applications and problem solving of increasing complexity, and require ongoing assessment of students' understanding for the purpose of guiding instruction and student revisions of their work.

3. *Students learn more effectively if they understand how they learn and how to manage their own learning.* A "metacognitive" approach to instruction can help students learn to take control of their own learning by having a set of learning strategies, defining their own learning goals, and monitoring their progress in achieving them. Teachers need to know how to help students self-assess their understanding and how they best approach learning. Through modeling and coaching, teachers can teach students how to use a range of learning strategies, including the ability to predict

outcomes, create explanations in order to improve understanding, note confusion or failures to comprehend, activate background knowledge, plan ahead, and apportion time and memory. Successful teachers provide carefully designed "scaffolds" to help students take each step in the learning journey with appropriate assistance, steps that vary for different students depending on their learning needs, approaches, and prior knowledge.

These key principles of learning are evident in the research that has emerged on effective teaching. Looking across domains, studies consistently find that highly effective teachers support the process of meaningful learning by:

- Creating *ambitious and meaningful tasks* that reflect how knowledge is used in the field
- Engaging students in *active learning,* so that they apply and test what they know
- Drawing *connections to students' prior knowledge* and experiences
- Diagnosing student understanding in order to *scaffold the learning process* step by step
- *Assessing student learning continuously* and adapting teaching to student needs
- Providing clear *standards,* constant *feedback,* and opportunities for work
- Encouraging *strategic and metacognitive thinking,* so that students can learn to evaluate and guide their own learning

ADAPTING STRATEGIES TO KINDS OF LEARNING

Having identified some general principles about learning and teaching, it is important to acknowledge that effective teaching strategies differ with the kind of learning. As Bransford, Darling-Hammond, and LePage (2005) point out, the appropriateness of using particular types of teaching strategies depends on

(1) the nature of the materials to be learned; (2) the nature of the skills, knowledge, and experiences that learners bring to the situation; and (3) the goals of the learning situation and the assessments used to measure learning relative to these goals. These variables are represented in the model seen in Figure 1, developed by James Jenkins. One important point of the model is that a teaching strategy that works within one constellation of these variables may work very poorly if one or more factors are changed.

For our discussion, the kind of learning sought is especially critical to examine: Does it aim for rote understanding and recall, or does it aim for the kind of meaningful learning that would allow learners to use what they've

FIGURE 1
The Tetrahedral Model of Learning

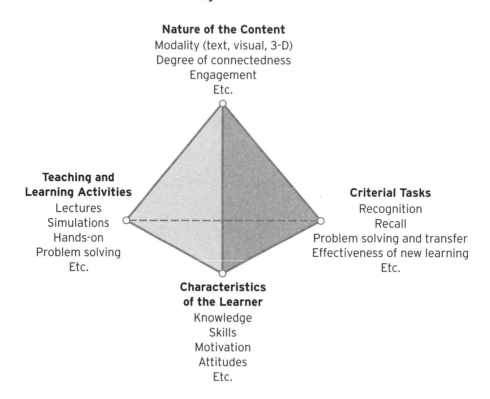

Nature of the Content
Modality (text, visual, 3-D)
Degree of connectedness
Engagement
Etc.

**Teaching and
Learning Activities**
Lectures
Simulations
Hands-on
Problem solving
Etc.

Criterial Tasks
Recognition
Recall
Problem solving and transfer
Effectiveness of new learning
Etc.

**Characteristics
of the Learner**
Knowledge
Skills
Motivation
Attitudes
Etc.

learned to solve problems? For example, what if we wanted to teach students about veins and arteries?[1] The text presents the facts that arteries are thicker than veins and more elastic, and they carry blood rich in oxygen from the heart. Veins are smaller, less elastic, and carry blood back to the heart. What's the best way to help students learn this information? The Jenkins model reminds us that the answer to this question depends on who the students are, what we mean by "learning" in this context, and how we measure the learning that occurs.

If we want to ensure only that students remember certain key facts about arteries—for example, that they are thicker than veins and more elastic— then one strategy would be to use a mnemonic technique such as teaching students to remember the sentence "Art(ery) was *thick* around the middle so he wore pants with an *elastic* waist band." If students understand the vocabulary being used, this technique would "work" for remembering these specific facts.

Suppose, however, that we want students not only to remember certain facts but to *understand* why they are important with respect to bodily functioning. This involves a change in learning goals and assessments, as well as teaching and learning strategies. To learn with understanding, students need to learn *why* veins and arteries have certain characteristics. For example, arteries carry blood from the heart, blood that is pumped in spurts. This helps explain why they would need to be elastic (to handle the spurts). In contrast, veins carry blood back to the heart and hence need less elasticity due to a lessening of the spurts.

Learning to understand relationships such as why arteries are elastic and arteries are less so should facilitate subsequent transfer. For example, imagine

---

[1] *This example is drawn from Bransford, Darling-Hammond, and LePage (2005), pp. 18–20, and was modified with help from John Bransford, for clearer explication of the biological principles involved.*

that students are asked to design an artificial artery or vein. Would it have to be elastic? Students who have only memorized information have no grounded way to approach this problem. Students who have learned with understanding know the functions of elasticity and hence are freer to consider possibilities such as relatively nonelastic materials that can still handle differences in pressure (adapted from Bransford & Stein, 1993).

This example illustrates how memorizing versus understanding represent distinctive kinds of learning, and how changes in these goals require different types of teaching strategies. To understand how arteries function, students would have to examine how they work *in the context* of the cardiovascular system and other bodily functions. They would need to *link* this knowledge to other knowledge they have acquired about physical properties of matter (aspects of force and gravity that are implicated in the need to pump fluid from the legs to the heart), and they would likely need opportunities to *construct or analyze* models of how this operates. The details of teaching strategies also vary with the knowledge, skills, attitudes, and other characteristics that students bring to the learning task. For example, younger students may not know enough about pumping, spurts, and elasticity to learn with understanding if they are simply told about the functions of arteries. They may need to see dynamic simulations that display these properties and consider examples that draw on aspects of the world that are already familiar (such as how elastic works in a rubber band). Seeing and experiencing things concretely is often an important prerequisite to learning to use information in more abstract or general ways.

Research examining whether "something works" should take into consideration each perspective of the Jenkins framework. In the box are a few critical questions to help position the teacher.

Seeing and experiencing things concretely is a prerequisite to learning to use information in more abstract ways.

TEACHING WITH LEARNING IN MIND

What kind of content is worth having students spend their time learning?

What are the goals for learning?

Are the assessments of learning consistent with the goals?

Who is being taught?

How might teaching techniques need to change for students with differing sets of prior skills and knowledge?

A sophisticated understanding of the content, the learner, and the goals of instruction is important for effective teaching. As we proceed, we highlight these concerns as we discuss general strategies for teaching and learning for understanding and describe how they play out in a number of subject matter domains.

HOW CAN WE TEACH FOR MEANINGFUL LEARNING?

Brigid Barron and Linda Darling-Hammond

THE NEED FOR INQUIRY-BASED LEARNING TO SUPPORT TWENTY-FIRST-CENTURY SKILLS

Enthusiasm for approaches to instruction that connect knowledge to the contexts in which it will be applied has been on the upswing since the 1980s. Recommendations from an array of organizations have emphasized the need to support twenty-first-century skills through learning that supports inquiry, application, production, and problem solving. More than a decade ago, the SCANS Report (Secretary's Commission on Achieving Necessary Skills, 1991) suggested that for today's students to be prepared for tomorrow's workplace they need learning environments that allow them to explore real-life situations and consequential problems. These arguments have been echoed in scholarly research (for example, Levy & Murnane, 2004), national commission reports (such as NCTM, 1989; MLSC et al., 1996), and policy proposals (see NCREL EnGauge, 2003; Partnership for 21st Century Skills, 2002), urging instructional reforms to help students gain vital media literacies, critical thinking skills, systems thinking, and interpersonal and self-directional skills that allow them to manage projects and competently find resources and use tools.

For these capacities to be nurtured, the reports argue, students must be given opportunities to develop them in the context of complex, meaningful projects that require sustained engagement, collaboration, research, management of resources, and development of an ambitious performance or product. The rationale for these recommendations has come in part from research demonstrating that students do not routinely develop the ability to analyze, think critically, write and speak effectively, or solve complex problems from working on constrained tasks that emphasize memorization and elicit responses that merely demonstrate recall or application of simple algorithms (Bransford, Brown, & Cocking, 1999; Bransford & Donovan, 2005). In addition, there is a growing body of research indicating that students learn more deeply and perform better on complex tasks if they have the opportunity to engage in more "authentic" learning.

A set of studies have found positive effects on student learning of instruction, curriculum, and assessment practices that require students to construct and organize knowledge, consider alternatives, apply disciplinary processes to content central to the discipline (such as use of scientific inquiry, historical research, literary analysis, or the writing process), and communicate effectively to audiences beyond the classroom and school (Newmann, 1996). For example, a study of more than twenty-one hundred students in twenty-three restructured schools found significantly higher achievement on intellectually challenging performance tasks for students who experienced this kind of "authentic pedagogy" (Newmann, Marks, & Gamoran, 1995). The use of these practices predicted

Students do not routinely develop the ability to analyze, think critically, write and speak effectively, or solve complex problems from working on constrained tasks that emphasize memorization and elicit responses that merely demonstrate recall or application of simple algorithms.

student performance more strongly than any other variable, including student background factors and prior achievement.

This is promising, but the checkered history of efforts to implement "learning by doing" makes clear the need for greater knowledge about how to successfully manage problem- and project-based approaches in the classroom (Barron et al., 1998). The kind of teaching suggested by these descriptions is not straightforward and requires knowledge of the characteristics of successful strategies and highly skilled teachers to implement them. In this chapter, we focus on the design and implementation of inquiry-based curriculum that engages children in extended constructive work, often in collaborative groups, and subsequently demands a good deal of self-regulated inquiry.

INQUIRY-BASED LEARNING

The family of approaches that can be described as *inquiry-based* includes project-based learning, design-based learning, and problem-based learning.

The research we review spans the K–12 years, college, and graduate education and can be found across core disciplines and in interdisciplinary programs of study[1]. Two major conclusions emerge:

> **Small group inquiry approaches can be extremely powerful for learning.** To be effective, they need to be guided by thoughtful curriculum with clearly defined learning goals, well-designed scaffolds, ongoing assessment, and rich informational resources. Opportunities for professional development that include a focus on assessing student work increase the likelihood that teachers will develop expertise in implementing these approaches.

---

[1] *The research literature on these approaches includes detailed cases studies, pre- and post-single sample designs, and experimental or quasi-experimental designs.*

Assessment design is critical. Designing good assessment is an important issue for *revealing* the benefits of inquiry approaches as well as for *promoting* the success of learning. Specifically, if one looks only at traditional learning outcomes, such as memorization of information or responses to multiple-choice questions, inquiry-based and traditional methods of instruction appear to yield similar results. Benefits for inquiry learning emerge when the assessments require application of knowledge and measure quality of reasoning. Consequently, we also take up a discussion of *performance assessment* and its role in both supporting and evaluating meaningful learning.

Our discussion within this chapter is organized into four sections.

First, we provide a historical perspective on inquiry-based learning in the context of the ongoing calls to develop inquiry and collaborative capacities in learners.

Next, we summarize research on collaborative small group learning. Our review focuses primarily on studies that offer data on the outcomes of cooperative or collaborative learning approaches. However, we also look at the kinds of interaction between children that lead to deeper learning and better group problem solving, and what we have learned about how teachers can support productive interactions.

In the third section, we summarize what we know about the forms of inquiry-based approaches (project, design, and problem-based) with respect to learning outcomes, supportive activity structures, and classroom norms.

Finally, we close with common design principles and recommendations about approaches to assessment.

AN HISTORICAL PERSPECTIVE ON INQUIRY-BASED LEARNING

Projects as a means for making schooling more useful and readily applied to the world first became popular in the early part of the twentieth century in the

United States. The term *project* represented a broad class of learning experiences. In early works one sees the label applied to activities as diverse as making a dress, watching a spider spin a web, and writing a letter. The key idea behind such projects was that learning was strengthened when "whole heartedness of purpose was present" (Kilpatrick, 1918).

Enthusiasm and belief in the efficacy of such approaches for school-aged children has waxed and waned, with project-based learning having been rejected as too unstructured during several eras of "back to the basics" backlash, or policymakers having argued that applied projects are only needed for vocational training. Critics of the progressive movement held that discovery learning approaches led to "doing for the sake of doing" rather than doing for the sake of learning. There is a growing consensus that authentic problems and projects afford unique opportunities for learning, but that authenticity in and of itself does not guarantee learning (Barron et al., 1998; Thomas, 2000).

The key is how these complex approaches are implemented. For example, in the curricular reforms of the post-Sputnik years, initiatives using inquiry-based approaches (typically called "discovery learning" or project learning) were found to produce comparable achievement on basic skills tests while contributing more to students' problem-solving abilities, curiosity, creativity, independence, and positive feelings about school (Dunkin & Biddle, 1974; Glass et al., 1977; Good & Brophy, 1986; Horwitz, 1979; McKeachie & Kulik, 1975; Peterson, 1979; Resnick, 1987; Soar, 1977). This kind of meaning-oriented teaching, once thought to be appropriate only for selected high-achieving students, proved to be more effective than rote teaching for students across a spectrum of initial achievement levels, family income, and cultural and linguistic backgrounds (Braddock & McPartland, 1993; Garcia, 1993; Knapp et al., 1995).

However, new curriculum initiatives focused on inquiry using complex instructional strategies were found more often to promote a significant increase in learning gains among students taught by the early adopters—teachers who were extensively involved in designing and piloting the curriculum and who were given strong professional development. These effects were not always sustained as curriculum reforms were "scaled up" and used by teachers who did not have the same degree of understanding or skill in implementation.

At the present time, there is still controversy over whether inquiry-oriented approaches are effective and efficient for developing the student's basic knowledge of a domain. Implementation issues continue to be a concern for both practitioners and researchers and complicate research. Examples include studies that have suggested that "direct instruction"—usually understood as traditional lecture-based approaches—is preferable to "discovery learning." The sources of confusion are shown in a study by Klahr and Nigam (2004), which taught middle school students to set up controlled experiments and then measured the students' knowledge of experimental design and their ability to set up experiments that could appropriately control for potentially confounding variables. They labeled their conditions "direct instruction" and "discovery learning." However, both conditions included features of discovery learning, including the chance for students to explore the materials and try together to set up experiments. In their discovery learning condition, the researchers simply instructed the participating sixth graders to design experiments to evaluate variables related to the speed of a ball traveling down a ramp. In the direct instruction approach, the children were taught about the importance of not confounding variables in the context of demonstration experiments. This lesson was given after they had tried to set up experiments on their own.

Although the researchers' conclusions suggested that the direct-instruction approach yielded better learning, they failed to acknowledge that this approach included both a great deal of experimentation and some direct instruction. In addition, critics of the study's conclusion point out that in a real classroom situation children would be given much more guidance and scaffolding than took place in their discovery-learning condition. Thus the study does not prove that classroom-based inquiry approaches are do not work but only that they are more successful when combined with necessary instruction. This combination of appropriately timed direct instruction with the results of inquiry has also been found in other studies to be superior to either approach alone (see, for example, Bransford, Brown, & Cocking, 1999, box on p. 46). We return to this important principle later in the chapter.

Classroom research does indicate that well-designed, carefully thought-out materials and connected classroom practices are needed to capitalize on inquiry-based approaches. Without careful planning, students may miss opportunities to connect their project work with key concepts underlying a discipline. For example, Roth (2006) found that in an engineering-based curriculum for elementary school students engineering principles were unlikely to be discovered simply by successfully engineering solutions to problems such as building bridges or towers. Similarly, Petrosino (1998) described his observation of students building rockets in a science curriculum highlighting interesting products and a high level of engagement but no growth in learning the principles of flight. However, a slight variation in the task that required students to determine the variables related to how far a rocket will travel led to a dramatic increase in students' conceptual knowledge relative to the original project.

In recent years, the research base on inquiry approaches has grown to include both comparative studies and more descriptive classroom investigations of teaching and learning processes. There is a growing consensus on the importance of a number of design principles that characterize successful inquiry-based learning environments and that can be used by teachers as they embark on developing or enacting new curriculum. We summarize the relevant research base beginning with collaborative approaches to learning and then moving to three specific approaches to designing inquiry experiences: project-based learning, design-based learning, and problem-based learning. (See Table 1 of the Appendix for a summary of design principles that have emerged from classroom research.)

COLLABORATIVE SMALL GROUP LEARNING: EVIDENCE AND BEST PRACTICES

The technique of having small groups of students work together on learning activities has its roots in part in an experiment that was aimed at supporting friendships across ethnic groups following desegregation (Aronson & Bridgeman, 1979). This effort was based on theories of interpersonal relationship formation developed in the field of social psychology (Deutsch, 1949), and it proved successful not only at developing relationships but also at improving achievement.

Cooperative small group learning is one of the most studied pedagogical interventions in the history of educational research. E. G. Cohen (1994b) defines cooperative learning as "students working together in a group small enough that everyone can participate on a collective task that has been clearly assigned" (p. 3). This definition includes what has been called cooperative learning, collaborative learning, and other forms of small group work. This context for learning has been the subject of hundreds of studies and several meta-analyses (P. A. Cohen, Kulik, & Kulik, 1982; Cook, Scruggs, Mastropieri, & Castro, 1985; Hartley, 1977; Johnson, Maruyama, Johnson, Nelson, & Skon, 1981; Rohrbeck, Ginsburg-Block, Fantuzzo, & Miller, 2003). Overall these analyses come to the same conclusion: there are significant learning benefits for students when they are asked to work together on learning activities as compared to approaches where students work on their own (Johnson & Johnson, 1981, 1989).

For example, in a comparison of four types of problems presented to individuals or cooperative teams, researchers found that teams outperformed individuals on all types and across all ages (Quin, Johnson, & Johnson, 1995). Problems varied in terms of how well defined they were (a single right answer versus open-ended projects such as writing a story) and whether they were more or less reliant on language. Individual experimental studies have shown that groups outperform individuals on learning tasks, and further that individuals who work in groups do better on later individual assessments as well (Barron, 2000b, 2003; O'Donnell & Dansereau, 1992).

There are desirable outcomes for students in other areas of their lives as well, including improvement in student self-concept, social interaction, time on task, and positive feelings toward peers (P. A. Cohen et al., 1982; Cook et al., 1985; Ginsburg-Block, Rohrbeck, & Fantuzzo, 2006; Hartley, 1977; Johnson & Johnson, 1989). Ginsburg-Block and colleagues (2006) focused on the relationship between academic and nonacademic measures. They found that both social and self-concept measures were related to academic outcomes. Larger effects were found for interventions that used same-gender grouping, interdependent group rewards, structured student roles, and individualized evaluation procedures. They also found that low-income students benefited more than high-income students, and urban students benefited more than suburban. Racial and ethnic minority students benefited even more from cooperative group work than nonminority students, a finding that has been repeated over several decades (see Slavin & Oickle, 1981). Ginsburg-Block and colleagues (2006) conclude that those dimensions of group work that support academic outcomes also yield social and self-concept benefits.

Most recently, the focus has gone beyond the practical benefits of collaboration for individual learning to recognize the importance of helping children develop the capacity to collaborate as necessary preparation for all kinds of work. For example, the Science for All Americans, Project 2061 (American Association for the Advancement of Science, 1989) suggests that a core practice of scientific inquiry is collaborative work; schools should be preparing students for this kind of work through classroom activities that require joint efforts.

The collaborative nature of scientific and technological work should be strongly reinforced by frequent group activity in the classroom.

Scientists and engineers work mostly in groups and less often as isolated investigators. Similarly, students should gain experiences sharing responsibility for learning with each other. In the process of coming to understandings, students in a group must frequently inform each other about procedures and meanings, argue over findings, and assess how the task is progressing. In the context of team responsibility, feedback and communication become more realistic and of a character very different from the usual individualistic textbook-homework-recitation approach [AAAS, 1989, p. 202].

Challenges of Small Group Work in Classrooms

Although there is much consensus about the desirability of developing collaboration skills, and research is clear about the general benefits of small group interaction for learning, this does not mean that helping small groups engage in high-quality discussion and sharing is easy. Research has identified at least three major challenges for cooperative learning in classrooms: (1) developing norms and structures within groups that allow individuals to work together; (2) developing tasks that support useful cooperative work; and (3) developing discipline-appropriate strategies for discussion that support rich learning of content.

A number of studies have pointed out the importance of structure for positive group outcomes. Yager, Johnson, and Johnson (1985) examined the effect of structured and unstructured oral discussions with mixed-ability second-grade cooperative learning groups. Groups were randomly assigned and stratified on the basis of sex and ability level. Each class consisted of three twelve-minute sections: teacher instruction, oral discussion, and class discussion. During the oral discussion, the unstructured group was told to work together on the material introduced by the teacher; the structured group received roles of learning leader and learning listener. The role of the leader was to give a synopsis of the day's lesson, and the listeners were to ask questions to push the leader to give a full explanation. The structured group achieved higher scores on unit tests given at day nine and day eighteen, and on the retention test given eighteen days after the end of the unit. Given that the assessments were taken individually, the researchers concluded there is group-to-individual transfer of knowledge.

Gillies (2004) also studied structured and unstructured groups in ninth-grade math classes in Australia. The students in the structured groups were trained in cooperative social skills before working in groups on the mathematics unit. The unstructured groups were told to work together but not given any further direction. All students received a teacher-created math assessment at the end of the unit and a questionnaire recording their perceptions of the group process. The students in the structured group performed better on the math assessment and exhibited more cooperative and on-task behavior than did the unstructured groups.

Calling students' attention to how their group is functioning appears to facilitate better group outcomes. In a study of group processing, Yager, Johnson, Johnson, and Snider (1995) observed positive gains in achievement for low-, middle-, and high-ability third graders who were given processing time to discuss how their group was working and what could be done to improve their efficacy. The control group also engaged in cooperative group work without the opportunity for group processing, thus illuminating how specific cooperative learning interactions produce more positive outcomes.

The nature of the task also appears to matter. For example, Nystrand, Gamoran, and Heck (1993) did a study across nine schools and fifty-four ninth-grade English classes of the effects of small groups on achievement. They noticed that, in this sample, those who stayed in small groups longer had lower achievement. It turned out that these students were in groups assigned to tasks that amounted to "collaborative seatwork," not permitting student autonomy and student production of knowledge. The lowest-rated groups on these dimensions were those assigned grammar work rather than analysis of

Teachers must maximize opportunities to concretely connect the work to key concepts

literature. These groups scored lower on the final assessment than those who were in groups that allowed them "to interact over the substance of their problem, defining tasks as well as solutions, and constructing interpretations" (p. 20). The researchers argued that adolescents need tasks allowing them to "compare ideas, develop a train of thought, air differences, or arrive at a consensus on some controversial issue" for them to deepen their knowledge and understanding (p. 22).

Once groups know how to work together, and they have a task worth working on, they still need to learn how to have content-rich discussions that are productive of serious learning. A review of nineteen studies that focused on the nature of small group discussions in science (Bennett, Lubben, Hogarth, Campbell, & Robinson, 2005) concluded that the studies consistently show that "students often struggle to formulate and express coherent arguments during small group discussions, and demonstrate a relatively low level of engagement with tasks." The authors note that five of the seven most highly rated studies make the recommendation that teachers and students need to have explicit opportunities to learn the skills associated with developing arguments and with effective small group discussion.

In a separate review of ninety-four studies, which focused on better understanding the conditions for high-quality discussion,[2] the same group of

---

[2] With respect to methods, of the ninety-four studies twenty-eight were experimental designs, and twelve of those were randomized clinical trials. The remainder were case studies that used a variety of approaches to collect data: video, audio, interviews, observations, questionnaires, or tests.

authors (Hogarth, Bennett, Campbell, Lubben, & Robinson, 2005) concluded: "A successful stimulus for students working in small groups to enhance their understanding of evidence has two elements. One requires students to generate their individual prediction, model or hypothesis which they then debate in their small group (internally driven conflict or debate). The second element requires them to test, compare, revise or develop that jointly with further data provided (externally driven conflict or debate)."

Findings of this kind suggest that teachers should play an active role in helping groups learn to coordinate their work on productive tasks and learn how to talk about what they are perceiving in terms that reflect the modes of inquiry in the discipline.

Designing Activities for Productive Collaboration

A great deal of work has been done to specify the kinds of tasks, accountability structures, and roles that help students collaborate well. It is generally agreed that tasks requiring interdependence of team members, accountability structures at the group and individual level, and opportunities to reflect on group progress and interaction are key elements. In Johnson and Johnson's summary (1999b) of forty years of research on cooperative learning, they identify five "basic elements" of cooperation that have emerged as important across multiple models: positive interdependence, individual accountability, face-to-face promotive interaction, social skills, and group processing (pp. 70–71).

A number of activity structures have been developed to support group work. Table 3 in the Appendix of this book summarizes well-known techniques for arranging group work. They range from cooperative learning approaches where students are simply asked to help each other complete individually assigned traditional problem sets to approaches where students are expected to collectively define projects and generate a single product that reflects the continued work of the entire group. Many approaches fall in between these two extremes. Some of these approaches assign children to management (e.g., E. G. Cohen, 1994a, 1994b), conversational (King, 1990; O'Donnell, 2006), or intellectual roles in the group (Cornelius & Herrenkohl, 2004; Palincsar & Herrenkohl, 1999, 2002; White & Frederiksen, 2005).

As the table suggests, different lines of work emphasize one or another dimension of the group work process. For example, Slavin (1991) argues that "it is not enough to simply tell students to work together. They must have a reason to take one another's achievement seriously" (p. 73). He developed a model focusing on external motivators that reside outside the group, such as rewards and individual accountability established by the teacher. His meta-analysis found that group tasks with structures promoting individual account-ability produce stronger learning outcomes (Slavin, 1996).

E. G. Cohen's review of research (1994b) on productive small groups focuses more on internal group interaction around the task, arguing that the means for accomplishing what rewards and accountability offer the group process may vary with the type of task and interaction. Cohen and her col-leagues developed Complex Instruction, one of the best-known and well-researched approaches. Complex Instruction uses carefully designed activities that require diverse talents and interdependence among group members. Teachers are helped to pay attention to unequal participation that often results from status differences among peers and are given strategies that allow them to bolster the status of infrequent contributors (E. G. Cohen & Lotan, 1997). In addition, roles are assigned that support equal participation: recorder, reporter, materials manager, resource manager, communication facilitator, and harmonizer. A major aspect of the approach is development of "group-worthy tasks" that are both sufficiently open-ended and multifaceted in their cognitive demands that they require and benefit from the participation of every member of the group. Tasks that require a variety of skills such as research, analysis, visual representation, and writing are well suited for this approach.

There is strong evidence about the success of Complex Instruction strategies in promoting student academic achievement (Abram et al., 2001;

E. G. Cohen, 1993, 1994a, 1994b; Cohen & Lotan, 1995; Cohen et al., 1999, 2002). In recent studies, evidence of this success has been extended to the learning gains of new English language learners (Lotan & Valdes, 2006).

In other approaches, roles are linked to specific kinds of cognitive engagement. For example, Cornelius and Herrenkohl (2004) described a classroom unit on sinking and floating that engaged children in experimentation. Students presented their theories, methods, and findings to the whole class. The audience members (their peers) were given roles to ask questions about the presenter's theories and predictions, the results, or the relationships between theories and results. Roles of this sort reveal to students what elements of the scientific process—theorizing, prediction, their relationship to data collection and findings—are important to attend to and how they should be considered. Thus the structure and modes of inquiry of the discipline (Schwab, 1978; Shulman, 1987) are made visible, and the means for evaluating scientific rigor are introduced to students.

White and Frederiksen (2005) have developed both cognitive and social roles. Students take turns being in charge of managing cognitive aspects of group work such as theory, evidence, synthesis, and application. Other students manage social processes such as collaboration, equity, communication, mediation, and reflection. Roles are taught explicitly and written guides developed to help students understand them. This makes visible and learnable those processes of thinking and behavior that would often be invisible. The notion of making thinking visible through collaborative interactions between students and teachers has also been described as "cognitive apprenticeship" (Collins, Brown, & Newman, 1989). A key aspect of an apprenticeship approach is giving students opportunities to engage in parts of a task while also giving them a view of the whole task or problem.

Another example of a successful approach to role-based collaboration comes from the domain of computer science. A collaborative approach to learning to program, called PAIR programming, has been studied using a quasi-experimental approach at the undergraduate level (McDowell, Werner, Bullock, & Fernald, 2006). In this case, the practice of working in pairs actually came about from the workplace, where a collaborative approach called Extreme Programming has been developed. In Extreme Programming, partners create code together, sitting shoulder to shoulder. One partner is designated as "the driver" and creates the code and is in control of the keyboard. The other partner is looking over her shoulder, reviewing the code to identify errors in syntax and logic or design mismatches. This approach is now being tried out in middle schools (Werner, Campe, & Denner, 2005).

Not only do students who learn in pairs generate higher-quality programs but they learn as much as students who do all their work alone, are more likely to take another class in the discipline, and are more likely to pass it (McDowell et al., 2006). Students who learned in pairs enjoyed the work more and were more confident. Perhaps most important, those students who worked in pairs during the introductory course were more likely one year later to have declared a major related to computer science than students who were taught in the traditional way, working alone. The effect was particularly strong for women, who are underrepresented in the field of computer science. Although it is assumed that collaborative work enhances motivation or confidence, few studies have looked at these outcomes explicitly. This work makes an important contribution to our understanding of the affective outcomes of collaborative learning.

What Does Productive Collaboration Look Like?

Recent research has gone beyond summative assessments of the benefits of group work to try to understand why collaboration benefits learning and what differentiates more and less successful approaches to collaboration. A number of social processes have been identified that help to explain why group work supports individual learning. They include opportunities to share original insights (Bos, 1937), resolve differing perspectives through argument (Amigues, 1988; Phelps & Damon, 1989), explain one's thinking about a phenomenon (King, 1990; Webb, Troper, & Fall, 1995), provide critique (Bos, 1937), observe the strategies of others (Azmitia, 1988), and listen to explanations (Coleman, 1998; Hatano & Iganaki, 1991; Schwartz, 1995; Shirouzu, Miyake, & Masukawa, 2002; Webb, 1985).

Research on the interactions that can occur within collaborative learning situations makes the important point that it is not simply the act of asking children to work in groups that is essential but rather the *possibility* that certain kinds of learning processes can be activated (E. G. Cohen, 1994b). Research that attends explicitly to variability in group interaction has yielded information about what productive collaboration looks like, and conversely what less-than-ideal collaboration looks like. In an experimental study comparing the problem solving of groups and individuals at the sixth-grade level, Barron (2000b) found that groups outperformed individuals, and that when students were given a new analogous problem to solve, those who had first solved the problems in groups performed at a significantly higher level.

However, more detailed analyses revealed that among the sixteen trios of students there was a great deal of variability in how well the students collaborated, and the quality of collaboration—how they talked and interacted with one another—was related to their group score and later individual scores (see the box "More and Less Successful Groups"). If a collaboration is going well, (1) many students will be involved in the discussion as contributors and responders; (2) the contributions are coordinated rather than consisting of many independent unrelated conversational turns; (3) there are few instances of off-task behavior; and (4) students attend to each other and to their work in common, as indicated by eye gaze and body position. These are good markers of *mutual engagement*, an important element of collaborative work. As discussed in the next section, it is also possible to look at the quality of the content of the discussion, for example, what Engle and Conant (2002) call disciplinary engagement—that is, the extent to which the students' conversation reflects the issues and practices of a discipline's discourse.

MORE AND LESS SUCCESSFUL GROUPS

Barron (2003) analyzed group interaction through videotapes of sixth-graders working in triads to solve a complex math problem. She contrasted teams who were more and less successful in solving the problem. Children were asked to solve the problem posed to the main character in a staged, fifteen-minute video adventure called "Journey to Cedar Creek," the first episode in the series *The Adventures of Jasper* (CTGV, 1997). The problem posed to the students was to make a decision about whether Jasper had enough time to make it home in his new boat before sunset; the boat had no running lights. To make this decision, students needed to determine (1) the number of miles to be traveled on the return trip, (2) the length of time the return trip would take, and (3) the time he would arrive back to his home dock, or the number of hours available for travel before the sunset. Students were given a storyboard with eighteen stills from the movie that helped them remember relevant scenes and quantitative information.

Part of the analysis involved coding children's conversation. The quantitative analyses established that groups who differed in their level of joint success did not differ on a number of variables that might plausibly account for the observed difference. These variables included prior achievement, the number of turns, and the number of times correct proposals were brought into the group. What differed between more and less successful groups was how peers responded to ideas. More successful groups responded to correct proposals by engaging them in further discussion or accepting and documenting them. In contrast, less successful groups had a high probability of responding to ideas with silence or rejecting them without rationale. Further analyses suggested that the conversations in less successful groups were not as aligned topically as those in more successful groups. Frequently, when a peer generated a correct proposal the conversation that was occurring just previously was not closely related to the proposal. A reasonable hypothesis is that this would make it harder for peers to recognize the significance of the proposal. However, almost half the correct proposals were directly related, and most were still not accepted or taken up in the conversation.

A second part of the analysis involved describing what was happening between children as proposals were made for solving the problem. Qualitative analyses of the conversation of four triads illustrated the broader interactional contexts in which proposals were made and responded to. These portraits depicted the challenges that arose for some triads as participants attempted (or did not) to coordinate individual perspectives into a joint problem-solving space.

In the less successful cases, relational issues arose that prevented the group from capitalizing on the insights fellow members had generated: competitive interactions, differential efforts to collaborate, and self-focused problem-solving trajectories. Behaviorally these issues manifest in violation of turn-taking norms, difficulties in gaining the floor, domination of the workbook, and competing claims of competence ("I know what I'm doing!" "No, I do!"). Although constructs such as status (E. G. Cohen & Lotan, 1995) may be called on to explain these patterns, it is informative to attend to the dynamic shifts observed. It was apparent that both speakers and listeners played consequential and interdependent roles in uptake and documentation of ideas. For example, indirect or mitigated (Linde, 1988) contributions were especially problematic in the context of self-focused peers, as when a soft-spoken suggestion was made when a partner was thinking aloud to himself. On the other hand, persistence and resistance to dominating efforts were effective strategies to combat a self-focused partner, although they may have come at some cost to continued engagement or even a future desire to work together.

Groups that did well engaged the ideas of participants, had a low rate of ignoring or rejecting ideas, paid attention to attention, and echoed the ideas of one another.

(continued)

Their successful achievement of a joint problem-solving space was especially reflected in much "huddling" around the workbooks and mutual gazing.

These nonverbal synchronies suggest an intense level of joint ownership over the production and representation of the work. It was not that more successful groups were immune to problems of coordination but rather that members used strategies that resulted in a joint focus of their attention. For example, when documenting solutions, the writer might "broadcast" his or her writing orally and thus make it available for monitoring by other students in the group. In addition, some groups explicitly monitored the group's joint attention and addressed possible disruptions to it. Thus, successful coordination was accomplished through a variety of strategies that included use of external representations (sharing pictures, writing, models), conversational devices (reading aloud, discussing, questioning, or calling for attention to an idea), and physical moves (huddling, sharing materials, maintaining eye contact).

How Can Teachers Support Productive Collaboration?

The classroom teacher plays a critical role in establishing and modeling practices of productive learning conversations. Aspects of the larger classroom learning environment shape small group interactions. Observing a group's interactions can yield a substantial amount of information about the degree to which the work is productive, as well as an opportunity for formative feedback and support for aligning understandings and goals among group members. Computer-based tools can also be useful in establishing ways of working and supporting productive collaborative exchanges. One of the best and most documented examples is the Computer-Supported Intentional Learning (CSILE) project (Scardamalia, Bereiter, & Lamon, 1994), which includes a knowledge gathering and improvement tool to support inquiry and norms for knowledge building discourse. Beyond any specific tool or technique, a particularly important role for the teacher is to establish, model, and encourage norms of interaction that reflect good inquiry practices.

A paper by Engle and Conant (2002) documents how this can be done by analyzing the productive disciplinary engagement of a group of elementary school students. This group work took place in a research-based experimental classroom designed as part of A. L. Brown and Campione's Community of Learners project (1996). They studied students' collaborative work in the context of a jigsaw approach to developing knowledge about animal species and their mechanisms of reproduction and defense. The jigsaw method divides topics among students so that each class member becomes an expert in a subtopic. Experts then teach their group members what they know so that the group benefits from the distributed work. In this case, groups of four or five students wrote proposals to study a specific animal species. The groups were then assigned an animal on the basis of the quality of their group proposal. The final product of the group was a written report, done by all members of the group. Individual students became expert on a specific subtopic such as reproduction strategies or defense mechanisms and contributed chapters that focused on these subtopics. After they shared this knowledge with their group, the entire group wrote the introduction and conclusion. Engle and Conant's analysis (2002) focuses on a single group who became highly and persistently engaged in an unplanned controversy over classifying killer whales as belonging to the species of dolphin or whale (they were assigned to research the whale). The controversy resurfaced a total of eight times across the eight-week project. They sought to understand what supported the students' persistence and their disciplinary engagement.

The controversy was sparked by contradictory claims offered by various experts (in books and among the trainers they met during a field trip to Marine World) and was sustained because different claims were adopted by opposing group members. Students' passionate engagement was reflected in intensive emotional displays, persistence in having their ideas heard, additional research, and continued attention over weeks. A key aspect of their discourse that afforded productive learning conversation rather than devolving into an argumentative shouting match was the appropriation of scholarly moves such as use of various kinds of evidence to justify their claims. In addition, analysis of talk made it clear that although at times students spoke over one another and competed for floor time, they held themselves accountable to the contributions others made. This was indicated by the proportion of turns in which students associated particular group members with controversy-relevant claims, or evidence. The authors call this process "positioning."

Their analyses stress the importance of understanding the classroom environment, the curriculum, and the guidance of the teacher as a system; they highlighted four principles, described here with examples of how the teacher, Ms. Wingate, communicated them to students and realized them through activities and resources:

Problematize subject matter by encouraging students to define problems and treat claims and explanatory accounts, even those offered by "experts," as needing evidence. Ms. Wingate encouraged students to question all sources. Rather than ignoring differences across sources, Ms. Wingate drew attention to them: "One book says one thing, and other books say another thing . . . you need to figure out which one is right" (Engle & Conant, p. 431). She helped them see the importance of looking for converging sources: "Compare sources, and see if they are the same" (p. 431). She also reminded students that they had used this same strategy in a recent history unit.

Give students authority to address such problems by identifying them with claims, explanations, or designs in ways that encourage them to be authors and producers of knowledge. Ms. Wingate explicitly communicated her enthusiasm for debate and productive conflict. For example, when a student communicated to her that a research group was having a big fight about research, she said "I love that!" (p. 431). She also marked the expectation that each student would become an expert in a subtopic, which she defined as "the person who knows everything about that" (p. 432). She also emphasized that the students would become more knowledgeable than she: "And you guys are researching a lot of things that I don't know things about. And so when you find information, I'm going to ask you questions about it, just like anyone in the classroom is, who doesn't know things about it" (p. 432).

Hold students accountable to others—such that they are responsible for addressing others' viewpoints even if they disagree—and to shared disciplinary norms, such that they pay attention to evidence, using practices of the discipline. Ms. Wingate encouraged the students to incorporate a range of sources into their research. She suggested they use "as many books as you can, and experts, and the computer, and write to the science desk, and do as many things as you can" to learn about their research areas (p. 433). Students were also constantly made aware of the requirement that they help their group members learn: "Let's say, Ron, you become an expert of panther babies, and Jamal becomes an expert on panther protection. You'll need to teach Jamal everything you know about babies, and he'll teach you everything he knows about protection, so when you go to the jigsaw group, you'll need to talk about the whole panther, not just the panther babies" (p. 433). A final type of accountability that was key to this group's learning was accountability to having evidence and being able to cite sources. Ms. Wingate established early on that they would need to keep track of where they found information: "You may find some information in this movie, that's going to be important to you at some other time. And if you ever want to say where you got your evidence, you can look back in your book, and say 'Ah, I saw it in *Hawaii: Threatened Paradise*. . . .' So it's really important that we start writing down where we get our information" (pp. 434–435).

Provide students with relevant resources such as models, public forums, or tools that support discussion. Informational resources such as books, magazines, films, access to experts, and field trips were critical in allowing students to find a broad range of topics, contradictions, and perspectives. These discrepancies were important for driving debate but also for developing students' reasoning and sophistication in using numerous types of evidence. In addition, throughout this unit and other units Ms. Wingate offered models of how to build up arguments with evidence. For example, one student explained how to engage in debate based on evidence from an earlier unit on the use of DDT to fight malaria:

"So maybe I decided malaria [was worse] and Ms. A decided DDT was. Ms. A might say 'I think DDT because of this,' and then I would raise my hand because I have something to say to that. I'd either want to BACK her up and say 'yeah and also this' (gestures a point), or I'd want to say 'oh NO, I don't think that, because I think Malaria is worse, because of THESE reasons' (gestures multiple reasons)" [pp. 427].

Another important resource was time. Students were given plenty of time to investigate this question and opportunities to share the group's current thinking and disagreements with one another and with Ms. Wingate, the class, and a student teacher. Ms. Wingate repeatedly reflected back what she heard: "It sounds like there's not a group decision on this" and later, "I think you have got different sides of an argument that both sides I feel like have good points" (p. 440). She encouraged less vocal students to weigh in and consistently asked for evidence.

Project-based, problem-based, and design-based learning demand strong scaffolding, assessment, and flexibility

In Sum . . .

A great deal of research has shown that collaborative approaches to learning are beneficial for individual and collective knowledge growth, including development of disciplinary practices. Studies also indicate that such approaches can help students develop affective qualities, such as confidence and motivation. Research is also beginning to show that teachers can support expression and development of collaborative capacities through careful design of activities, assessments, and methods for establishing and maintaining classroom norms that support productive joint work. We now turn to research on specific approaches to activity design that engage students in inquiry and sustained project work.

RESEARCH ON INQUIRY LEARNING APPROACHES

The design of most inquiry-based approaches is based on insights from cognitive theories about how people learn and the importance of students both making sense of what they learn and processing content deeply so that they truly understand it (Bransford, Brown, & Cocking, 1999). There are many ways to accomplish these goals, and this has given rise to several distinct genres of approaches. In this review we summarize research on three of the more well-researched strategies: project-based learning, problem-based learning, and design-based learning, which share both similarities and differences.

Project-Based Learning

Project-based learning (PBL) involves completing complex tasks that typically result in a realistic product, event, or presentation to an audience. Thomas (2000) defines productive project-based learning as (1) central to the curriculum; (2) organized around driving questions that lead students to encounter central concepts or principles of a discipline; (3) focused on a constructive investigation that involves inquiry and knowledge building; (4) student-driven, in that students are responsible for making choices and for designing and managing their work; and (5) authentic, by posing problems that occur in the real world and that people care about.

Implementing Project-Based Learning–Districtwide

According to Robert J. Van Maren, superintendent of the Bonner Springs/Edwardsville School District, in Bonner Springs, near Kansas City, Kansas, "It's essential that learning not only be fun, but also be something that teachers and kids can get passionate about. I've never seen anyone be passionate about testing, but as a result of No Child Left Behind and other like initiatives, that's what we've been forced to offer."

To change the paradigm, Van Maren championed a recent effort to bring the project-based Expeditionary Learning Schools (ELS) Outward Bound model to his own school district–a type of learning that's been very successful at other schools around the country. In this model, the focus is on learning "expeditions": long-term student investigations that, though keyed to state and federal academic standards, are designed to nurture a strong affinity for dynamic learning and a curiosity about the world beyond the classroom. In ELS, the focus is on learning by doing, as opposed to the more passive traditional class experience.

FINDING FUNDING

As a result of Van Maren's efforts, Kansas City's Ewing Marion Kauffman Foundation awarded five-year, $150,000 grants to four of the district's schools–three elementary schools and one middle school–to support their transformation into Expeditionary Learning Schools. That brought the total number of ELS in the Kansas City area to eleven, giving the region the opportunity to become the flagship of the movement.

Van Maren believes this is where their schools are headed–and that they'll get there without compromising national and state standards in the process. "I'm an old science teacher, and I know that kids learn by doing, not by sitting there doing worksheets or practice tests," he said. "This grant allows us to use the best pedagogy available to teach using an investigative style, so kids can discover the linkages between what they're learning–not just math for math's sake, or science for science's sake. We believe that the test scores will take care of themselves."

By test scores, or almost any other method of accounting, ELS has a successful track record in education reform. After it had been in operation for just six years, Congress hailed it as a national educational model, and schools from coast to coast were signing up. In 2003, the Bill & Melinda Gates Foundation awarded ELS a five-year, $12.6-million grant to create twenty small college-preparatory high schools.

That track record was one reason the Kauffman Foundation chose to fund ELS. Another was diversity. "In Kansas City, we have a huge range of school settings—large, small, rural, urban, suburban, wealthy, not wealthy—so we looked hard to find an innovative program that could accommodate our needs," said Margo Quiriconi, the organization's director of research and policy. "Their model has been successfully implemented in almost every kind of school imaginable."

GETTING BUY-IN

The success is in part due to an ELS mandate regarding program buy-in: Before a school can apply, the school board must unanimously approve it, and 80 percent of school staff must agree on the proposal.

"Even though this is a school-based model, not a district-based model, we can't pick a school if we don't have support from the top down," said Corey Scholes, a former K-8 principal who is now the ELS representative working with the Bonner Springs schools. "Changing an entire school culture is really hard work. You just can't do it without the support of both administration and the teachers. The Bonner Springs school system showed an intense dedication to the model."

Joseph DiPinio, principal of grant recipient Robert E. Clark Middle School, was a staunch supporter from the beginning. "As part of the grant process, we visited Expeditionary Learning Schools around the country, and in every instance I walked away with the thought, 'That's how I want my school to be,'" he said. "When you see something good for kids, you want to figure out a way to make that happen, but the costs for the professional development and the school design are so extensive. We wouldn't have been able to afford to do this comprehensively on our own."

"My passion has always been professional development for teachers, and now I get the pleasure of working on site with teachers twenty-five days a year," Scholes said. "I would have sawed off my left arm to have this kind of support when I was a principal."

Though excitement about the new venture is evident, Bonner Springs's superintendent acknowledges that the next five years will be challenging.

"Change is difficult, and it's always easier to just keep doing what you've always done," Van Maren said. "But we want different results. We want our kids to reach a new level of potential and be competitive with kids all over the world. Just as important, we want to bring the joy and passion back into the classroom. We want to create a learning experience that kids and teachers will never forget."

MORE INFORMATION

- For more on the Expeditionary Learning Schools Outward Bound model, go to www.elschools.org.
- A video about the ELS program at King Middle School in Portland, Maine, can be seen at www.edutopia .org/expeditionary-learning-maine-video.
- To read about King's program, see "Expeditionary Learning (page 40)"

Adapted from Edutopia article "River Journeys and Life Without Bathing: Immersive Education," by Laura Scholes. Originally published May 15, 2007.

There are a number of research strands that contribute to our understanding of the effects of project-based learning. One has examined the strong success of whole-school models such as Expeditionary Learning, which create an entire curriculum grounded in "intellectual investigations built around significant projects and performances" (Udall & Rugen, 1996, p. xi). Expeditionary Learning schools' approach to project-based learning also focuses on teamwork, community building, and connections beyond the school. They use a pedagogy that emphasizes performance-based assessment, reflection on learning, and revision of work to meet standards in the discipline. Evaluation of schools that have implemented this model has found substantial gains in student learning as measured by standardized test scores, as well as an increase in student motivation and teachers' confidence in their ability to reach all students (ELOB, 1997, 1999a, 1999b; New American Schools Development Corporation, 1997).

Another group of schools using project-based learning as the center of the curriculum, the Co-nect schools, which add an emphasis on technology, were found to exhibit larger value-added student achievement gains on standardized tests than a group of comparison schools in Memphis, Tennessee (Ross et al., 1999) and to exhibit gains comparable to the district average in Cincinnati, Ohio (CPS, 1999). These whole-school efforts to implement project-based learning approaches include a broad range of organizational and pedagogical strategies that make it difficult to isolate the "effects" of project-based learning in a controlled, experimental fashion. At the same time, they allow us to examine PBL in an authentic context, where the principles that drive the approach—student-centeredness, authenticity, disciplinary inquiry—extend to decisions about all the other aspects of the school organization. In that sense, these examples may be viewed as a comprehensive test of the principles that guide project-based learning.

Generally, project-based learning sees students who engage in this approach benefit from gains in factual learning that are equivalent or superior to gains for those who engage in traditional forms of instruction (Thomas, 2000).

The goals of PBL are broader, however. The approach aims to enable students to transfer their learning more powerfully to new kinds of situations and problems and to use knowledge more proficiently in performance situations. There are a number of studies demonstrating such outcomes in both short- and long-term learning situations.

For example, Shepherd (1998) describes the results of a unit in which an experimental group of fourth and fifth graders completed a nine-week project to define and find solutions related to housing shortages in several countries. In comparison to the control group, this group of students demonstrated a significant increase in scores on a critical-thinking test, as well as increased confidence in their learning. Other short-term, comparative studies of traditional vs. project-based approaches have demonstrated such unique benefits for projects as an increase in problem definition (Gallagher, Stepien, & Rosenthal, 1992), growth in use of arguments to support reasons (Stepien, Gallagher, & Workman, 1993), and the ability to plan a project after working on an analogous problem-based challenge (A. Moore, Sherwood, Bateman, Bransford, & Goldman, 1996) all of which are skills needed in real-world contexts.

A more ambitious, longitudinal comparative study by Boaler (1997, 1998) followed students over three years in two British schools that were comparable with respect to students' prior achievement and socioeconomic status but that used either a traditional curriculum or a project-based curriculum. The traditional school featured teacher-directed whole class instruction organized around texts, workbooks, and frequent tests in tracked classrooms. Instruction in the other school used open-ended projects in heterogeneous classrooms. Using a pre- and posttest design, the study found that students had comparable learning gains when tested on basic mathematics procedures; those who in addition participated in the project-based curriculum did better on conceptual problems presented in the National Exam. Significantly more students in the project-based school passed the National Exam in year three of the study than those in the traditional school. Boaler noted that, although students in

Expeditionary Learning

At King Middle School, in Portland, Maine, which has adopted the Expeditionary Learning Outward Bound model of personalized, project-based learning, celebrations with everyone from parents to community members are an important part of the learning process. At least twice a year, students, who stay with the same group of teachers for two years (a practice called looping), undertake four- to twelve-week interdisciplinary projects, each of which concludes with an event.

Besides incorporating such subjects as art, science, and language arts, the projects include well-considered use of computer technology, which has been aided by the state of Maine's decision to provide all seventh and eighth graders with Apple iBook laptop computers.

Culminating events have come in a number of forms: a performance of an original play; a presentation to younger students of a geology kit; and production of a CD-ROM, book, or video—all of which incorporate state curriculum standards. Projects at King have included an aquarium design judged by local architects; a CD narrative of Whitman's "O Captain! My Captain!" by students learning English; *Voices of U.S.* (a book of immigrant stories); a guide to shore life of Casco Bay; original music composition and production; documentaries on learning with laptops; a claymation video explaining Newton's Laws; a Web site on pollution; and a CD-ROM on Maine's endangered species.

Ann Brown, the eighth-grade science teacher who oversaw the claymation video production, likes the effect of such projects on the students. "I think it makes for an interesting way for kids to represent their learning," she said. "It's a lot more interesting than having them simply write about it or draw pictures of it, because they really have to think about how to communicate with an audience and use text and images that make sense to people who haven't studied what they've studied."

UNDERSTANDING AND REPRESENTATION

"The goal for us at King Middle School is to create opportunities for all kids to do representational work about their learning," stated David Grant, King's technology teaching strategist. He works with both students and teachers to ensure that any video or computer or Web production furthers the curriculum. "It's in the making of things that kids actually do their learning," he said. "When you start to make something, you look at it, you reflect upon it, and you begin to be informed by your own representation. And then in that way, you either go out into the world to get more data to support your ideas or you begin to think about something new in your mind and you start to re-represent. And that's how the learning gets deep."

It's also how one can tell whether students understand the concepts they're talking about. "I'm sitting right down at the computer with the kid and I'm saying, 'Well, how does that show us Newton's Law?' And they might have gotten that answer right on the test. But when you sit down and look at their representation and you hear from them what they're trying to say, and you pull it apart a little bit, you wind up in this space where you really get to see what they know and what they don't know. And that's always where we want to be working from—what they know and what they don't know. And working with these media allows that to happen."

QUALITY LEARNING FOR EVERYONE

Brown likes the fact that video requires students to work in teams and learn from each other. "That adds to the final product because the different angles produce different ways of approaching the same problem. You get pieces of the best ideas coming together, so the final product is that much better, and they're also learning from each other and thinking differently."

King put an end to tracking and special education "pullout" classes at about the same time it adopted the project approach to learning and began emphasizing the use of technology. Since then, test scores have shot up—a major accomplishment for a student population that is 60 percent low-income and 22 percent refugee and that comes to school speaking twenty-eight languages. Following years of below-average scores on the state achievement test, King students began outscoring the state average in six out of seven subjects in 1999, and they even moved into the top third in some subjects.

Principal Mike McCarthy, a National Principal of the Year in 1997, believes that giving all students—not just those at the top of the class—the highest-quality and most challenging education makes the difference at King. "I've heard people describe what a Gifted and Talented classroom would look like. It should include field experiences. It should include technology. It should include independent work. It should include work that's in-depth. That's basically what our school is. Everyone has access to that kind of learning."

The close relationship of students and their families with teachers through looping also plays a significant role in students' success, McCarthy added. "That means they can get heavily invested in each other. And I think that's part of the reason we produce such great work. One kid said a few years ago, 'Nobody feels stupid around here anymore.' I think that was one of our highest achievements."

MORE INFORMATION

- A video on King Middle School's Expeditionary Learning program can be seen at www.edutopia .org/expeditionary-learning-maine-video.
- For more on the Expeditionary Learning Schools Outward Bound model, go to www.elschools.org.

Adapted from Edutopia article "Laptops on Expedition: Embracing Expeditionary Learning," by Diane Curtis. Originally published Jan. 19, 2004.

the traditional school "thought that mathematical success rested on being able to remember and use rules," the PBL students had developed a more flexible, useful kind of mathematical knowledge that engaged them in "exploration and thought" (Boaler, 1997, p. 63).

Another comparative study came about as part of an independent evaluation of a five-year project that created opportunities for students to develop multimedia projects. The Challenge 2000 Multimedia Project in Silicon Valley involved students on a variety of projects that led to presentations of their work at regional fairs. To assess the effectiveness of these experiences, researchers created an additional performance task that asked these students and a comparison group to develop a brochure informing school officials about problems faced by homeless students (Penuel, Means, & Simkins, 2000). The students in the multimedia program earned higher scores than the comparison group on all three measures derived from the design task: content mastery, sensitivity to audience, and coherent design. There were no differences on standardized test scores of basic skills.

Many other studies have recorded student and teacher reports of positive changes in motivation, attitude toward learning, and skills as a result of participating in PBL, including work habits, critical thinking skills, and problem-solving abilities (see, e.g., Bartscher, Gould, & Nutter, 1995; Peck, Peck, Sentz, & Zasa, 1998; Tretten & Zachariou, 1995). Some have found that students who do less well in traditional instructional settings excel when they have the opportunity to work in a PBL context, which better matches their learning style or preference for collaboration and activity type (see, e.g., Boaler, 1997; Meyer, Turner, & Spencer, 1997; Rosenfeld & Rosenfeld, 1998). One interesting study observed four PBL classrooms in the fall and spring of a school year, finding much larger increases in five critical thinking behaviors (synthesizing, forecasting, producing, evaluating, and reflecting) and five social participation behaviors (working together, initiating, managing, intergroup awareness, and intergroup initiating) for initially low-achieving students over the course of the year than for initially high-achieving students (Horan, Lavaroni, & Beldon, 1996).

Problem-Based Learning

Problem-based learning approaches are a close cousin of project-based learning and are often configured as a specific type of project that aims to teach problem definition and solution strategies. In problem-based learning, students work in small groups to investigate meaningful problems, identify what they need to learn in order to solve a problem, and generate strategies for solution (Barrows, 1996; Hmelo-Silver, 2004). The problems are realistic and ill structured, meaning that they are not perfectly formulated textbook problems but rather are like those in the real world with multiple solutions and methods for reaching them. In addition, research that has sought to establish the characteristics of "good" problems suggests that they should resonate with students' experiences, promote argumentation, foster opportunities for feedback, and allow repeated exposure to concepts.

Much work on this approach has been associated with medical education. For example, physicians-in-training are presented with a patient profile, including a set of symptoms and a history, and the small group's task is to generate possible diagnosis and a plan to differentiate possible causes by conducting research and pursuing diagnostic tests. The instructor typically plays a coaching role, helping to facilitate the group's progress through a set of activities that involve understanding the problem scenario, identifying relevant facts, generating hypotheses, collecting information (interviewing the patient, ordering tests), identifying knowledge deficiencies, learning from external resources, applying knowledge, and evaluating progress. The steps in the cycle may be revisited as work progresses (for example, new knowledge deficiencies may be noticed at any point and more research might be carried out). Meta-analyses of studies of medical students have found that, across studies, students who are enrolled in problem-based curricula score higher on items that measure clinical problem solving and on actual ratings of clinical performance (Albanese & Mitchell, 1993; Vernon & Blake, 1993).

Similar problem- or case-based approaches have been used in business, law, and teacher education to help students learn to analyze complex, multifaceted situations and develop knowledge to guide decision making (see, e.g., Lundeberg, Levin, & Harrington, 1999; Savery & Duffy, 1996; S. M. Williams, 1992). This method of learning is guided in part by our understanding of the important role of analogy in learning and transfer (Gentner & Markman, 1997; Holyoak & Thagard, 1997; Kolodner, 1997). In complex domains, reasoning by analogy to familiar cases is an important strategy for making sense of new situations.

In all problem-based approaches, students take an active role in knowledge construction. The teacher plays an active role in making thinking visible, guides group process and participation, and asks questions to solicit reflections. The goal is to model good reasoning strategies and support the students to take on these roles themselves. At the same time, teachers also offer instruction in more traditional ways such as lectures and explanations crafted and timed to support inquiry. In a case study of an expert problem-based learning teacher/facilitator, Hmelo-Silver and Barrows (2006) found that the teacher's primary means of shaping the groups' progress was through questioning that helped focus students' attention and supported generation of causal explanations. Continued questioning helped students create accurate mental models of the patient's condition and pushed them to link their hypotheses to the patient's symptom profile. It is of note that in medical school settings each group often has continued access to a facilitator. In most K–12 schools, a single teacher has to find ways to move from group to group, making this approach more challenging.

Studies of the efficacy of problem-based learning suggest that, like other project-based approaches, it is comparable, and sometimes superior, to more traditional instruction in facilitating factual learning, but it is better in supporting flexible problem solving, application of knowledge, and hypothesis generation (for a meta-analysis, see Dochy, Segers, Van den Bossche, & Gijbels, 2003). Additional quasi-experimental studies have demonstrated that students who participate in problem-based experiences generate more accurate hypotheses and more coherent explanations (Hmelo, 1998b; Schmidt et al., 1996), are more able to support claims with well-reasoned arguments (Stepien et al., 1993), and show larger gains in conceptual understanding in science (D. C. Williams, Hemstreet, Liu, & Smith, 1998).

These gains and others have been identified in a line of research undertaken by the Cognition and Technology Group at Vanderbilt University over more than a decade. In one early study, for example, more than seven hundred students from eleven school districts engaged in a set of problem-based projects through the Jasper series, which presents videotaped problems that include a package of information to be used in solving problems that are posed. For the five sites that employed matched control groups, the researchers determined that participants experienced larger gains than the comparison students in all five areas measured: mathematics concepts, word problems, planning capabilities, positive attitudes about mathematics, and teacher feedback.

Design-Based Learning

A third genre of instructional approaches has grown out of the idea that children learn deeply when they are asked to design and create an artifact that requires understanding and application of knowledge. It is believed that design-based projects have several features that make them ideal for developing technical and subject matter knowledge (Newstetter, 2000). For example, design activity supports revisions and iterative problem solving as projects require cycles of

defining → *creating* → *assessing* → *redesigning*

The complexity of the work often dictates the need for collaboration and distributed expertise. Finally, a variety of valued cognitive tasks are employed such

Tomorrow's Engineers—Building a Competitive Robot

Every spring, thousands of students meet at regional events to put their creations through their paces in a competition that, like many others, involves teamwork, problem solving, and perseverance—but unlike some, imagination, creativity, professionalism, and maturity as well. The students who participate in the annual FIRST Robotics Competition (FRC), and their mentors, also tend to have a lot of fun.

Started by engineer and inventor Dean Kamen, FIRST (For Inspiration and Recognition of Science and Technology) is about inspiring and motivating students to become engaged in math, science, engineering, and technology. Each year, teams of students, teachers, sponsors, and professional engineers respond to the FIRST challenge by designing and building a robot.

"To passively sit in a classroom is a nineteenth-century format," Kamen has said. "In this next century, you're going to have to be creative, or you're not going to make it."

HANDS-ON SCIENCE AND ENGINEERING

The regional and final national competitions are the culmination of six intense weeks during which students, working with high school teachers and professional engineers, design and build a remote-control robot from a standard kit of hundreds of parts. The robot must be able to complete specific tasks and maneuver through a specially designed course—both of which change every year. More than ten thousand students, on thirteen hundred teams from twenty-three countries, competed in the various FIRST competitions in 2007. (In addition to FRC, there is a competition for nine-to-fourteen-year-olds and another for high school students that uses a smaller, more accessible parts kit.)

"Mentoring plays a big role in the process right from the start," says Lori Ragas, senior teams coordinator for FIRST. From the first brainstorming session to the last match at one of the regionals or the national competition, professional engineers work side-by-side with the high school students, explaining the functions of different parts, providing feedback on design options, and rolling up their sleeves to repair a faulty part or tinker with a design element.

A recent winner of the engineering design award, the team from Poudre High School, in Fort Collins, Colorado, devoted the first week and a half after announcement of the design challenge to what teacher and robotics coach Steve Sayers called "pure strategy," where everyone—from the first-year participant to the veteran team member, from parents to professional engineers—put forth design ideas. From those best ideas came a basic design, which the team spent the next five weeks refining, fabricating, and testing on a prototype of the actual competition course.

Although much of the work each year revolves around design and engineering, Sayers, who was a chemical engineer before making the switch to teaching, pointed out that a successful team requires an eclectic mix of students with a variety of skills and interests.

"If a student wants to be on the team, the first questions I ask them are, 'What do you enjoy doing? What are you good at?'" said Sayers, adding that there's "something for everyone" on the Poudre High robotics team. Students interested in computers do the programming or computer-aided design and animation work. Those with artistic abilities design everything from team T-shirts to flyers to the look and feel of the robot itself. Writers create the design documentation. The list of responsibilities goes on and on. No one job, Sayers was quick to add, is more important than any other.

"Everyone is an equal part of the team," he said. "We all just respect each other for the different roles we play."

SKILLS FOR THE FUTURE

Mark Leon, NASA's robotics education project manager, has been working with high school robotics teams since 1998. NASA's reason for supporting robotics education (both financially and by providing mentors to schools throughout the country) is simple: "We need to build robots that are smarter, robots that can survive for long periods of time without being in communication with NASA," Leon said. "We're getting these students excited about robotics engineering, helping them to choose math and technology careers so they can contribute back to this country, so they can be part of the workforce that builds the next generation of robotic explorers."

But the benefits to students—and to any future employers—go beyond the science and engineering skills students gain from participating in the program. Respect, cooperation, and learning to be a team player are just a few of the life skills students learn through the robotics program. Those are skills, team members and adult advisers agree, that students will carry with them, whatever career they choose.

Janet Tsai, who was on the Poudre High team for two years, put it this way: "We're all working towards a common goal. And to get to that common goal, we all need to work together and listen to everyone's ideas. You can't just remain contained in your own little bubble and hope that everyone else knows what's going on too."

Tyson Wormus, a three-year veteran of the Poudre High team, had a similar experience. "I've become a lot more confident through the work with this program," he said. "I can present ideas without many qualms, and I've learned to listen to other people's ideas."

For students like Tsai, participation in the FIRST program affords an up-close look at what life as an engineer is all about. "The hands-on experience I gained from working on this project has just been absolutely phenomenal," she said. "It's really neat the way the students design and fabricate the robot. It really shows you what you can do." Because of her participation in FIRST, Tsai said, she is considering majoring in science or engineering when she gets to college.

Tsai is not unusual in her reaction. A recent survey of FIRST Robotics Competition participants concluded that, relative to a comparison group of non-FIRST students with similar backgrounds and academic experiences (including math and science), they are:

- Far more likely to attend college full time (88% vs. 53%)
- More likely to expect to earn at least a master's degree (77% vs. 69%)
- Roughly 10 times as likely to have an apprenticeship, internship, or co-op job as a college freshman (27% vs. 2.7%)
- Twice as likely to major in science or engineering (55% vs. 28%)

Source: "More than Robots: An Evaluation of the FIRST Robotics Competition Participant and Institutional Impacts." Prepared by Alan Melchior, Faye Cohen, Tracy Cutter, and Thomas Leavitt, Center for Youth and Communities, Heller School for Social Policy and Management, Brandeis University, Waltham, Massachusetts (http://www.usfirst.org/uploadedFiles/Who/Impact/Brandeis_Studies/FRC_eval_finalrpt.pdf, accessed Oct. 22, 2007)

MORE INFORMATION
- A video about Poudre High School's 2001 Robotics Team can be seen at www.edutopia.org/poudre-high-school-robotics.
- For more on the FRC and other FIRST competitions, visit www.usfirst.org.

Adapted from Edutopia article "Building a Better Robot: A Robotics Competition Introduces Students to Engineering," by Roberta Furger. Originally published Dec. 3, 2001.

as setting constraints, generating ideas, prototyping, and planning through storyboarding or other representational practices. These are all critical twenty-first-century skills.

Design-based approaches can be found in science, technology, art, engineering, and architecture. Nonschool-based projects organized around contests such as the FIRST robotics competitions (www .usfirst.org) or the Thinkquest competition (www .thinkquest.org) also stress design using technological tools and collaborative project work. For example, Thinkquest is an international competition in which teams of students from nine to nineteen years old come together to build Web sites designed for youth about an educational topic. Teams of three to six are mentored by a teacher who gives general guidance

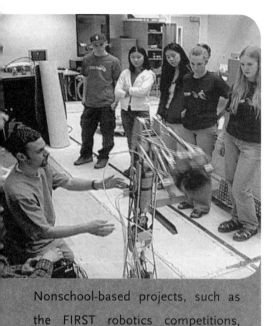

Nonschool-based projects, such as the FIRST robotics competitions, stress student teamwork and strategy

throughout the several months of the design process but leaves the specific creative and technical work to the students. Teams receive and offer feedback during a peer review of the initial submissions, and then they use this information to revise their work. To date, more than thirty thousand students have participated; there are currently more than fifty-five hundred sites available in the online library (http://www.thinkquest.org/library/). Topics range from art, astronomy, and programming to issues such as foster care or use of humor for mental health; almost anything is fair game.

Despite the wide range of applications of learning through design, much of the research-based curriculum development and assessment has taken place in the domain of science (Harel, 1991; Kafai, 1994; Kafai & Ching, 2001; Lehrer & Romberg, 1996; Penner, Giles, Lehrer, & Schauble, 1997). For example, a group from the University of Michigan has been developing an approach called Design-Based Science (Fortus, Dershimer, Marx, Krajcik, & Mamlok-Naaman,

2004), and a Science by Design series that includes four high school units focused on constructing gloves, boats, greenhouses, and catapults. A separate group from the Georgia Institute of Technology has been developing an approach they call Learning by Design, also used in science (Kolodner, 1997; Puntambekar & Kolodner, 2005).

Within the relatively small body of research that uses control group designs, the research on learning reported by Kolodner and colleagues (Kolodner, Camp, et al., 2003) shows large and consistent differences between the Learning by Design (LBD) classes and their comparisons. Their measures assess groups' ability to complete performance tasks before and after instruction. Each task has three parts: (1) students design an experiment that would constitute a fair test; (2) they run an experiment and collect data (the design is specified by the researchers; and (3) they analyze the data and use them to make recommendations. The researchers also score group interaction from videotaped records on seven dimensions: negotiation during collaboration, distribution of the work, attempted use of prior knowledge, adequacy of prior knowledge, science talk, science practice, and self-monitoring. They report that the Learning by Design students consistently outperform non-LBD students on collaborative interaction and aspects of metacognition (for instance, self-monitoring).

In another design experiment that included a comparison sample, Hmelo, Holton, and Kolodner (2000) asked sixth-grade students to design a set of artificial lungs and build a partially working model of the respiratory system. They found that the design condition led to better learning outcomes than students exposed to traditional instruction. They also noted that the design students learned to view the respiratory system more systemically and understood more about structure than function, and more about the functions of the system than causal behaviors. They argue that design activities are particularly good for helping students develop understanding of complex systems because they can be presented as a united whole whose structure is adapted

Build San Francisco Institute: Immersing Students in Civic Education

The Build San Francisco Institute, a yearlong design program co-sponsored by the Architectural Foundation of San Francisco (AFSF) and the San Francisco Unified School District (SFUSD), has as one of its core principles that subjects such as math, history, and writing have a larger context; they are essential tools for conceptualizing, understanding, sketching, and building relevant and compelling real-world projects. "In a military academy, they don't teach trigonometry; they teach navigation," explained Build SF co-founder Richard Hannum. "Because you need trig for navigation, you learn it."

A BRIDGE TO THE REAL WORLD

Offering accredited courses with titles such as Architectural Design and Urban Sociology, today's Build SF is the offshoot of an after-school and summer program launched thirteen years ago. In 2004, as a part of the SFUSD's Secondary School Redesign Initiative, the program was expanded to an all-afternoon, five-day-a-week schedule; two of those days are devoted to working with mentors from some of San Francisco's leading architecture, interior-design, engineering, and contracting firms, along with certain city agencies involved in urban planning.

The curriculum was designed to develop student interest in architecture-related fields and, more fundamentally, to immerse them in the process of meshing civic and business interests. "It's not about building little architects," said Hannum, a Bay Area design-firm principal as well as one of AFSF's founders. "Rather, we use architecture as a vehicle to give kids with no community context an insight into, and a voice in, the public process."

The ability to provide a bridge between education and business is why Janet Schulze, principal at San Francisco's John O'Connell High School of Technology, is a Build SF booster. The program, she said, "is the fastest way to integrate academic skills into a real-world setting."

Schulze praised the effort San Francisco's design community dedicates to the program, particularly in terms of offering mentorships. "I'd love to see the medical and finance communities do something like it," she added.

"STUDIO" MEANS STUDY

At Build SF's downtown studio, the decibel level is much higher than what would be acceptable in most high school classrooms. "This place does develop a certain hum," admitted Alan Sandler, the foundation's executive director. "It's supposed to be like a busy office." AFSF programs director

Will Fowler characterized the ambience as "the real sound of learning. It shocks and delights them that they are encouraged to talk to each other."

Use of the term *studio* rather than the word *classroom* is also not accidental. According to Fowler, "We want the kids to understand that Build SF is more a design studio than it is a school."

None of this is to say that this early part of the school year isn't anarchic for both pupils and teachers. "It's always frustrating at the beginning," Hannum said. "It takes kids time to get over the idea that they have to raise their hands to speak. I tell them, 'We're not in class. We're adults, and if you have something to say, say it.'" Fowler believes it takes about six weeks for the lessons to begin to sink in. "By January," he says, "they will be a well-oiled machine."

Build SF's insistence on treating kids like adults also takes getting used to on the instructional side. Accustomed to dealing with hundreds of kids in a traditional high school setting, Boston-area refugee Casey Brennan admitted she was nervous in 2005 when she began instructing at Build SF. "We were trained never to leave kids alone. When Will Fowler first told me to walk away, it was difficult."

"There is only one rule," Fowler explained. "When Casey says, 'Listen up,' they have to listen up."

RISING TO CHALLENGES

Another central precept of Build SF is that participants be exposed to the unvarnished realities of life in the highly competitive and often-contentious world of design and architecture. One recent project involved creating a series of historically themed tiles for the city's newly redesigned Pier 14. The students had to first design the tiles and then present and "sell" their ideas to the Port Commission—a process that took several iterations, and not a little frustration, before the commission was satisfied. Then the Build SF team had to master the complex process of tile production, from drawing, tracing, and painting to glazing and firing, as well as overseeing installation.

The class also had to realistically assess the talents of each member and assign tasks accordingly. Some of the students less accomplished as artists or designers came into their own as key team leaders whose organizational skills could help the project advance—"our version of middle management," Fowler said with a smile.

Some projects, such as designing and building a bridge with sets of Lego blocks, are meant to get kids from different schools comfortable with one another. "Students tend to spend their entire school careers with the same kids from the same neighborhoods," the AFSF's Sandler said about the goal of opening up new vistas. "When they come here and leave their baggage behind, they're able to develop a different, adult persona."

Comings and goings at the Build SF studio go on throughout the afternoon as students arrive from their morning high school classes, go to work on their various projects, or move on to their assigned mentorships. Some stay all afternoon; others depart for after-school activities at their respective high schools. This open-endedness might strike some critics as an easy way to ditch school. For the Build SF team, however, it is a critical part of the program. "Maybe for the first time in their school careers, kids have to be responsible for their own time," Sandler said. "Our key motto is 'Trust the kids'—treat them as professionals, and they will rise to the challenge each and every time."

MORE INFORMATION
- For more on the Build San Francisco Institute, go to www.afsf.org/program_buildsf.htm.
- A video on the program can be viewed at www.edutopia .org/learning-design.

to specific purposes (Perkins, 1986). Echoing the findings of other classroom research, Hmelo and colleagues (2000) argue that design challenges need to be carefully planned. In this case they argue they should be designed functionally, and they stress the importance of dynamic feedback, allowing students to engage in multiple iterations of design, and giving adequate time to the entire system of classroom activities. In particular, they suggest that teachers working on design projects pay attention to:

- Finding a balance between having students work on design activities and reflecting on what they are learning, so that they can guide their progress. Incorporating reflective activities is important to encourage an understanding-based approach.
- Learning how to integrate real-world knowledge without letting it overwhelm the class with irrelevant aspects of the world that might take the students on unproductive tangents.
- Determining how to maintain extended engagement in a manner that emphasizes principled understanding rather than completion.

Much of the research on learning through design-based projects has been less experimental and more naturalistic, either focused on single-case pre- and postresearch designs or longer-term design experiments where close observation of learning processes and outcomes is accompanied by changes to the curriculum or additions of support for its implementation. For example, Fortus and colleagues (2004) carried out a study with ninety-two students that tracked their learning across three Design-Based Science units. Their units included designing a structure for extreme environments, designing environmentally friendly batteries, and designing safer cell phones. Each unit contained multiple design and learning cycles. The research team found that both higher- and lower-achieving students showed strong evidence of progress in learning the targeted science concepts, and that students applied the concepts well in their design work. They also noted a positive effect on motivation and sense of ownership over designs at both individual and group levels.

Unfortunately, because there was no control group, it is difficult to make strong claims about the relative efficacy of this approach compared to more traditional approaches.

The Cognition and Technology Group at Vanderbilt also documented strong gains in learning for students in a five-week design project aimed at teaching basic principles of geometry in the context of architecture and design (Barron et al., 1998). Students were asked to help design a playground and then create two- and three-dimensional representations for a playhouse they would explain in public presentation to experts. Students of all ability levels made significant gains in their ability to use scale and measurement concepts on their blueprints and to answer traditional test items measuring scale, volume, perimeter, area, and other geometric concepts. Of the thirty-seven designs submitted, 84 percent were judged accurate enough to be built, a result considered a high rate of achievement. (See the box "Successful Inquiry Learning Guided by Design Principles" [p. 57] for a description of the project and how it was supported.)

Design programs build bridges between education and the business world

CHALLENGES OF INQUIRY APPROACHES TO LEARNING

Many challenges have been identified with management of project-based, problem-based, and design-based learning opportunities, as the pedagogies required to implement these approaches are much more complex than teachers' direct transmission of knowledge to students via textbooks or lectures. In fact, inquiry approaches to learning have frequently been found to be highly dependent on the knowledge and skills of teachers engaged in trying to implement them (Good & Brophy, 1986). When these approaches are poorly understood, teachers often think of inquiry or other student-centered approaches as "unstructured," rather than appreciating that they require extensive scaffolding and constant assessment and redirection as they unfold.

Research on these approaches signals a number of specific challenges that emerge when students lack prior experience or modeling regarding particular aspects of the learning process. With respect to disciplinary understanding, students can have difficulty generating meaningful questions or evaluating their questions to understand if they are warranted by the content of the investigation (Krajcik et al., 1998), and they may lack background knowledge needed to make sense of the inquiry (Edelson, Gordon, & Pea, 1999). With respect to general academic skills, students may have difficulty developing logical arguments and evidence to support their claims (Krajcik et al., 1998). As for management of the work, students often find it hard to figure out how to work together, manage their time and the complexity of the work, and sustain motivation in the face of setbacks or confusion (Achilles & Hoover, 1996; Edelson et al., 1999).

Teachers may also encounter challenges as they try to juggle the time needed for extended inquiry, learn new approaches to classroom management, design and support inquiries that illuminate key subject matter concepts, balance students' needs for direct information with their opportunities to inquire, scaffold the learning of many individual students, offer enough (but not too much) modeling and feedback for each one, facilitate learning among multiple groups, and develop and use assessments to guide the learning process (Blumenfeld et al., 1991; Marx et al., 1994, 1997; Rosenfeld & Rosenfeld, 1998; Sage, 1996).

In design projects, students take ownership of their education and it becomes more meaningful to them

Without supports to learn these complex skills, teachers may be unable to use inquiry approaches to learning to their best advantage, engaging students in "doing" but not necessarily in disciplined learning that has a high degree of transfer.

How Can Teachers Support Productive Inquiry?

Clearly, successful inquiry-based approaches require planning and well-thought-out approaches to collaboration, classroom interaction, and assessment. Some research has focused especially on how to support these approaches well. For example, Puntambekar & Kolodner (2005) describe two studies designed to advance our understanding of the kinds of support students need to learn content in the context of design projects. They knew from earlier classroom research (Gertzman & Kolodner, 1996) that simply furnishing students with rich resources and an interesting problem (say, design a household robot with arthropod features) was not enough. Students needed help understanding the problem, applying science knowledge, evaluating their designs, explaining failures, and engaging in revision. Students often neglected to use informational resources unless explicitly prompted.

To address these problems, the researchers introduced a design diary that was intended explicitly to introduce design process ideas and to support four phases of design work: understanding the challenge, gathering information, generating a solution, and evaluating solutions. The goal of the eighth-grade, three-week curriculum was to help students learn about coastal erosion. Students were given a challenge of designing a solution to this problem for a specific coastal island off the coast of Georgia. To experiment with solutions, they had access to stream tables as well as informational resources on videotape and the Internet. In addition to implementing the journal, they carried out careful assessment of students' learning and observation of classroom interactions. In this first study, the learning outcomes were disappointing. However, the researchers' insights about how to support students were generative.

For example, they noted that the teacher missed many opportunities to advance learning because she could not listen in to all small group discussions and had decided not to have whole group discussions. They also noted that the students needed more specific prompts for justifying design decisions.

In the second study, they designed and implemented a broader system of tools and processes, which greatly improved the learning outcomes—notably, more structured diary prompts that asked for design rationales and explanations, and insertion of whole class discussions at strategic moments. They also added new activity structures that required students to publicly defend designs earlier in the process; they called these "pin up sessions," drawing on ideas from architectural studio learning. In these sessions, students present their ideas by pinning their drawings of their design plans to the wall as a poster and then explaining them to the class in order to get feedback. For each idea, students were asked to give a justification from informational resources or experimental evidence they themselves collected (Kolodner et al., 2003; Puntambekar & Kolodner, 2005). These processes of helping students keep track of and defend their thinking were very helpful. In addition, the *redundancy* of learning opportunities afforded by the several forms of support was a key in helping students focus on learning concepts and connecting them with their design work.

The playground design project described earlier (Barron et al., 1998), which used a combination of problem-based, project-based, and design-based learning approaches, generated an additional set of design principles:

- Define learning-appropriate goals that lead to deep understanding
- Offer scaffolds that support both students' and teacher's learning
- Ensure multiple opportunities for formative self-assessment and revision
- Design social organizations that promote participation and result in a sense of agency

Application of these principles is described in the box "Successful Inquiry Learning Guided by Design Principles."

SUCCESSFUL INQUIRY LEARNING GUIDED BY DESIGN PRINCIPLES

A curriculum project featuring multiple activities was developed by the Cognition and Technology Group to develop fifth-grade students' mathematical problem-solving ability, representational capacities, and understanding of concepts such as area and scale. The sequence began with a design challenge presented in the context of a video-based anchor from the Jasper series. In this series, fifteen-minute videos were encoded on videodisks, featuring narratives ending with *problem-solving challenges* that could be addressed by data embedded in the movie. This design invited students to formulate problems, find relevant data, and generate quantitative methods to solve them (CTGV, 1997). In addition, embedded within the fifteen-minute narrative were explanations that gave ideas for how to approach problems that supported teachers' and students' knowledge building. These carefully designed, video-based problems modeled aspects of inquiry and encouraged development of key subject matter knowledge. They were followed by thematically related, real-world projects that students could implement as a means of deepening their learning and engaging their motivation.

In one version of this sequence, the goal for students was to learn about measurement, drawing to scale, and how to produce drawings that someone could build from. Students begin by solving a challenge presented in "Blueprint for Success." In Blueprint for Success they meet two students, Christina and Markus, who visit an architect's office for career day. The story begins with a dramatic scene in which a friend is playing in the street and is hit by a car. Although the accident was not serious and the friend is going to be fine, the incident prompts a local developer to donate land. The developer comes to the architect's office while Christina and Markus

(continued)

are visiting. Christina and Markus suggest that a playground be built on the donated property to create a fun spot for children to play. The developer agrees with this idea and invites the children to design the equipment and park layout, and to complete the needed blueprints. The story ends with a summary of the materials that have been donated by the local businesses and a challenge to children in the classroom to develop the plan. Specifically the challenge is to:

- Create a design or model of the playground for the builders
- Make a site plan of the lot, the playground, and each piece of equipment
- Generate a front and side view of the equipment with relevant angles, lengths, and depths

At the end of the story, students find out that community organizations and businesses have agreed to donate building supplies, including 280 feet of fence, 32 cubic feet of sand, sliding boards for a slide, and all the wood and fine gravel to cover the lot. The students are asked to specify how much wood, gravel, and sliding board they will need. In addition, students are given a list of safety requirements that detail appropriate ranges of angles, depth of gravel needed, and distances required between pieces of equipment. These materials and safety requirements then become constraints for students to attend to as they complete their designs.

Reflecting the first design principle, the learning goals and activities are closely aligned. To succeed in this challenge, students must resolve issues such as what it means to draw to scale; how to maximize area, given constraints on perimeter; and figure out how to create blueprints of equipment that show the measurements of all the relevant dimensions. Their playground scale drawings are assessed and revised through several cycles, and their subject matter learning is supported through a variety of multimedia resources created specifically to address particular concepts such as scale, area, and volume.

Only after each member of the group has demonstrated mastery of these concepts through his or her playground design is the student allowed to continue on to the next phase where the design activity might result in an actual product. For the project-based component, students are asked to design a play structure for a local community center. From the outset of the problem-based work, children are aware that their work on "Blueprint" is preparing them to design a playhouse for young children that may actually be built and donated to community centers in local neighborhoods; there is considerable excitement generated by the idea that their design might actually end up being used by young children. Students also know that for their design to have a chance of being built they must make an accurate blueprint and scale model. Specific design constraints for the playhouse are imposed:

- Children who are four and five years old will play in it.
- Only two sheets of wood, each 4 feet by 8 feet, can be used to build the playhouse. The walls, roof, and trim must all come from this wood. The design should use as much of the two sheets of wood as possible.
- The playhouse must have three walls and a flat roof.
- The floor space that the playhouse covers must be between 10 and 20 square feet.
- Any openings for doors and windows must be safe. They must be larger than 7 inches or smaller than 4 inches to prevent children from putting their head into an opening and getting stuck. There should not by any V-shaped openings.

Finally, students are told that they will explain the blueprints and scale models they create on videotape so that they can be evaluated for accuracy and consistency with problem constraints. The evaluators in this case are not their teachers but an outside audience known as "Jasper Central." This structure frees the teacher to join with the students and serve in the role of coach. The final presentation is an important aspect of the projects. It gives students an opportunity to reflect on issues such as what it means to explain one's thinking, and how to convince someone of the accuracy of a plan, as well as issues such as what makes a presentation engaging. The guidelines for the presentation:

- Every member of your group must speak during the presentation.
- The presentation should be five to ten minutes long.

(continued)

- You must convince Jasper Central of the following:
  - The design uses as much of the available wood as possible, but no more than the available wood. The playhouse is safe for four- and five-year-old children. The playhouse is fun to play in. Use your imagination and be creative.
- Students spent approximately one week designing their playhouses, preparing their blueprints, and developing their presentations. The presentations are evaluated for accuracy, safety, and consistency, and for how well they communicate important design features. Here is an example of one group's presentation.

PRESENTATION OF FINAL PLAYHOUSE DESIGN MODELS

All three presenters in unison: Good morning, students.

Presenter one: Hello, I'm Mr. Robert. I'm going to talk about the blueprint today. First I'd like to say, we started out with 4 by 8 pieces of plywood so each wall should by 4 by 4, 4 feet across and 4 feet up. Our scale is 6 inches for one block [points to scale on blueprint]. Now I'll talk about the front. The window is 9 inches across and 1 foot down. So, that should mean that there is a block and a half going across and there are two blocks going down. That's the same for this one. Now I'll talk about the door. The door is 3 feet high, so it should be six blocks up, and three blocks across. Now the side views. Both of them have two windows, 1 foot going across and 1 foot going up. Also, I'd like to talk about the extra wood. The extra wood in the parenthesis means how many there is. It shows it right here, they're in the windows. Like this: there's four of them, it shows it right here. And then right here it can show that there are two of them right here and right here [points to two window spaces], and then, like this big space, this is the door, it shows that it has one of these, and then the number tells the number of them so you can look right here at the parts that are extra wood and you can find where these are. Now I put "important" by this right here, I put the shutters, are 3 inches each, um, so the architect would know um, how long to paint um, how long to draw um. Thank you.

Presenter two: Hi, I am Mr. Sircar and I'm here to talk to you about our front view and top view. Let's start off with our window; you can see that our window has been 9 inches wide and 1 foot long, on both. The reason we picked 9 inches is because, so children could stick out their heads and, and see out, see outside, and so they would not get their head stuck, and because, the requirement sheet said that any openings would have to be more wider than 7 inches. Now, see our door. Our door has been 2 feet wide and 3 feet long. The reason we picked 2 feet wide is so that children wouldn't have to squeeze in, and the reason we picked 3 feet long is because so children wouldn't have to duck. . . . Now you can see that our top view has been just four by four [picks up three-dimensional scale model and orients top to audience]. . . . You can see there has been grass, pencils, a school, and a flag. The way we got those extra pieces of wood has been from our seven holes, One, two, three, four, five, six, seven [turns music stand to show audience each as he counts]. We got those extra pieces from our extra ply-wood, our grass, our pencils, the name of the school, and our flag. Thank you.

Presenter three: Hi, my name is Mrs. Duncan, and y'all already met me today. Now, I'm going to talk about our left side, our right side of our school house. We have grass that is green and we have windows, and we got shutters from this extra credit, extra wood [points to blueprint]. And now I am going to talk about left side. We have grass green, we have extra wood again [points to blueprint where extra wood is detailed], and we have windows. I'm going to talk about why we built our school house. We built our school house for ages four- and five-year-old children. They can play school, learn, and do all kinds of other things. Thank you.

In unison: Class dismissed!

The system of activities, assessments, and resources described here reflects the four design principles. First, learning-appropriate goals that lead to deep understanding were defined. Both the problem-based and project-based activities required and supported specific mathematical concepts. Second, multiple types of scaffold that could support both student and teacher learning were provided through the embedded teaching sequences within "Blueprint for Success" and through extra resources that illustrated concepts of scale, volume, and related concepts. Third, there were multiple opportunities for formative self-assessment and revision given to both individuals and groups. Students' drawings were scored, and they were revised until they had met a standard of accuracy. Fourth, motivation, a sense of agency, and continued engagement were supported by collaborative structures, a chance to design something that might be built, and the opportunity to present to an outside audience supported.

This project-based learning planner assists teachers in their efforts to create effective projects. The guide came from LEARN, a nonprofit educational foundation based in Quebec.

PBL Project Planner

I ASK MYSELF . . .	ANSWER
Vision stage:	
1. What are my subject/learning objectives?	1.
2. What are my interdisciplinary subjects and competencies?	2.
3. What inquiry question/investigation will meet no. 1, no. 2?	3.
Inquiry stage:	
1. How will I hook or trigger the student's interest in the inquiry question? What scenario will I use?	1.
2. What kinds of information can I expect to be brought out of our class brainstorming session? What kind of misconceptions do I expect to encounter?	2.
3. What rubric(s) will I use? Will I design it myself or with my students?	3.

I ASK MYSELF . . .	ANSWER
Build stage:	
1. How will I organize the brainstorming session? How will we categorize and sort the information we come up with?	1.
2. What kind of teams will work best for this project? (i.e., number of members, roles, responsibilities)	2.
3. What information and computer technologies are necessary in order to accomplish these tasks? Do I need to review or teach any of these skills?	3.
4. What research techniques will we need? Do I need to review or teach any?	4.
5. What kind of final products would lend themselves well to this type of investigation?	5.
6. At what stage will I ask for product updates? What format will these updates be in? (i.e., journal entry, oral presentation, etc.)	6.
Showtime stage:	
What kind of showcase will be most appropriate to display the student's knowledge acquisitions? (i.e., museum display, PowerPoint presentation, play in front of an audience, etc.)	1.
Transition stage:	
Will I ask my students to give an oral reflection or a written reflection of their learning, and thoughts on this project?	1.

Source: LEARN, www.learnquebec.ca.

The Critical Importance of Assessment

As the discussion suggests, collaborative and inquiry approaches to learning require that we consider classroom activities, curriculum, and assessment as a system in which each interdependent aspect is important to an environment that promotes flexible knowledge development. Indeed, our ability to assess—both formatively and summatively—has enormous implications for what we teach, and how effectively. At least three elements of assessment are especially important for meaningful learning of the kind we have been describing:

Designing *intellectually ambitious performance assessments* that define the tasks students will undertake in ways that allow them to learn, and apply the desired concepts and skills in authentic and disciplined ways

Creating guidance for students' efforts in the form of *evaluation tools* such as assignment guidelines and rubrics that define what constitutes good work (and effective collaboration)

Frequently using *formative assessments* to guide feedback to students and teachers' instructional decisions throughout the process

The nature of assessment plays a significant role in shaping the cognitive demands of the work students are asked to undertake. Research suggests that thoughtfully structured performance assessments can support improvement in the quality of teaching, and that inquiry-based learning demands such assessments both to define the task and to properly evaluate what has been learned (Black & Wiliam, 1998b). In addition to finding beneficial influences of performance assessments on teaching practices (Chapman, 1991; Firestone et al., 1998; Herman, Klein, Heath, & Wakai, 1995; Lane et al., 2000; Stecher et al., 1998), some studies have also found that teachers who are involved in scoring performance assessments with other colleagues and discussing their students' work declare the experience helpful in changing their practice to become more problem-oriented and more diagnostic (see Darling-Hammond & Ancess, 1994; Falk & Ort, 1997; Goldberg & Rosewell, 2000; Murnane & Levy, 1996).

A number of studies have found an increase in performance on both traditional standardized tests and performance measures for students in classrooms that offer a problem-oriented curriculum that regularly features performance assessment. For example, in a study of more than two thousand students within twenty-three restructured schools, Newmann, Marks, and Gamoran (1995) found much higher achievement on complex performance tasks for students who experienced what these researchers termed "authentic pedagogy," instruction focused on active learning in real-world contexts calling for higher-order thinking, consideration of alternatives, extended writing, and an audience for student work.

There are many ways in which authentic assessments contribute to learning. For example, exhibitions, projects, and portfolios are occasions for review and revision toward a polished performance. These opportunities help students examine how they learn and how they can perform better. Students are often expected to present their work to an audience—groups of faculty, visitors, parents, other students—to ensure that their apparent mastery is genuine. Presentations of work also signal to students that their work is important enough to be a source of public learning and celebration; they are an opportunity for others in the learning community to see, appreciate, and learn from student work. Performances create living representations of school goals and standards so that they remain vital and energizing, and they develop important life skills. As Ann Brown (1994) observed: "Audiences demand coherence, push for high levels of understanding, require satisfactory explanations, request clarification of obscure points. . . . There are deadlines, discipline, and most important, reflection on performance. We have cycles of planning, preparing, practicing, and teaching others. Deadlines performance demand the setting of priorities—what is important to know? [p. 8]"

Planning, setting priorities, organizing individual and group efforts, exerting discipline, thinking through how to communicate effectively with an audience, understanding ideas well enough to answer the questions of others . . . all of these are tasks people engage in outside of school in their life and work. Good performance tasks are complex intellectual, physical, and social challenges. They stretch students' thinking and planning abilities while also allowing student aptitudes and interests to serve as a springboard for developing competence.

In addition to designing tasks that are intellectually powerful, teachers need to guide students as to the quality of work and interactions they are aiming for. The benefits of clear criteria given in advance have been documented by many studies (for example, Barron et al., 1998). E. G. Cohen and her colleagues tested the idea that clear evaluation criteria could improve student learning by improving the nature of the conversation (Cohen, Lotan, Abram, Scarloss, & Schultz, 2002). They found that introducing evaluation criteria led groups to spend more time discussing content, discussing the assignment, and evaluating their products than groups who were not given criteria. They also found that individual learning scores were significantly correlated with the amount of evaluative and task-focused talk.

The criteria used to assess performances should be multidimensional, representing the various aspects of a task rather than a single grade, and should be openly expressed to students and others in the learning community rather than kept secret in the tradition of content-based examinations (Wiggins, 1989). For example, a research report might be evaluated for its use of evidence, accuracy of information, evaluation of competing viewpoints, development of a clear argument, and attention to conventions of writing. When work is repeatedly assessed, the criteria guide teaching and learning— students become producers and self-evaluators while teachers become coaches. A major goal is to help students develop the capacity to assess their own work against standards, and to revise, modify, and redirect their energies, taking initiative to promote their own progress. This is an aspect of self-directed work and self-motivated improvement required of competent people in many settings, not least a growing number of workplaces.

Use of performance tasks is also important so that we can adequately assess the benefits of problem- and project-based approaches for learning and application of knowledge. For example, Bransford and Schwartz (1999) and Schwartz and Martin (2004) have demonstrated that the outcomes of different instructional conditions might look similar on "sequestered problem solving tasks" but much less so on assessments that gauge students' "preparation for future learning." The preparation for future learning tasks asked students to read new material that was composed to include opportunities to learn. On this kind of task, they found that students who had been in a learning condition where they were first asked to invent a solution to a problem were more likely to learn from the new material than students who had been given traditional instruction consisting of explanations, examples, and practice.

In Table 2 of the Appendix we summarize types of assessment that can be used in long-term inquiry approaches. As the table shows, assessment venues can be construed broadly to include rubrics that are applied to artifacts, whole class discussions, midcourse design reviews, performance assessments, and new transfer problems. The best project-based approaches use a combination of informal ongoing formative assessment and project rubrics that can both communicate high standards and help teachers make judgments about the multiple dimensions of project work. For rubrics to be useful, they must include scoring guides that specify criteria, ideally written for both teachers and students. More research on designing and using such assessments is needed.

Finally, formative assessment is a critical element in learning generally, and it is especially important in the context of long-term, collaborative work. Formative assessment is designed to provide feedback to students so that they can then revise their understanding and their work. It is also used to inform teaching so it can be adapted to meet students' needs. The benefits of formative assessment for learning have been documented in a classic review article (Black & Wiliam, 1998a), which documented that substantial learning gains result from giving students frequent feedback about their learning, especially when that feedback comprises specific comments that can guide students' ongoing efforts.

An important aspect of ongoing assessment is development of students' capacity to assess their own work, so that they internalize standards and become meta-cognitive in their thinking about their own learning. The power of these approaches has been illustrated in many studies (see, e.g., Black & Wiliam, 1998; Magnusson & Palincsar, 2004; Palincsar & Brown, 1984; Paris, Cross, & Lipson, 1984; Schoenfeld, 1992). A useful illustration can be seen in a comparison group study that evaluated the impact of self-assessment on student learning in twelve inquiry-based middle school science classrooms featuring inquiry cycles in which students investigated concepts of force and motion through experiments and computer simulations. The experimental groups used half their time in discussion structured to promote self- and peer-assessment of cognitive goals and processes, while the control group used this time for general discussion of the concept. The study found that students involved in self-assessment showed significantly larger gains on both a conceptual physics test and project scores, and that students with low pretest scores showed the largest gain on all of the outcome measures (Frederiksen & White, 1997). An analysis of formal and informal self-evaluation processes in Australia and England (Klenowski, 1995) concluded that an integrated practice of self-assessment leads students to take a greater responsibility for their own learning, thus cultivating a shift toward intrinsic motivation and internal locus of control.

Research on formative assessment suggests that feedback is more productive when it is focused on student process, rather than product, and keyed on the quality of the work (task-involving) rather than quality of the worker (ego-involving), offering comments instead of grades for students to consider (Black & Wiliam, 1998a; Butler, 1988; Deci & Ryan, 1985). Shepard (2000) suggests that the focus on process and task allows students to see cognitive prowess not as a fixed individual trait but as a dynamic state that is primarily a function of the level of effort in the task at hand (see also Black & Wiliam, 1998a, 1998b). This can support their motivation as they sustain confidence in their own ability to learn.

This is compatible with recent research underscoring the influence of a student's identity as a learner on his or her engagement and approaches to learning. How students see themselves in relation to activities and disciplines can influence the goals they adopt and the strategies they pursue (Boaler & Greeno, 2000; Gee, 2003; Gresalfi & Cobb, 2006; Nasir & Kirshner, 2003). It has been hypothesized that as students become engaged as producers of complex products and organizers of long-term projects, they begin to recognize within themselves capacities that lead them to identify as authors, designers, critical consumers, and analysts (Barron, 2006a, 2006b; Mercier, Barron, O'Connor, 2006). These identities, or possible selves (Markus & Nurius, 1986), in turn can lead to development of learning goals that support continued engagement (Nasir, 2005). The highly engaging nature of inquiry-based approaches is often noted. If these approaches are supported by formative self- and peer-assessments and opportunities for feedback and revision, positive identity construction is reinforced, which may be as important to long-term learning outcomes as near-term knowledge gains (Barron, 2006a, 2006b; Hidi & Renninger, 2006).

It is important to note that there are a set of related practices of importance in the activities we have described: integration of assessment and instruction, systematic use of iterative cycles of reflection and action, and ongoing opportunity for students to improve their work. The practices are grounded in a conception of learning as developmental and a belief that all students will learn from experience and feedback, rather than being constrained by innate ability. As Black and Wiliam (1998a) remark of one of the studies they reviewed:

> An initiative can involve far more than simply adding some assessment exercises to existing teaching—in this case the two outstanding elements are the focus on self-assessment and the implementation of this assessment in the context of a constructivist classroom. On the one hand it could be said that one or other of these features, or the combination of the two, is responsible for the gains, on the other it could be argued that it is not possible to introduce formative assessment without some radical change in classroom pedagogy because, of its nature, it is an essential component of the pedagogic process [p. 9].

Even though formative assessment may be introduced as part of a "radical change in classroom pedagogy," it also creates fundamental changes in teachers' ability to teach effectively. As Darling-Hammond, Ancess, and Falk

(1995) observed in a study of five schools' use of performance assessments to drive high-quality learning, "As [teachers] use assessment and learning dynamically, they increase their capacity to derive deeper understanding of their students' responses; this then serves to structure increased learning opportunities" (p. 131).

CONCLUSION

This section has presented classroom approaches that support sustained inquiry and collaborative work. It is clear that such approaches are critical for preparing students for future learning. The research to date suggests that inquiry-based approaches can be productive and an important way to nurture communication, collaboration, and deep thinking, but it is also challenging to implement them. A major hurdle in implementing these curricula is that they require simultaneous changes in curriculum, instruction, and assessment practices—changes that are often foreign to teachers as well as students (Barron et al., 1998; Blumenfeld, Soloway, Marx, Krajcik, Guzdial, & Palincsar, 1991). Teachers need time—and a community—to support their capacity to organize sustained project work. It takes significant pedagogical sophistication to manage extended projects in classrooms so as to maintain a focus on "doing with understanding" rather than "doing for the sake of doing" (Barron et al., 1998). In the chapters that follow, we examine how meaningful learning that operates from these principles can be pursued in the fields of literacy, mathematics, and science.

READING FOR UNDERSTANDING

2

P. David Pearson, Gina N. Cervetti, and
Jennifer L. Tilson

As we have noted, learning has multiple goals that often require differing approaches. Like other kinds of learning and performance, reading can be experienced in more than one way, from the most mechanical of decoding processes to the most critical of analytic processes. Sometimes—all too often, in fact—reading instruction seems to be based on a conceptualization of reading as a single line of development from simpler to more complex thinking tasks: *first* students develop phonemic awareness and concepts about print; *then* they move into phonics and decoding skills; *then*, once they have the words right, they can do text-based (or lower-level) comprehension; and finally, once they have the facts straight, they can move on to more interpretive, analytic, or critical stances toward text.

On the basis of research and theory, we take a different approach to reading development and instruction. We argue that from the first day readers set eyes on print—indeed, even as they listen to their parents or teachers read text aloud—they must orchestrate movements between many approaches and many stances toward the printed page. Sometimes, such as when the words are obscure to them, readers will operate as if "breaking the code" to translate letters into sound were all that mattered. At other times, they will focus on finding links between the message they are getting from the text and the experiences and knowledge they have stored in their memories, and when they do, we can say that they are taking the stance of a "meaning-maker." At still other times, often when prodded by a teacher to do so, they can deal with questions such as why poetry "hooks" our aesthetic mind and why informational texts are easier to understand when the text is supported with visual images, such as pictures and graphs. When they do, they are focusing on the stance of the "text user," who wants to be sure that the form of the text matches its communicative function. And finally, readers, even young readers, can be encouraged to adopt a critical stance toward text, to be "text critics" by asking questions about why authors depict characters or issues in particular ways—and what effect those depictions have on readers.

This flexible conceptualization of reading, adapted from the work of Freebody and Luke (1990), guides this chapter and is incorporated into our model of *mindful engagement*. Our claim is that when we encourage students to take on these different stances or roles as readers, we help them engage deeply and thoroughly with text in ways that encourage deep understanding and learning.

THE ROLE OF THE READER IN INTERACTING WITH TEXT

The clearest exposition of the range of roles readers can play as they read text is captured in the Four Resources Model (Freebody, 1992; Freebody & Luke, 1990), which explains how readers traverse four "necessary but not sufficient roles"—code breaker, meaning maker, text user, and text critic:

> **Code breaker:** Readers *break the code* of written language by recognizing and using fundamental features and architecture, principally the alphabet, sounds in words, spelling patterns, and structural conventions.

Meaning maker: Readers *participate in understanding and composing* meaningful written, visual, and spoken texts, taking into account each text's interior meaning systems in relation to their available knowledge and their experiences of other cultural discourses, texts, and meaning systems.

Text user: Readers *use texts functionally* by traversing and negotiating the labor and social relations around them, that is, by knowing about and acting on the cultural and social functions that various texts perform in school, work, and social situations, and understanding that these functions shape how texts are structured, their tone, their degree of formality, and their sequence of components.

Text critic: Readers *critically analyze and transform texts* by acting on knowledge that texts are not ideologically natural or neutral; they represent particular points of view while silencing others. They also influence people's ideas, and their designs and discourses can be critiqued and redesigned in novel and hybrid ways [Luke & Freebody, 1999, n.p.; emphasis ours].

These roles can be thought of as describing key goals of classroom literacy programs. They have guided the official curriculum in at least one Australian state, Queensland (see Luke & Freebody, 1999). All of the goals are important. From the perspective of this model, the competent reader is not the one who has settled on a single resource or role to use on all occasions but the one who recognizes that according to the occasion certain resources will occupy center stage and others will play supporting roles from the wings. So breaking the code is likely to be a part of any encounter with text, but it plays a starring role only if the code is obscure (as it would be with really unfamiliar words and patterns) or if knowledge is weak (so readers must struggle through the code to get to even a semblance of word meaning). Critical resources may not be engaged at all unless a student has been guided by a teacher to interrogate the authority of the text, or unless a writer questions the personal values a reader happens to bring to the page in a way that provokes conflict or outrage. We do students and our society a disservice when we fail to offer a curriculum in which all four of these roles are promoted and students receive guidance in determining how to travel back and forth among them.

DEVELOPING MINDFUL ENGAGEMENT

Reading for these several purposes depends not only on a set of academic skills but also on student interest and motivation, and on the reading context. Consequently, we use a somewhat framework for examining reading for understanding that entails both motivational and cognitive aspects of teaching and learning, and the individual and social faces of reading. We call this framework *mindful engagement*.

This framework builds on what we know about learning in general, as well as learning to read in particular. As Bransford, Brown, and Cocking (1999) note in *How People Learn*, learning well depends on (1) how prior knowledge is incorporated in building new knowledge, (2) how knowledge is organized, and (3) how well learners can monitor and reflect on their learning. These important ideas are extended by work on engagement in reading comprehension by Guthrie (Guthrie & Wigfield, 2000) and on teaching for cognitive engagement by Taylor and Pearson (Taylor, Pearson, Peterson, & Rodriguez, 2003). Both Guthrie and Taylor reinforce the notion of mindful engagement—of an active, intentional reader who does all that is necessary to render text meaningful, integrate new understandings with existing knowledge structures, and monitor all the processes and routines required to build and maintain that knowledge.

Discussing books with their peers deepens a student's connection with the text

The *mindful* part of mindful engagement is meant to evoke the cognitive and reflective aspects of reading. Among the things we have learned about reading is that knowledge is both a cause and a consequence of comprehension. Thus prior knowledge influences how well a reader can comprehend a given text; but that very text, once understood, changes the reader's knowledge base, to allow the reader to understand even more ideas the next time she sets eye on print. In short, the text has the capacity to actually alter knowledge structures. In addition, comprehension involves ongoing monitoring to evaluate its consistency with existing knowledge, and readers can invoke specific strategies to fix things up when the going gets tough. Mindful reading involves strategic behavior and monitoring that supports comprehension, connection making, and critique (Afflerbach, Pearson, & Paris, in press; Duke & Pearson, 2002).

The *engagement* part of mindful engagement reminds us that interest, motivation, and personal investment shape and are shaped by the act of comprehending (Guthrie & Wigfield, 2000). We can cope strategically and successfully with very obscure topics if we really want to learn the information. Sometimes our awareness that we have worked through a patch of text successfully gives us the will and stamina to continue, even (maybe especially) in the face of tough material. At still other times, the realization that we engaged together in the task of comprehending a text gives us the motivation to persevere, and feedback from our peers that they appreciate our contribution to some public purpose keeps us on task and a part of the learning community (Afflerbach et al., in press).

In this chapter, we attempt to answer the question, "If reading for understanding can be viewed in terms of mindful engagement, what do we know about instructional contexts that support this kind of involvement?" Our review of research examining the relationship between understanding and learning suggests that (1) the motivational aspects of reading engagement are supported by "immediate" contexts that provoke short-term interests in the moment (such as wanting to be a part of the group) as well as enduring involvement through stimulating ideas, goals, and tasks; and (2) the cognitive aspects of mindful engagement are supported by contexts that demand strategic behavior and intentionality in order to make deep connections among knowledge, experience, and text. We examine three key lines of reading research:

If reading for understanding can be viewed in terms of mindful engagement, what do we know about instructional contexts that support this kind of involvement?

- Research that attempts to improve comprehension and learning by engaging students in *rich talk about text*
- Research that attempts to *teach* cognitive and metacognitive *strategies directly* and intentionally
- Research in which *reading is used as a tool to enhance the development of knowledge and inquiry* in disciplines such as science and social studies

RICH TALK ABOUT TEXT

Many approaches to literacy instruction focus on conversation around text as a key aspect of learning to read for meaning. The belief that social interaction through language is critical to developing the cognitive habits of highly skilled readers follows in part from Vygotsky's notion (1978) that individuals appropriate practices from social contexts and make them part of their personal repertoire. The key element in Vygotsky's theory of learning is that "all the higher functions originate as actual relationships between individuals" (1978, p. 57). In other words, people must interact around ideas if they are to incorporate them into their own thinking repertoire. Vygotsky's work also incorporates the notion that talking about ideas actually helps people organize and clarify their thinking and develop conceptual frameworks that make further learning possible.

Discussion with peers serves as both a forum through which students can sharpen their cognitive skills and deepen their involvement and a motivation for engagement in reading. Thus another key ingredient in fostering the kind of active reading that we term *mindful engagement* is the presence of meaningful social interaction with peers around texts. What distinguishes these approaches is the focus on authentic, student-to-student dialogue about rich texts that mirror important ideas in students' lives, our society, and the various cultural groups students represent and live within.

The positive effects of thoughtful and cognitively challenging discussion on reading achievement have been documented in studies with varying methodologies, ranging from ethnographic description (such as Gambrell & Morrow, 1996; Kong & Pearson, 2003; Raphael & McMahon, 1994) to natural experiments (Nystrand, Gamoran, Kachur, & Prendergast, 1997; Taylor et al., 2003). Taylor and colleagues documented the central role played by teachers in orchestrating student engagement. They found that the most critical ingredient in determining higher achievement in the high-poverty classroom was a teacher who (1) adopted a coaching, modeling, and facilitating stance toward teaching; (2) emphasized a great deal of student responsibility for learning, with less teacher talk and more student talk; (3) employed high-level questions about texts; and (4) elicited more active student responses—reading, writing, and doing rather than listening (Taylor et al., 2003). Relying on qualitative and quasi-experimental evidence, Gambrell and Morrow (1996) also add another element, peer collaboration, as a factor that supports motivation and cognitive development alike.

The importance of student responsibility for learning and peer collaboration is reminiscent of the findings we reviewed earlier regarding inquiry approaches generally. In the context of literacy development, researchers have documented the utility of a number of specific pedagogical approaches for promoting engaged discussion about texts as a key feature of reading for meaning. Among these approaches are Book Club/Book Club Plus, Shared Inquiry, and Instructional Conversations, instructional strategies further discussed below that approach reading as the basis for dialogic interaction with others, all of which can be used flexibly by teachers to encourage higher-order talk about various kinds of texts (see Wilkinson, 2005; Wilkinson, Murphy, & Soter, 2005; Wilkinson & Reninger, 2005 for reviews of this work). Collaborative Reasoning and Collaborative Writing (discussed later) are related approaches that add the element of disciplined argumentation to the conversations and written products peers are engaged in.

In all of these frameworks, it is expected that over time students will assume a degree of control over their own learning, and that they will work toward improving their peer conversations through intentional reflection. It is also worth noting that most of these approaches recommend that the texts used with students be conceptually related through important ideas and over-arching themes. The approaches also share a common belief that higher-order talk—that is, discussions going beyond the literal meaning of a text to engage students in analysis, critique, and evaluation—about related texts is important in fostering increased engagement. This can lead in turn to better comprehension of any particular text in the set as well as texts that students will later encounter on their own. In short, a carefully organized environment for encouraging authentic talk around text can help students grapple with cognitively challenging ideas.

Research-Based Programs
Book Club
A prototype for highly engaged talk about literary texts is Book Club (Raphael, Florio-Ruane, & George, 2001; Raphael & McMahon, 1994). Book Club and its successor, Book Club Plus, are "conceptual frameworks" (2001, p. 1) around which teachers can organize literacy activities and instruction, to give students with varied reading abilities the opportunity to engage in conversation and writing around texts. The framework, which was collaboratively developed by researchers and teachers and is implemented through a professional

development network, was devised with the aim of offering educators a structure that draws on important aspects of literacy learning yet is flexible enough to adapt to particular situations in order to meet the needs of a variety of learners and goals. The key principle is that thinking is made public and forms the basis for a dialogic interaction around texts. Furthermore, the ultimate goal is for students to gain understanding of themselves as members of a social group that is engaged in many cultural practices. Students learn about self and others through reading and conversations about literature, particularly if the literature engages the important themes of human experience—friendship, betrayal, life, death, happiness, sadness, conflict, and harmony (with both nature and humans).

The Book Club framework includes teacher instruction, reading, writing, literature discussion, and group reflection and sharing. A major component involves students' working on their own, primarily in heterogeneous small groups. The literature discussion element, the "Book Club" for which the program is named, is a student-led group during which students discuss ideas that arose during their reading of the text and writing in a reading journal, ask questions of each other to clarify points of confusion as well as discuss themes in the text, and make connections between the text and their lives. These elements are initially separate segments, but they tend to blend together as students become more confident in recording and expressing their ideas as they read (Raphael & McMahon, 1994). As a unit of thematically related study progresses, students are encouraged to make intertextual connections among the texts they have read. Book Club Plus extends the Book Club model, adding time for teacher-directed instruction in leveled texts using the Guided Reading approach (Fountas & Pinnell, 1996), bringing to students a more explicit focus on teacher-directed strategy instruction that can then be applied in their reading and discussion during Book Club.

Through analysis of student writing over the course of a school year, as well as case studies of conversations occurring in classrooms using Book Club,

Raphael and colleagues (2001) demonstrate the growth in critical thinking that occurs when students engage in these conversations around text. For example, when teachers blindly scored writing samples from several points in the year from one struggling student, all agreed that there was significant change on a number of dimensions (Raphael et al., 2001). From transcripts of Book Club conversations, the authors note important changes in the degree to which discussion adheres to the text, types of questions posed by students, and the willingness of students to admit confusion about the text and seek clarification as indicators of increased engagement with reading.

Shared Inquiry

Shared Inquiry discussion, an approach most closely associated with the Junior Great Books Foundation, is another model in which students engage in discussion around literature. The program emphasizes students' taking an active inquiry approach to reading, reasoning with others about the text, and engaging in discussion that includes higher-level inferential questioning. In this approach, students read a shared text, recording their reactions, questions, and points of confusion as they read. Then the teacher or other students pose questions about genuine points of ambiguity in the texts that are subject to interpretation. Students discuss the text, using evidence from the text to support their assertions. Finally, students respond to the text in writing. Like so many other approaches in this family, Shared Inquiry emphasizes inferential reasoning, questioning, and student-to-student talk. It also includes the role of writing as a means to organize and push thinking about the text.

The efficacy of the Shared Inquiry approach is documented in two quasi-experiments in the Chicago Public School system (Kerbow, 1997). The researcher demonstrated that students in fifth and eighth grades who participated in Shared Inquiry discussions with Junior Great Books texts performed better than students in a control group on tests of critical thinking and reading comprehension (Kerbow, 1997). These results suggest the effectiveness of high-level discussion with peers around important ideas in texts as a significant factor in increasing students' ability to read for meaning.

Instructional Conversations

One of the best-documented conversational approaches, Instructional Conversations, begins with the acknowledgment that the discussions we want to promote have existed since the time of Socrates (Goldenberg, 1993; Rueda, Goldenberg, & Gallimore, 1992; Tharp & Gallimore, 1991). Instructional Conversations (ICs) are "discussion-based lessons geared toward creating richly textured opportunities for students' conceptual and linguistic development" (Goldenberg, 1993, p. 317). They can be based on any text. The objective of these conversations is to use the class discussion as a forum to bring ideas to light and to refine them through collaborative consideration.

These discussions, which may appear quite natural to an observer but in fact take a great deal of careful planning and orchestration on the part of the teacher, are about relevant ideas or concepts, are focused, are responsive to students' input, and encourage a high level of participation (Goldenberg, 1991). ICs stand in direct contrast to the recitation model of discussion, wherein the teacher initiates a question, a student responds, and this response is evaluated by the teacher, who then initiates the next questioning cycle (Cazden, 1988). Instead, ICs encourage students to construct knowledge collaboratively, beginning with what is known. As with Shared Inquiry discussions, the teacher's role is not to furnish answers but instead to model the language of academic discussion for students by clarifying, mediating turn taking when necessary, and probing students to think even more deeply about relevant aspects of the conversation.

Research on classrooms using IC techniques, particularly classrooms with a high number of English language learners, is promising. Through discourse analysis, researchers have documented a high level of focus in the conversations, engagement among students, use of student background knowledge, and responsiveness in typical IC sessions (Goldenberg, 1991; Rueda, Goldenberg, & Gallimore, 1992). In a 1999 study, Saunders and Goldenberg demonstrated that fourth- and fifth-grade students who were engaged in Instructional Conversations outperformed students in a control group on tests of story reading comprehension. Combined with use of written literature logs, ICs demonstrate an even greater effect for English language learners, although there was no added significance for English-proficient students in this condition.

Collaborative Reasoning and Writing

Another approach, Collaborative Reasoning (see Clark, Anderson, Archodidou, Nguyen-Jahiel, Kuo, & Kim, 2003), is noteworthy on two counts. First, it appropriates the "adversarial" motif from formal debate by encouraging students to "take sides" on some important moral or ethical question promoted by a selection (typically a story) in which the characters encounter a problem that entails privileging one "good" over another (for example, stealing a bicycle to ride for help in order to save a life, or stealing something to get money to give to someone with no money for food). Students work collaboratively to develop the arguments (claims and evidence) they will use in a class debate about the main issue. On measures of reading comprehension, writing fluency and organization, and reasoning, the evidence favors Collaborative Reasoning (CR) over approaches that discuss the same texts in a more conventional manner.

CR researchers have demonstrated that students become rhetorically skilled as a result of participation in the discussions (Anderson et al., 2001) and are able to transfer their understanding to their writing. Reznitskaya, Anderson, McNurlen, Nguyen-Jahiel, Archodidou, and Kim (2001) compared learning outcomes after five weeks for students in three classrooms that participated in Collaborative Reasoning with those in three classrooms that did not. Students in the Collaborative Reasoning classrooms wrote persuasive essays that included more relevant arguments, counterarguments, rebuttals, formal argument devices, and text-based information.

Sharpening discussion around contentious ideas, when ideas from all participants are taken seriously, may increase the quality of reasoning and writing students engage in. In another study of collaborative writing Dale (1994) examined what factors in group interactions affect the success of writing groups. The writing assignments given to ninth-grade students (who were working in coauthoring triads) were pertinent to their lives and designed to engender cognitive dissonance: arguing for or against mandatory study hall or adolescent access to birth control. After explicitly modeling coauthoring with the classroom teacher and teaching specific lessons on the genre of writing students were to use, Dale found that the more successful groups engaged each other's ideas more fully—seeking elaboration, clarification, evaluation, and alternatives in the discussion of the possible directions for their group paper—and engaged in more cognitive conflict. This allowed them to see more perspectives, in a sense to "see" the cognitive processes of their group members through their communication, which leads to greater learning (Damon, 1984).

In terms of the three big ideas that frame this volume, discussions of this sort (1) account for and capitalize on prior knowledge, (2) promote coherent knowledge frameworks for ideas encountered in the readings and further developed in discussion or writing, and (3) encourage students to monitor their reading by employing two key resources: the ideas in the texts and the knowledge they bring to the task.

Rich Talk About Text and Mindful Engagement

All of these instructional approaches promote mindful engagement in reading (and, in some cases, writing) through rich, intellectual conversation with peers about texts. This kind of social interaction around texts motivates reading and is a forum in which to learn about what mindful engagement looks like. In terms of the three big ideas that frame this volume, discussions of this sort (1) account for and capitalize on prior knowledge, (2) promote coherent knowledge frameworks for the ideas encountered in the readings and for ideas further developed in discussion or writing, and (3) encourage students to monitor their reading by employing the two key resources available to them: the ideas in the texts they read and the knowledge they bring to the task.

Teaching as Coaching

In all four of the approaches reviewed, the teacher assumes a range of supportive roles—model, coach, and facilitator—while resisting the traditional role of dispenser of wisdom and knowledge. In Instructional Conversations, for example, rather than the teacher posing questions with the intent of finding out how well students have understood the text, she guides the students toward considering many aspects of important concepts and ideas reflectively and carefully. Students are accountable to the group for thinking deeply about what they read and for identifying and considering themes carefully. This type of social interaction around challenging ideas promotes greater attention to reading for meaning and shifts the classroom focus to coconstruction of ideas among readers.

Making Thinking Public and Coconstructing Understandings About Text

In all of the instructional approaches reviewed, the students construct their understanding of the text by making their thinking public through use of language, learning that it is important to be aware of and seek clarification when one does not understand. For example, one of the elements that differentiate a Shared Inquiry discussion from a traditional recitation model of classroom interaction is the presence of genuine wondering in the questions that are posed by teachers and students alike. Students are engaged in reading in this approach because of the emphasis on returning to the text to untangle important ideas and ferret out the motivations for characters' actions that have multiple possible explanations. Because of this genuine opportunity for coconstruction of understanding about the text, students can become more active participants in discussion about their reading.

Discussing Important Ideas in Thematically Related Texts

Students discuss socially and culturally significant texts with others within a community of readers. The underlying message for students in all of these classrooms is that texts constitute the means to consider important themes, concepts, and ideas with others in order to come to a deeper understanding about the world. The Book Club framework, for example, not only gives students an opportunity to interact with peers in conversations where genuine questioning of the text is valued and encouraged but also uses thematically related texts to deepen students' understanding of the themes in the literature they read.

Illustrating the Value of Talk About Text for Mindful Engagement

To illustrate the power of social interaction around texts to promote mindful engagement, we offer a vignette from an article by Damico and Riddle (2004), which details Riddle's experience in learning to design instruction that engaged students in authentic discussion of complex topics related to social justice. In the vignette, students voice their questions and ideas about an important theme in related texts. The discussion took place in Riddle's fifth-grade classroom. For this unit of study, she carefully selected a set of thirteen related texts (biographies, picture books, films, and songs) that centered on the issues of freedom and slavery. Thus Riddle was enacting the principle of using thematically related texts to help students grapple with big ideas. After reading two of these texts, a student raised a question that sparked a lively, extended discussion.

> Aaron: Does anybody really know what freedom means?
>
> [. . .]
>
> Teacher: OK, Aaron. Why are you asking that question?
>
> Aaron: The reason I am asking this question is because everybody, every person that has said something, I am all hearing the same things almost.
>
> [. . .]

Teacher: OK. I am writing down your question because I think it is really good, so give me a second. Does anybody really know the definition of freedom? And is it true? Is there anybody who can respond to Aaron's question?

Aaron's question indicated that he saw connections among comments that his classmates had raised in discussions, the texts at hand, and a central theme. Reflecting on the big ideas in related texts set a context in which Aaron could pose this question. In addition, the teacher's role in this initial interchange is not a didactic one; she has taken more of a coaching role in order to facilitate students' construction of meaning around the texts. This is evident through her response to Aaron's question, her recording of the question, and how she turns the discussion back to the students. The teacher encourages students to interact with each other around the question that Aaron has raised. Although she is regulating some turn taking, the students have conceptual control over the conversation.

As the discussion continued, other students had further ideas to contribute.

Neil: OK, to answer Aaron's question, freedom is defined in the dictionary, but the dictionary doesn't have to mean that that is the only definition. Lots of people have different opinions. Just because *Webster's* says that freedom means something, that could or could not be true, because we all have our opinions. And like freedom is . . . actually I don't think any of us can really define it in the way that we best could because we never really have had the point in our lives where we have been totally free yet.

Aaron: That's what I am trying to do.

Teacher: OK, who is the next person to go? Alicia?

Alicia: My opinion is that there are various definitions of freedom. It depends on who you are talking to. If you are talking to somebody who has less freedom than you, it might mean something different for them than somebody with more freedom.

In this portion of the discussion, students are clearly interacting with each other as well as with the teacher. They are making their thinking public by explaining their ideas and adding dimensions of meaning to the concept of *freedom*. As Damico and Riddle note, Neil questions the dictionary as a source and explains the importance of relating one's own experience to text. Similarly, Alicia points out the importance of social context and raises the idea that there can be differing amounts of freedom. Through sharing their ideas, students are beginning to coconstruct understandings about the text. These understandings both reflect the texts and go beyond them.

Strategy Instruction

One of the key understandings to emerge from research on basic reading processes in the early years of the cognitive revolution (circa 1975 to 1980) is that good readers are not only better at reading and comprehending text; they are also much more intentional, strategic, and mindful about their reading when the situation calls for it. A vast pedagogical enterprise called "strategy instruction" emerged from this understanding that good readers did not just "do reading" but were thoughtful about their own understanding (or lack of understanding) in developing plans for fixing comprehension when it went awry.

This recent ascendancy of strategy instruction in reading curriculum is due, at least in part, to a positive review of research on this approach in the report of the National Reading Panel (2000), which concluded that the experimental evidence was strong enough to merit the teaching of several effective strategies. Indeed, over the past thirty years, increasing evidence has supported explicit teaching of cognitive (how to do X) and metacognitive (how to monitor whether X helped with comprehension) strategies, because their effects have been thoroughly documented in numerous independent reviews

(Dole, Duffy, Roehler, & Pearson, 1991; Duke & Pearson, 2001; Pressley, 2000; Rosenshine & Meister, 1994). Converging evidence for a range of cognitive and metacognitive strategies has emerged in reading (see Almasi, 2003; Pearson & Gallagher, 1983), writing (Graham & Perin, 2007), mathematics (Schoenfeld, Chapter Three of this book), science (Zimmerman & Stage, in Chapter Four of this book), cognitive psychology (see, e.g., Paris, Lipson, & Wixson, 1983, 1994), and special education (see Deshler & Shumaker, 1986; Graham & Harris, 2005a, 2005b).

Applications of this research in reading have been driven by two related questions:

> What strategies do skilled readers use to make sense of text, especially when they find themselves in a "tricky" situation (for instance, dense, inaccessible text, or a difficult comprehension task)?
>
> If you teach those very same strategies to less skilled readers, does their comprehension improve?

The particular configuration of cognitive and metacognitive strategies for reading varies slightly with the research synthesis, but the family resemblance among the efforts is strong. The list from the National Reading Panel (NRP; 2000) report illustrates the core members of the "family":

Comprehension monitoring
Cooperative learning
Graphic organizers
Story structure
Question answering
Question generation
Summarization
"Suites" of strategies that combine several components

To be sure, some of the entries in the NRP list may not be all of the same ilk; for example, cooperative learning seems more of an instructional format medium than a strategy for comprehending text, and comprehension monitoring seems more metacognitive than cognitive—and thus widely applicable. In spite of these quibbles, the differences among the various lists are more matters of style and preference than substance (see Duke & Pearson, 2002; Pearson, Roehler, Dole, & Duffy, 1992; Pressley, 1998). In short, there is a high degree of consensus about what should be taught in the name of strategy instruction. More important, the empirical evidence for single strategy instruction (see Duke & Pearson, 2002; National Reading Panel, 2000) is substantial and consistent: students who learn specific strategies can apply them, resulting in increased comprehension of the texts to which they are applied and transfer to the comprehension of new passages.

The major strategy "suites" in reading instruction, which combine multiple strategies into a coherent approach, are Reciprocal Teaching (Palincsar & Brown, 1984; Rosenshine & Meister, 1994) and Transactional Strategies Instruction (Brown, Pressley, Van Meter, & Schuder, 1996). The goal of these suites or routines is that students who use them consistently will achieve "(a) better understanding of the texts to which the routines are applied, and (b) the development of an infrastructure of processes that will benefit encounters with future text, especially texts that students must negotiate on their own" (Duke & Pearson, 2002, p. 225). Reciprocal Teaching calls for instruction of a routine that includes prediction, questioning, seeking clarification, and summarizing as a set of strategies that help students construct meaning from text. Transactional Strategies Instruction (TSI) includes a large number of cognitive and interpretative strategies—among them thinking aloud, constructing images, creating themes, predicting, clarifying, analyzing story grammar or text structure, making connections, summarizing, questioning, and reading to identify literary elements such as theme and plot—and emphasizes the metaphor of a tool kit from which students pick strategies that fit the situation at hand (as described in Duke & Pearson, 2002).

Both Reciprocal Teaching and Transactional Strategies Instruction have social dimensions. In reciprocal teaching, teachers turn over responsibility for conducting the discussions and monitoring their quality and focus as soon as possible. In TSI, teachers and students work together to select and enact strategies for a given text. Thus making meaning in both approaches is a community process.

The empirical evidence for both Reciprocal Teaching and TSI is quite encouraging. Rosenshine and Meister (1994) concluded, after reviewing sixteen studies, that Reciprocal Teaching is effective at improving comprehension of text. The effect was visible for both standardized tests, and to an even greater extent for experimenter-developed comprehension tests. P.J. Moore (1988) reached a similar conclusion after reviewing a number of studies. Transactional Strategies Instruction (see Pressley, 1998) has also been documented as effective in both qualitative and quasi-experimental studies.

On the question of how to teach strategies, after reviewing scores of studies of both the individual strategy and "suite" variety, Duke and Pearson abstracted a set of steps that typically occur in explicit strategy instruction:

- Naming and describing the strategy—why, when, and how it should be used
- Modeling the strategy in action—either by teacher or student, or both
- Using the strategy collaboratively—in a sort of group think-aloud
- Guiding practice using the strategy with gradual release of responsibility
- Using the strategy independently—with no teacher guidance, either individually or in small student-led groups

Metacognitive Strategies

Another crucial aspect of strategy instruction is work on metacognition, or the ability to think about and monitor one's own learning so as to improve it. As Baker (2002) notes: "There is a sequence of development from other-regulation to self-regulation. This notion provides the framework for virtually all instructional programs in which the goal is to enable students to take responsibility for their own learning" (p. 78). Baker emphasizes that motivation and social interaction influence metacognition, just as they do other kinds of learning. Further, metacognitive strategies add "will" to "skill" in extending what students can accomplish by learning specific cognitive tactics (see Paris, Lipson, & Wixson, 1983; Paris, Wasik, & Turner, 1991).

Many studies have documented how explicit teaching of metacognitive strategies can improve learning for a range of students. This research has often studied the thought processes of experts and then organized them for teaching to novices engaged in that work. An example in the area of literacy learning illustrates both how metacognitive strategies are studied and applied and how they help students improve their learning. The theoretical base begins with Vygotsky (1978), who suggested that talking things through, internally or aloud, actually helps people learn by helping them organize and manage their thought process. In fact, studies of writers have found that they engage in an internal dialogue in which they talk to themselves (sometimes even muttering aloud) about audience, purpose, form, and content. They ask and answer for themselves questions about who they are writing for, why, what they know, and how ideas are organized as they plan, draft, edit, and revise. They guide their thinking with metacognitive strategies that help them write purposefully.

This basic research has led to strategies for teaching writing that help novice writers learn how to engage in this kind of self-talk and self-monitoring as they go through similar processes. In one study, teachers of fourth- and fifth-grade learning-disabled and nonlearning-disabled students were taught how to implement these strategies in their classroom by analyzing texts, modeling the writing process, guiding students as they wrote, and giving students opportunities for independent writing over the course of a year (Englert, Raphael, & Anderson, 1992). Analyses were conducted for an intervention

Focusing on Literacy

J.E.B. Stuart High School, in suburban Falls Church, Virginia, once ranked among its district's lowest performers on state exams. Today, a focus on literacy has helped transform Stuart into an internationally recognized model of achievement. The school has received awards from the International Center for Leadership in Education, the Education Trust, and the Bill & Melinda Gates Foundation, among other organizations.

The most recent accolades came from the National Association of Secondary School Principals, which chose Stuart's principal, Mel Riddile, as 2006 Principal of the Year and named Stuart a Breakthrough High School in 2003.

More important, the school's reading-proficiency scores on the Virginia Standards of Learning tests rose from 64 percent in 1998 to 94 percent in 2004.

ADDRESSING THE FUNDAMENTALS

Just over half of Stuart's nearly fifteen hundred students come from low-income homes, and two-thirds speak English as a second language. Spanish, Vietnamese, Somali, Chinese, Urdu, and other languages blend with English in Stuart's halls. The student body is so diverse—41 percent Hispanic, 25 percent white, 21 percent Asian, 10 percent black, and 3 percent "other"—that *National Geographic* has featured it as a microcosm of the changing U.S. society.

In 1997, when Riddile arrived at the school, teachers identified the biggest obstacles to student achievement as rampant absenteeism and poor reading skills. Students missed an average of twenty-three days annually, and three-fourths of them read at least two years below grade level.

By 2003, increased vigilance and automated 6:00 A.M. wake-up calls had reduced the average absentee rate to seven days. However, improving reading levels necessitated a cultural shift that was driven by Riddile's insistence that all teachers teach reading.

Riddile started by hiring a literacy coach and amassing data. Each spring, the specialist administers the Gates-MacGintie reading test to eighth graders in Stuart's primary feeder school; those who score poorly also undergo individual screening. Although all freshmen take a required literacy course that includes online, individualized instruction, struggling readers get an additional course—taught by a literacy expert—for remediation on history, science, and other core subjects. Students who need extra help also receive tutoring. Stuart's A/B schedule affords ample time for difficult subjects: classes alternate from day to day, and most class blocks are just over ninety minutes long.

TEACHER DEVELOPMENT

Student progress is closely monitored throughout the school. Academic success, Riddile believes, "is not about the ability of our students. It's about our ability to teach them." As a former social studies teacher, he understood some staffers' initial resistance to thinking of themselves as reading instructors. "We had new state standards, they had content to cover, and nobody ever taught them how to teach reading," Riddile said. But data convinced them they needed to adapt to students' learning styles.

Professional development begins with a college course and continues at the school. The literacy coach observes teachers in their classrooms, modeling strategies and offering discreet follow-up suggestions. She also conducts quarterly in-service training for all teachers new to Stuart, so they learn core strategies such as the text-comprehension exercise K-W-L (know, want, learn), which asks students to jot down what they know about a subject before reading, what they want to know as they read and discuss, and finally what they've learned or still want to learn.

Some teachers admit being hesitant to try the new strategies at first but see positive results in students' grasp of concepts. "We've found a strong correlation between literacy and math," said math chair Stuart Singer. "We don't spend our time exclusively with numbers."

Monthly faculty meetings feature staff development in numerous kinds of literacy. The music department led a program on dynamic markings, the symbols based on Italian words that indicate expression on a score. In a faculty meeting, Colin McDaniel, who teaches an upper-level ESL class, conducted a content-area lesson in Nepali—which he learned in the Peace Corps—so that colleagues could experience the challenges confronting English language learners.

Over the years, a common instructional language has emerged at Stuart. "This gives students a structure," said literacy coach Louise Winney, adding that it also creates consistency, essential for reluctant readers.

The coach receives coaching as well as the teachers. The school district schedules training for literacy-class teachers at all grade levels as part of an intensified, systemwide literacy focus dating back at least five years.

REACHING OUT

To strengthen alignment, Stuart works with its feeder schools. For example, once a month, ESL instructor Nancy Svendsen leads as many as forty-five student volunteers to nearby Bailey's Elementary School, where they read to kindergartners. A week in advance, group members choose a picture book and polish their teaching techniques. Reading *Goldilocks and the Three Bears* to young Rayhan Alam, junior Tony Truong broke off to point to an illustration and ask, "Which one is the little bear? Who do you think you'll see on the next page?" Han responded, "Maybe Goldilocks?"

The cognitive strategy of questioning helps "build a bridge from this book to that kid," explained Svendsen, who started the program to help her students develop better reading, speaking, and leadership skills.

"We're very lucky, because we have good programs and teachers who have big expectations for the students," says Nelly Samaniego, liaison to the school's Hispanic Parent Teacher Student Association, a subset of the larger PTSA.

Parents are also involved. The nonprofit J.E.B. Stuart Scholarship Foundation, spun off from the PTSA, awards $500 to $2,000 to up to thirty-five students a year. "Some of our kids are not here legally, so they can't get aid from government," career specialist Carol Kelley explained. "Even kids who are legal have trouble affording school." Yet currently at least 90 percent of Stuart's graduates go on to postsecondary education.

MORE INFORMATION

A video on literacy strategies in a Las Vegas school can be viewed at www.edutopia.org/las-vegas-c-p-squires -elementary.

Adapted from Edutopia article "Reading Rules: The Word of the Day Is 'Literacy,'" by Carol Guensburg. Originally published Feb. 2006.

group and a matched comparison group of students selected from a larger pool of students from seven urban schools participating in a broader research study. In each group, half of the students were learning disabled and half were not. The study found that the groups whose teachers had received the special training engaged in more self-regulating metacognitive strategies and were more able to explain their writing process. This ability was positively and significantly related to measures of their academic performance in reading and writing. Although there were significant differences in the writing knowledge of learning-disabled and nonlearning-disabled students within the comparison group, the learning-disabled students whose teachers had special training were just as able to describe and use the writing strategies—such as the ability to organize, evaluate, and revise their papers appropriately—as were the regular education students in the comparison group. Sometimes, the learning-disabled students who received this strategy instruction even outscored the regular education students.

Strategy Instruction and Mindful Engagement

Through its focus on monitoring learning, strategy instruction supports mindful engagement in its dual commitment to both short-term and more enduring motives for achieving deeper understanding. The knowledge-experience-text connection is strengthened in this process; students learn to monitor the meaning of text against the standards of their knowledge and experience to see if it passes muster. Motivation is enhanced as students learn that they can solve their own problems while reading and as they work with their peers to understand and interpret texts.

Strategy instruction reflects the three learning principles we began with—drawing on prior knowledge, organizing knowledge, and monitoring learning—in several ways. The most obvious connection is in the ways students are taught to monitor their comprehension. They learn to make sure that the current meaning they have constructed for a text at any moment meets the constraints of both the text and their own knowledge, and they learn to guide their ongoing attempts to achieving deeper understanding. Indeed, no other pedagogical approach is as transparently dedicated to this enterprise. In addition, a number of strategies explicitly teach students how to access their prior knowledge as they read; readers are taught to constantly test their current sense of meaning of the text against their store of knowledge. Finally, the strategies organize knowledge about the act of reading or writing as they present models of *how* to understand or produce text, for example, by enunciating steps to follow, questions to guide the reading or writing process, guides to story structure, or processes to create graphic organizers, all of which implicitly or explicitly organize knowledge about texts and how they are created and interpreted.

> Strategy instruction reflects the three learning principles we began with: drawing on prior knowledge, organizing knowledge, and monitoring learning.

Reciprocal Teaching sessions are intended to take approximately thirty minutes and can include more than one student in the role of teacher in each session. Although typically conducted in small groups, Reciprocal Teaching has been conducted in one-to-one and whole group formats. The approach has been used with both good and struggling readers. Here are dialogues from Reciprocal Teaching with students struggling with the technique:

Teacher: What would be a good question about pit vipers that starts with the word "why"?

Student: (No response)

Teacher: How about, "Why are the snakes called pit vipers?"

[. . .]

Student: How do spinner's mate is smaller than. How am I going to say that?

Teacher: Take your time with it. You want to ask a question about the spinner's mate and what he does, beginning with the word "how."

Student:	How do they spend most of his time sitting?
Teacher:	You're very close. The question would be "How does spinner's mate spend most of his time?" Now you ask it.
[. . .]	
Teacher:	That was a fine job, Ken, but I think there might be something to add to our summary. There is more information that I think we need to include. This paragraph is mostly about what?
Student:	The third method of artificial evaporation.

(Palincsar & Brown, 1984; also quoted in
Rosenshine & Meister, 1994)

This next dialogue comes from a first-grade classroom employing Reciprocal Teaching.

Student 1:	My question is, what does the aquanaut need when he goes underwater?
Student 2:	A watch.
Student 3:	Flippers.
Student 4:	A belt.
Student 1:	Those are all good answers.
Teacher:	Nice job! I have a question too. Why does the aquanaut wear a belt? What is so special about it?
Student 3:	It's a heavy belt and keeps him from floating up to the top again.
Teacher:	Good for you.
Student 1:	For my summary now: This paragraph was about what aquanauts need to take when they go under the water.
Student 5:	And also about why they need those things.
Student 3:	I think we need to clarify *gear*.
Student 6:	That's the special things they need.

Teacher:	Another word for gear in this story might be equipment, the equipment that makes it easier for the aquanauts to do their job.
Student 1:	I don't think I have a prediction to make.
Teacher:	Well, in the story they tell us that there are "many strange and wonderful creatures" that the aquanauts see as they do their work. My prediction is that they'll describe some of these creatures. What are some of the strange creatures you already know about that live in the ocean?
Student 6:	Octopuses.
Student 3:	Whales?
Student 5:	Sharks!
Teacher:	Let's listen and find out. Who'll be our teacher?

(Palincsar & Brown, 1986)

The important role of the teacher as guide is evident throughout the dialogues. In addition to the modeling and scaffolding represented here, the teacher routinely reminds students of why these strategies are important and how they will help students in their reading. Two of the three fundamental principles of teaching for understanding are remarkably transparent. In both scenarios, teachers do much to highlight the relationship between old knowledge and new information and to encourage monitoring of learning. Less transparent is the focus on organizing new information into integrated knowledge frameworks. For that emphasis, the third context, integrated instruction, is more relevant.

INTEGRATED INSTRUCTION

A third approach to designing contexts for mindful engagement in literacy focuses on integrating reading and writing with subject-matter learning. Situating literacy instruction in subject areas, such as science or social studies,

Geo-Literacy: Immersive, Cross-Disciplinary Learning

At Tolenas Elementary School, in Fairfield, California, a recent third-grade class created an informational Web site that presents local history, geology, and geography in a format that makes use of digital photos, video footage, and audio and written interviews. In working on this considerable undertaking, the students developed a sense of what their teacher, Eva La Mar, calls "geo-literacy." She defines the term as "the use of visual learning and communication tools to build an in-depth understanding—or 'literacy'—of geography, geology, and local history."

CREATING A MASTER PLAN

Rush Ranch, the subject of the class project, is located in the San Francisco Bay Area and is a large area of marsh and land that was once a Native American village and later a working ranch. Now owned by the Solano County Farmlands and Open Space Foundation, Rush Ranch's remaining buildings have been converted into an information center and a blacksmith shop.

Successful geo-literacy projects take planning. Before beginning the project, La Mar worked with her students to develop an essential question to be answered through their interviews and other research: Why is the preservation of Rush Ranch important?

The class used books and Web sites to research the ranch. From these sources, they decided that the essential question might be answered by studying three aspects of the site in particular: the Native Americans who had lived on the land, the blacksmith's shop that stands on the property, and the plants and animals that live in the marshlands. The disciplines involved with these subjects would also facilitate cross-curricular learning.

Working in groups and keeping the essential question in mind (and on the board), students developed questions that they wanted to answer and noted items that they might want to photograph with digital cameras. They filled out planning sheets before visiting the ranch to be sure they got the information they were looking for.

SETTING CONTEXT

According to La Mar, geo-literacy focuses on local history, but not exclusively. Ideally, this type of learning lends a deeper understanding to larger themes of traditional curricula, such as U.S. history and world history.

La Mar says that the secret is finding a "bridge," a piece of prior knowledge that can be used to help students make the connection between a national event and a piece of local history. For the Rush Ranch project, she asked her students to learn about their own family histories and incorporate them into a timeline. The class then read a book about Bavarian immigrant Levi Strauss and other Gold Rush settlers. They discussed the reasons the settlers moved to California, comparing those reasons to the ones that brought their own families to Solano County.

Finding out students' prior knowledge means understanding their circumstances. Many of the students had never traveled outside of their community. So it was important, La Mar said, to use maps, movies, books, and Internet research to build their knowledge about the larger world before the project was even begun.

COMBINING DISCIPLINES

The Rush Ranch project also involved science: geology, geography, and the study of plants and animals. In presenting the information, students practiced research and writing skills as well. "Our students became the authors, the photographers, the videographers, and the local historians," La Mar said. They learned to examine ecology and other elements of science and geology, showing their interconnectedness with human settlement patterns and geography.

After the students shared their newfound knowledge, each used an AlphaSmart portable keyboard to type up findings. (La Mar's school allows teachers to check out a classroom set of the keyboards.) Students then took turns connecting their devices to one of the room's five desktop computers and watching as their writing appeared onscreen in a Microsoft Word document. These documents formed the basis of the students' Web writing.

Some of the work of creating the Web site was beyond third graders' abilities, La Mar said. To fill the gap, she enlisted help from Armijo High School's Women in Technology (WIT) program in creating panoramic shots and taking video footage. Students from Fairfield High School's multimedia program came to the classroom to help with object rotation, using QuickTime Virtual Reality (QTVR) software. This technology allows the Web site to show objects such as a black bear skull from many angles, giving the user a more complete experience. Fairfield multimedia teacher Kathy Link and Mike Keisling, who heads the WIT program, emphasized the benefits of this work for their students in terms of skill practice and volunteer experience, for future employment, college admissions, and scholarships.

GOING BEYOND

To assess her students' work, La Mar worked with them to create rubrics for the project. In addition, she inserted minilessons into the project to reinforce standards. Much of the impetus for the focus on standards comes from parents: although they appreciate the creative curriculum, they want to make sure their children continue to meet state and national standards. (In 2001 Tolenas Elementary School was one of four schools in Northern Solano County to reach California's target score of 800 of a possible 1000 on the Academic Performance Index. Only 18 percent of schools statewide reached that goal.)

Since this first project, La Mar's classes have done others like it. An important feature of her geo-literacy concept is its replicable nature. La Mar advises schools that want to participate to "pick a specific region, perhaps an old building, an old school house, or a park. Start with that and then build on it each year."

She added that the possibilities aren't limited to traditionally "historic" locations. "I first thought when I went to Solano County, 'What history is there?' But once you start digging in and you talk to local historians, you find some of the stories. Look for old trails. Look at the geography. . . . How many quarries do you have on your land? Where did the rock from those quarries go? What monuments are in the area, or what geological aspects? Start learning about the history of [your area]. It's quite fascinating."

MORE INFORMATION

- The Rush Ranch multimedia Web site created by Eva La Mar's class can be found at www.geolit .org/rushranch.
- To view a video about this project, visit www .edutopia.org/geo-literacy-project.
- For more on the Geo-Literacy Project model and other student projects, go to http://geolit.org.

Adapted from Edutopia article "Geo-Literacy: Using Technology to Forge New Ground," by Ashley Ball. Originally published June 2, 2003.

can create an engaging and authentic context for literacy learning and can invite meaningful involvement in reading and writing. Not only do subject-matter disciplines create a setting in which students can "practice" applying their discrete reading and writing strategies, they also foster opportunities for sophisticated and dynamic enactment of these strategies in the service of learning about the world.

Approaches to reading in contexts where the learning goals emphasize acquiring the knowledge or skills of another discipline may tend toward a more functional view of literacy, employing reading, writing, and discourse as a set of tools and processes that people use to acquire knowledge in other domains; or conversely they may treat subject-matter domains as opportunities to motivate or to authenticate literacy practices. Reading and writing in subject areas can be taught and applied as means to build knowledge and to partici-pate in the kinds of inquiry that are characteristic of the discipline. In addition, vocabulary and world knowledge stimulate further literacy development.

The literature on integrated instruction includes a growing body of instructional research (e.g., Guthrie & Ozgungor, 2002, and Hapgood, Magnusson, & Palincsar, 2004). This research is based on theory regarding the efficacy of integrated curriculum (see Gavelek, Raphael, Biondo, & Danhua, 1999; Yore et al., 2004) and a substantial body of professional wisdom embo-died by analyses of the very best practices of our very best teachers (Pressley, Wharton-McDonald, Rankin, Mistretta, Yokoi, & Ettenberger, 1996). Here, we focus on notable lines of instructional research that shed light on the potential of integrating subject-matter learning with literacy development.

Research-Based Programs
Concept-Oriented Reading Instruction (CORI)

Guthrie and his colleagues have demonstrated that a content-area focus can motivate meaningful involvement in reading and writing, through their work on Concept-Oriented Reading Instruction, or CORI (Guthrie, Anderson,

Alao, & Rinehart, 1999; Guthrie & Ozgungor, 2002). CORI is a framework for instruction that involves students in a series of activities around broad themes in science and social studies. The goal of CORI is to increase students' intrinsic motivation and sustained, strategic reading engagement. CORI is built around a knowledge goal in science or social studies; within that goal it supports firsthand experience, reading, strategy instruction, and opportunities for peer collaboration. CORI abets direct instruction of reading strategies, such as questioning, activating background knowledge, and summarizing—within a context that allows students to develop in-depth knowledge and become experts on a content-area topic. Guthrie and Ozgungor (2002) suggest that learning reading strategies is supported by students' developing bank of knowledge. The content context supports "both the cognitive and motivational aspects of reading engagement" (Guthrie & Ozgungor, 2002, p. 280). An important characteristic of CORI is coherence, or the linking of activities and content in ways that enable students to make connections between experience and reading, strategies and content, and literary and scientific texts.

An integrated curriculum strengthens literacy development and boosts knowledge in exciting ways

Guthrie and colleagues (1999) reported on a year-long study in five third- and fifth-grade classrooms that compared CORI students with those in traditionally organized classrooms. They found that the CORI program increased students' strategy use, conceptual learning, and text comprehension. In a related study, Guthrie and colleagues (2006) investigated the impact of integrated curricula involving firsthand experiences on reading motivation. The study involved ninety-eight students in four grade-three classrooms, all of which used the CORI model and offered reading strategy instruction. Two teachers created a high number of stimulating tasks (hands-on science) and two others created a low number. Findings supported the researchers' hypothesis that students who experience more interest-based reading episodes will have a greater increase in reading comprehension than students who experience fewer interest-based reading episodes. It is not just the number of experiences that matters, however. The researchers suggest "that for stimulating tasks to have lasting effects on motivation and comprehension they must be connected conceptually to further knowledge" (Guthrie et al., 2006, p. 234).

Guided Inquiry Supporting Multiple Literacies (GIsML)

Palincsar and Magnusson (2001) have a program of research regarding secondhand or text-based experiences in science. The research has concerned how secondhand (text-based) investigations can further common inquiry to advance students' understanding of science concepts and support students' ability to reason scientifically. The context of Palincsar and Magnusson's work is the Guided Inquiry Supporting Multiple Literacies (GIsML) program of professional development. In GIsML, teachers establish the classroom as a community of inquiry and engage students in cycles of investigation guided by specific questions. GIsML combines firsthand and secondhand experiences, particularly through use of a fictional scientist's notebook. The notebook models the posing of scientific questions, describes investigations of the fictional scientist, and reports data collected by the scientist. The notebook is designed to be used interactively by students. Students compare the results of their own investigations with those of the scientist and interpret data along with the scientist (Palincsar & Duke, 2004). The texts also model a scientist using secondhand materials, reading critically, interpreting data, and drawing conclusions. After students investigate scientific questions, they consult text to learn about others' interpretations.

In a quasi-experimental study comparing the learning outcomes of fourth-grade students studying light in classrooms using GIsML, with students in classrooms using considerate expository text (designed for easier understanding) the results indicated that text genre did make a difference in the knowledge that students developed from reading (Palincsar & Magnusson, 2001). Students learned more in the GIsML instruction using the scientist's notebook texts (they recalled more information and were better able to make inferences based on the text) than when they read the considerate expository text. Palincsar and Magnusson found the notebooks encouraged classroom conversations that reflected the inquiry process and fostered opportunities for students to engage in coconstruction of understanding about light.

Valle Imperial Project in Science (VIPS)

These approaches are also productive in use with English language learners. For example, a four-year instructional project in one rural California school district, the Valle Imperial Project in Science, combined modules from several kit-based inquiry-oriented science programs with a focus on writing through the use of science notebooks. Students used the notebooks to collect, record, analyze, and report data for their inquiry units, in English whenever possible. Using the notebooks was intended to help students develop knowledge of science content and enhance their English writing skills. The researchers found consistent positive relationships between the number of years that the EL students participated in the program (from zero to four) and their performance on standardized assessments of science, reading, writing, and mathematics administered in English (Amaral, Garrison, & Klentschy, 2002).

In-Depth Expanded Applications of Science (IDEAS)

Romance and Vitale (1992, 2001) developed the IDEAS model of integrated science and language arts instruction. IDEAS replaced the time allocated for traditional literacy instruction with a two-hour block of science instruction that included attention to reading and language arts skills. The science instruction was concept-focused and involved firsthand experiences, attention to science process skills, discussion, reading, concept mapping, and journal writing. Teachers implementing IDEAS typically engaged students in reading activities after hands-on activities, to ensure "that students had the learning experiences needed to make critical reading more purposeful" (Romance & Vitale, 1992, p. 547).

Romance and Vitale have demonstrated through a long program of research that IDEAS students outpace students receiving their regular language arts and science programs on nationally normed standardized measures (the Metropolitan Achievement Test-Science, Iowa Test of Basic Skills-Reading, and Stanford Achievement Tests-Reading). IDEAS students also consistently display significantly more positive attitudes and self-confidence toward both science and reading. Romance and Vitale suggest—and we concur—that there is reason to rethink the emphasis on basal reading materials, because they do not expose students to structured conceptual knowledge and do not prepare students for the kinds of reading they will ultimately have to do to understand ideas within academic disciplines.

Historical Reasoning and Argumentative Writing

Earlier in this chapter we described the power of collaborative reasoning and writing focused on argumentation for building students' reading comprehension and writing abilities. These principles extend to strategies that ground literacy development in the context of social studies. For example, De La Paz (2005) reports on a study of seventy eighth graders who participated in an integrated social studies and language arts unit designed to promote historical understanding and argumentative writing skills. Students in the experimental condition were taught a strategy for planning and composing argumentative essays in their English classes at the same time they learned historical reasoning in their social studies classes. The historical reasoning activities involved reading and reconciling primary and secondary documents to understand complex historical events. Compared to a control group, experimental students who mastered the writing and historical reasoning strategies were able to produce significantly better essays, that is, more historically accurate, more persuasive, longer, and with more arguments regardless of their initial learning profile.

Integrated Instruction and Mindful Engagement

All of these programs share a focus on using reading and writing to support acquisition of subject-matter knowledge and skills, and most have demonstrated positive effects on both literacy and content-area learning. Taken together, they shed light on reading for understanding and on the question of what is effective when literacy tools are put to use in service of learning in other domains. Among other things, these effective approaches point out the importance of a number of practices in support of mindful engagement.

Building Knowledge and Vocabulary to Advance Comprehension

The connection between background knowledge and comprehension is well established. We have long known that "the knowledge that readers bring to the text is paramount" in constructing meaning (Dole et al., 1991). We know that background knowledge improves comprehension (see McKeown, Beck, Sinatra, & Loxterman, 1992) and influences students' recall of information (Stahl, Hare, Sinatra, & Gregory, 1991). Background knowledge, or prior knowledge, comes in many forms—from specific to general—and includes word knowledge, which has also been reliably linked to reading comprehension. Studies have shown not only that students with a large vocabulary tend to be good comprehenders but also that vocabulary instruction can result in improved comprehension (Beck, Perfetti, & McKeown, 1982).

Situating literacy instruction in content areas is one way to build the kind of rich world knowledge that bears on comprehension. It also helps students develop extensive networks of generative, academic words. Several of the programs of research described

Subject-matter connections and firsthand experiences, like visiting a blacksmith, improve reading comprehension

here—most notably CORI and GIsML—use experiences within the subject area to build knowledge about the world that students then bring to bear on their understanding of related text. The GIsML project demonstrates how reading and writing can be used in subject areas to deepen students' understanding, to help students deepen, sharpen, and clarify their knowledge. Varelas and Pappas (2006) also demonstrated that students engaging in discourse about firsthand experiences and related texts developed their understanding of science ideas.

Using Reading and Writing in the Service of Disciplinary Knowledge

The CORI project yields particularly powerful evidence that connecting reading and writing to expertise in content areas can engage students and support strategic literate behavior. CORI researchers have demonstrated repeatedly that subject-matter connections and firsthand experiences result in more motivated and strategic literacy behavior and improved reading comprehension. The IDEAS project emphasizes development of expertise in important science topics and connection making among reading, writing, and science activities. It also emphasizes a systematic approach to comprehension of science texts through close reading and concept mapping. IDEAS researchers have found that the integrated program not only improved students' achievement in science and literacy but also improved their attitudes and self-confidence in both domains (see Romance & Vitale, 2001).

Using Content to Draw Students into Situations That Demand Higher-Order Meaning Making

Several programs of research have offered compelling evidence that growth in reading comprehension is accelerated when students are involved in reading real texts for authentic purposes with the goal of understanding the material well enough to use it for other purposes, such as making an argument or applying a concept in some way (Knapp, 1995; Taylor, Peterson, Pearson, & Rodriguez, 2002; Taylor et al., 2003). These studies have found that achievement is higher the more reading and writing are integrated, the more students discuss what they are reading, the more the teacher emphasizes deep understanding rather than literal comprehension of text, and the more discrete skills are taught in the context of meaningful reading rather than out-of-context reading. Integrating literacy with subject-matter learning promotes opportunities for deep processing of text, for connecting ideas across texts, and for making meaning of information through writing.

New knowledge students develop today, from a book or an experience, is the prior knowledge they bring to another activity tomorrow

The vignette about the "sticky glue" project demonstrates how the synergistic relationships among content-area activities, reading, and writing can motivate mindful engagement. In this vignette, reading and writing support students' acquisition of science knowledge and skills, while the science activities present authentic and engaging opportunities to read and write. Students move between text and experience as they gather and reconcile information from firsthand experiences and text in the interest of completing a design challenge. Students' experiences with ingredients and their reading of the reference text are multiple pieces and types of evidence that must be reconciled, that expand students' understanding of the core science idea (relationship between properties of ingredients and mixtures), and that constitute an authentic opportunity to learn and practice strategies for finding information in reference texts.

Students also use text as models for their investigations and their writing. Both the narrative account of the boy making hair gel and the handbook are models for how students might organize reports of their investigations to other members of their class and to other classes in the school. It is important to remember that science investigations allow students to develop deep and

AN INTEGRATED APPROACH TO READING, WRITING, AND SCIENCE

In Lucy Duncan's second- and third-grade classroom, students were given a set of ingredients (such as cornstarch, flour, and salt) and the design challenge of creating a mixture that could be used as glue. This challenge was part of a science unit on mixtures and dissolving.

Students embarked on the design challenge with the goal of creating a sticky glue mixture. Duncan began by asking them to gather information about the available ingredients in a firsthand way. Students observed the ingredients—first dry and then mixed with water—to learn more about the ingredients' properties and to begin selecting those that might help them create a sticky glue. In addition to observing the ingredients, students tested the stickiness of each ingredient. Students mixed each ingredient with water and then used the mixture to stick eighteen beans to an index card. The next day, students held the cards vertically and recorded how many beans stuck. The class created this chart to convey their findings.

Class Chart 1: The Sticky Beans Test

Ingredient	Evidence from Sticky Test (Number of Beans that Stuck)
Flour	18
Cornstarch	12
Salt	15

Students were then introduced to a reference book that includes information about the ingredients, such as where they come from, what they are used for, and some of their properties. Students practiced using a table of contents and index to search for information about specific ingredients and properties. They expanded their class chart to record the textual evidence next to their test results.

Class Chart 2: Evidence from the Sticky Beans Test and the Book

Ingredient	Evidence from Sticky Test (Number of Beans that Stuck)	Evidence from the Book
Flour	18	p. 19: hard when dry
Cornstarch	12	p. 13: used to glue paper around crayons
Salt	15	p. 25: sticky when damp

Students took the evidence from both their firsthand (experiment) and second-hand (text search) investigations into account as they made decisions about what to put in their first glue mixtures. Students made and tested these mixtures, recording the glue recipes as they worked.

Duncan then had students read a book about a boy who wanted to make hair gel. As the boy in the book tests possible hair gel ingredients, he decides on the properties he would like a hair gel to have—not only does he want his hair gel to make his hair stick up, but he'd also like it to be odorless and colorless. The book models the design process as the boy uses these desired properties to guide his choices about ingredients to include. The book also models recording of data and writing of procedural texts (that is, recipes). As students read the book, Duncan helped them practice the comprehension strategy of goal setting before reading, deciding to focus on what they could learn about their design process by reading a book about a boy who makes hair gel. After reading, students reflected on the design process used in the book, and how they could use this same property-driven design process to refine their glue mixtures.

Students then conducted tests of additional ingredients, focusing on new properties. Students decided that they would create a glue that is not only sticky but also strong. Students collected firsthand evidence about which ingredients are strongest—this time they glued a bent paperclip to an index card, and counted how many metal washers it could hold—and they looked back through the reference book to gather information about their ingredients. Students worked in groups to gather their strength data and recorded the group results on a new class chart.

(continued)

Class Chart 3: The Paperclip/Washers Test	
Ingredient	Evidence from Strength Test (Number of Washers the Paperclip Held)
Flour	10, 10, 11, 12, 13
Gelatin	9, 8, 11, 9, 7
Corn syrup	7, 9, 9, 10, 8

Students finished the glue activity by writing a recipe for strong glue that was based on the evidence they gathered, now from two separate firsthand investigations and two separate textual investigations.

coherent knowledge that supports future reading comprehension. We sometimes forget that the new knowledge students develop today, be it from a book or from an experience, is the prior knowledge they will bring to another science activity or another text tomorrow.

Finally, even though we can't always expect to be able to create such a perfect match between science activities and text as was illustrated in this vignette, we can select texts that support students' involvement in content area learning, and we can select content area activities that foster the opportunity for students to interact with text in a variety of ways. The context of a scientific investigation such as this one, in which students are immersed in the study of natural phenomena, generates a number of opportunities to learn from text that are grounded in the genuine desire to find out.

CONCLUSION

We have described three general contexts—social interaction around texts, strategy instruction, and integrated instruction—that have proved promising in creating classroom environments where students can engage mindfully with reading. All of these frameworks share the three characteristics described in *How People Learn*. They build on students' prior knowledge and help students connect their new learning to the learning of peers (for example, by encouraging students to discuss their questions about a text with peers). They emphasize the organization of knowledge by setting a rich learning context and by making explicit the links between important ideas and processes (for example, by situating reading instruction within the context of a scientific investigation). These frameworks all promote ample opportunity for students to reflect on and make sense of their learning (for example, by asking students to reflect on the reading strategies they employ to understand a text). All of these frameworks take steps to ensure that reading is not an isolated, disconnected activity but instead a tool that active learners use to find out about, inquire into, and make sense of the world.

Three general contexts—social interaction around texts, strategy instruction, and integrated instruction—have proved promising in creating classroom environments where students can engage mindfully with reading.

MATHEMATICS FOR UNDERSTANDING

3

Alan H. Schoenfeld

Throughout this book, we have returned to the idea that conceptions of learning undergird the several approaches to teaching that interest us here. In the previous section, we talked about the purposes of reading and roles for readers. Mathematics, too, can be viewed in many ways:

- A set of rules and procedures for solving problems and equations
- A discipline of formal logic, in which theorems are rigorously derived from axioms
- The "science of patterns," in which regularities are codified and explored
- The "language of science," a way of expressing regularities in the world around us, and more[1]

Perhaps most important, it can be experienced in two very different ways. For mathematicians, and for those students lucky enough to experience it this

---

[1] For very readable discussions of these aspects of mathematics, see Davis and Hersh (1981), Steen (1988), and Wigner (1960).

way in classrooms, mathematics is a form of sense making, a result of which is that the patterns, rules and procedures, and results all cohere in a meaningful way. It is a discipline in which one can explore, and make and verify discoveries. For most, however, mathematics has been experienced as a set of somewhat arbitrary rules and procedures to be memorized and applied. For that reason, this discussion begins with an image of what mathematics in school can be. It then turns to larger issues: what the goals of teaching for understanding should include, evidence that such goals are attainable, evidence of the consequences when instruction is not aimed at such goals, and a discussion of some of the conditions necessary for achieving the goals.

AN IMAGE

Imagine a class of third graders exploring the properties of even and odd whole numbers. The class has made various observations. The even numbers are the ones you get when you count by twos. Even and odd numbers alternate; there is an even number between each odd number and the next one, and there is an odd number between each even number and the next one.

The teacher asks the students to characterize even numbers and odd numbers. Ultimately, the students come up with definitions like this: "An even number of objects is one where you can pair things up (or count them off) two at a time, and when you're done, there are none left over."

"An odd number of objects is one where you try to pair things up two at a time, but when you're done, one object is left over." Looked at this way, a collection of ten objects is seen to be even but a collection of eleven objects is odd (see figures on page 115).

The teacher asks the students to add combinations of odd and even numbers, and to see what they notice. Among other things, the students have observed that whenever they add two odd numbers, the sum is an even number. The question that confronts the class is this: Will this *always* be true? How would they know this?

Ten is an even number because a set of ten items can be circled off two at a time, with none left over.

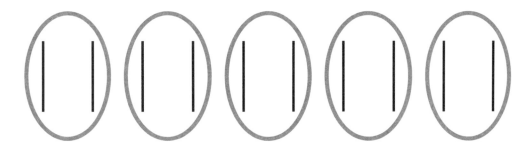

Eleven is an odd number because there is one item left over when you circle off items two at a time.

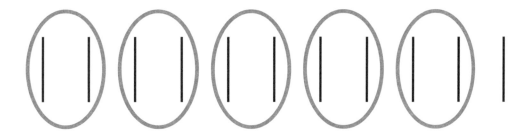

A serious debate ensues. Some students argue that is has to be true because it has worked every time they have tried it. Other students say, "But what about numbers we haven't tried? Maybe there are two odd numbers that add up to an odd number, and we just haven't found them yet." Yet other students argue that they can never know for sure: the odd numbers go on forever, so they can't actually try all the pairs to show that the sums are always even. Amid this conversation, the issue turns to *why* the sums have been even. Using the representation in the figure on page 117, a student shows why 7 + 9 is an even number:

Seven can be written this way:

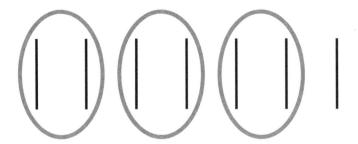

And nine this way:

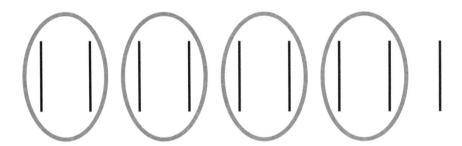

And if you position the nine backwards, like this,

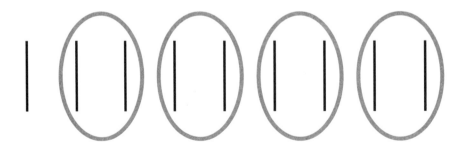

then the seven and the nine can be placed so that the "left over" singles are next to each other like this.

The two singles can now be circled together,

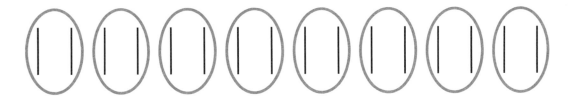

and when they are, the sum seven-plus-nine has no singles left over. So seven plus nine is an even number.

Interestingly, the student demonstrating that seven plus nine must be an even number began her presentation to the class with the specific case. However, by the time she is done, she realizes that her argument works in general, and she goes on to explain so to the class. No matter what two odd numbers you use, the first odd number must have a single object left over, and so must the second, and when you circle those two leftover objects together, then you have circled up all the numbers in the sum! After some discussion, the class agrees that the result is general: the sum of two odd numbers will always be an even number. It is worth noting that although it is not expressed in formal terms, the argument made by the students would hold up in "mathematical court" as a proof that the sum of two odd numbers is always even.

There are a number of things to be taken from this example, which is real (see, for instance, Ball & Bass, 2000; Stylianides, 2005). The first is that the students were engaged in real acts of sense making, of explorations of mathematical structure. They were asking *if* certain things were going to happen, and if so, *why*; and they were reflecting on the very nature of the enterprise. (They asked, in mathematical language: Is it possible to prove something for an infinite class of objects, when you can examine only finite subsets of them? This is a remarkably sophisticated question, and they resolved it in the positive!) The students' final argument, although expressed in third graders' language, is an ironclad mathematical proof. Thus their explorations did justice to the norms of mathematics as the "science of patterns" and can be formalized as a rigorous proof, should one desire.

This approach to mathematics (What properties does a set of objects have? Do there appear to be consistencies? If so, why do such consistencies appear? Must things always be that way? How does one know for sure?) lies at the core of doing mathematics, whether that mathematics is algebra, number theory (the formal domain of the current example), geometry (where most adults first encountered conjecture and proof, in high school), or probability and statistics; it underlies both pure and applied mathematics. Making sense of mathematical phenomena is what mathematicians *do*. As the example shows, students can learn to do it as well. With such sense making comes deep understanding, the goal of instruction.

Teaching for sense making demands a kind of interaction with the content that differs from the traditional "presentation and practice" mode of instruction. Mathematics education professor Deborah Ball, for example, who also works with elementary students, explicitly teaches her

Making sense of mathematical phenomena is what mathematicians *do*. Students can learn to do it as well. With such sense making comes deep understanding, the goal of instruction.

third-grade students the vocabulary of "conjecture" and "proof," and the habits of mind that go along with them; she creates a classroom climate in which students compare and contrast explanations on solid mathematical grounds (Schoenfeld, in press). Lampert (2001) elaborates on the kinds of planning and organization it takes to generate productive mathematical interactions in the classroom. Take a construct such as rate. How do fifth graders understand what it means for a car to be moving 55 miles per hour? How do they think about how far such a car would travel in a quarter hour, and how can one orchestrate discussion of these issues so that (1) students develop more robust understandings, and (2) the predilection to think through such issues carefully? Lampert elaborates on the values of teaching with problems as a vehicle for sense making.

Productive mathematical interactions in the classroom help strong sense making and deep understanding

Boaler (2002) characterizes analogous practices at the high school level. The National Council of Teachers of Mathematics (1991) describes the need for worthwhile mathematical tasks, productive discourse structures, and ways in which analysis of student understandings can feed into classroom instruction.

A rich set of mathematical goals for students thus includes both content and process. There is a broad consensus that, in terms of content, K–12 curricula should cover appropriate content related to number and operations, measurement, patterns, and functions; algebra, geometry, and statistics and probability; processwise, students should develop a range of problem-solving skills, notably the ability to engage in coherent chains of reasoning (and formally, proof); communicate mathematically, orally and in writing; make mathematical connections; and use mathematical tools of the trade (including specific mathematical representations) fluently. Moreover, the student should develop an appropriately mathematical disposition; mathematics should be seen as something that can and should make sense, and the student should expect to find it sensible, in the spirit of the example given here.

What has just been summarized in a paragraph is the gist of the National Council of Teachers of Mathematics' (2000) four-hundred-plus-page *Principles and Standards for School Mathematics,* which delineates broad goals for mathematics instruction. This is one of several recently produced documents outlining standards and approaches for mathematics teaching, all based on research on mathematical learning and effective teaching practices. What follows is a discussion of the origin of such documents, evidence of why they were necessary, and of whether the vision they present is attainable.

A BRIEF HISTORY: THE CONSEQUENCES OF ROTE LEARNING AND THE CONTEXT FOR CHANGE

Any brief historical discussion contains generalizations that capture broad truths and not everyone's experience. In particular, mathematics was the favorite school subject of the author of this chapter. I enjoyed mathematics, in large measure because it *did* make sense; I could see patterns, and could often figure out why things worked. From my perspective, mathematics (unlike other courses I took) required very little memorization; things fit together and all I had to do was understand the big ideas. I went on to become a mathematician.

My experience was atypical. For the vast majority of my classmates, mathematics did not make sense. It was a set of rules and procedures to be memorized and used. ("Ours is not to reason why; just invert and multiply".)

Here is a widely known example of what happens when students see mathematics as merely a set of rules to be applied, without making sense of the mathematical meaning. A problem on the 1983 National Assessment of Educational Progress mathematics assessment (NAEP; see Carpenter, Lindquist, Matthews, & Silver, 1983) asked:

An army bus holds 36 soldiers. If 1128 soldiers are being bussed to their training site, how many busses are needed?

NAEP data indicate that 70% of the students who took the exam did the computation correctly: 36 goes into 1128 a total of 31 times, with 12 left over. However, here is how students responded to the problem.

- 29% said the number of busses needed is "31 remainder 12;"
- 18% said the number of busses needed is "31;" and
- 23% correctly said the number of busses needed is "32."
- 30% did the computation incorrectly.

(Carpenter, Lindquist, Matthews, & Silver, 1983, p. 655)

The fact that so large a fraction of the students picked an answer that includes a remainder for the "number of busses" indicates that, whatever they were doing, they were *not* making sense of the situation. Rather, the students had learned, from their experience, that word problems were "cover stories" for arithmetic. What they did with word problems was identify the numbers and the relevant operations, perform the operations, and write down the answer (Schoenfeld, 1992). The fact that only 23 percent of students could both solve the equation correctly and make sense of what the situation really called for suggests why there has been substantial concern with the state of mathematics education in the United States, which has led to development of many reports about how it should be changed.

Lampert summed up the origins of students' (mis)understandings this way:

Commonly, mathematics is associated with certainty; knowing it, with being able to get the right answer, quickly ([D.] Ball, 1988; Schoenfeld, 1985; Stodolsky, 1985). These cultural assumptions are shaped by school experience, in which doing mathematics means following the rules laid down by the teacher; knowing mathematics means remembering and applying the correct rule when the teacher asks a question; and mathematical truth is determined when the answer is ratified by the teacher. Beliefs about how to do mathematics and what it means to know it in school are acquired through years of watching, listening, and practicing.

(Lampert, 1990, p. 31)

This experience of mathematics, as a body of facts and procedures to be *mastered,* often via rote memorization, took its toll over the years. Mathematics is hardly the most beloved of school subjects; indeed, it is unique among disciplines in having a term of discomfort ("math anxiety") attached to it in everyday language. The toll was seen in declining enrollments: as soon as people could stop taking mathematics, they did. Thus, the National Research Council reported that attrition rates in mathematics after ninth grade (the point at which mathematics became optional in most states) were at about 50 percent (Madison & Hart, 1990; National Research Council, 1989). Only half the students who took mathematics in ninth grade went on to take it in tenth; only half of those students went on to eleventh-grade mathematics, and so on (Madison & Hart, 1990). Although the United States had been producing adequate numbers of mathematicians and scientists, the capacity of the pipeline to continue doing so was in doubt.

It is worth noting that the American K–12 curriculum in the early 1980s focused largely on mastery of facts and procedures. In other nations, which did far better than the United States on international assessments such as the Third International Mathematics and Science Study (TIMSS), there was a greater focus on the conceptual underpinnings of the mathematics. In Japanese elementary classrooms, for example, researchers have documented how it is common for the whole class to spend an hour working on one or two carefully crafted conceptual problems. (For recent detailed descriptions, see Fernandez & Yoshida, 2004; Stigler & Hiebert, 1999). This more in-depth approach is typical of other high-achieving countries, which typically cover many fewer topics at each grade level and with a focus on much deeper meaning than is typical in the United States (McKnight et al., 1987; Schmidt, Houang, & Cogan, 2002.) These deeper inquiries also aim to ground mathematics in more authentic situations so that it is meaningful. In the study of "realistic mathematics" in The Netherlands and elsewhere, for example, students encounter meaningful applications of mathematics, in contexts designed to enhance understanding. Some of these approaches have been adopted for the design of standards-based materials in the U.S. market. Many of the new curricula took a "problem-based approach," and the Dutch collaborated in creating one of the new curricula, "Mathematics in Context."

In response to all of these pressures and more, the National Council of Teachers of Mathematics (NCTM) issued the 1989 *Curriculum and Evaluation Standards for School Mathematics,* known as the *Standards.* These were revised and updated in 2000, as NCTM'S *Principles and Standards for School Mathematics.* The broadened set of goals has already been described: meaningful engagement with powerful mathematics for all students; a focus on problem solving, reasoning, and sense making; emphasis on communication and connections. A major goal was to enlarge the base of those who studied mathematics, whether for reasons of general quantitative literacy (both for the workplace and for literate citizenship) or because of intended mathematical careers.

In the years since publication of *Principles and Standards,* under the influence of the Goals 2000 Act in the early 1990s and the No Child Left Behind Act in 2002, most states have produced their own standards. In some cases, such as California, there are forty or more standards at each grade level. With such large lists, the "big ideas" in the curriculum tend to be lost. Thus in 2006 NCTM produced the *Curriculum Focal Points for Prekindergarten Through Grade 8 Mathematics* as a brief successor volume to *Principles and Standards. Focal Points* is intended to help policymakers (and teachers) maintain a focus on the major ideas that should permeate the curriculum.

New Curricula, New Issues, and New Results

In early 1989 the National Research Council released *Everybody Counts,* a widely distributed public document that described the current state of mathematics education and called for change. Later that year, the NCTM released the

Math must be grounded in more authentic situations so that it is more meaningful to the student

Standards and began working toward the directions enunciated in it. NCTM, a teachers' organization, focused on helping its members understand what it might mean to "teach to the *Standards*." There was a significant problem, however: it is very difficult to teach in a manner consistent with the *Standards* when the teaching materials available are traditional rote textbooks. Commercial publishers were not interested in trying to produce new materials; the market was untested, and producing a new text series (text series in K–8 are marketed in chunks, such as K–4 and 5–8, not as books for each grade separately) is a very expensive and risky endeavor.

To stimulate creation of mathematics materials aligned with the *Standards*, the National Science Foundation (NSF) issued a request for proposals for development of *Standards*-based curricula. In the very early 1990s, about a dozen teams were funded to develop curricula at one of the elementary, middle school, or high school levels. Typically it took five years for development of an "alpha," or development, version of the new curricula, and a few more years for beta versions (those that had been piloted and revised) to appear. Thus the first cohorts of students to have worked their way entirely through tested versions of the curricula began to emerge in about the year 2000.[2] The first book bringing together curricular evaluations of the NSF curricula was published in 2003.

---

[2] *This chronology is worth noting, because the most vehement of the "math wars" were fought in the late 1990s. They were fought before any real data regarding the impact of the new* Standards-based curricula were available.

What the Data Say

Researchers have known for years that curricular effectiveness always depends on context. Curricula are implemented by teachers who have widely varied backgrounds and knowledge, sometimes in contexts that are supportive of the teacher's or the curriculum's goals, but often contexts that undermine them. (See, e.g., Borko, Eisenhart, Brown, Underhill, Jones, & Agard, 1992). Hence in assessing attempts to teach for understanding, it is difficult to tease out the impact of any particular variable such as curricular goals, teacher knowledge, available classroom materials, and contextual surround. Nonetheless, there are some broad trends and some specific results, which are summarized here. At the broadest level, there is growing evidence that under certain conditions entire school districts can move toward improved student performance on tests that demand real understanding, and even toward reduction of racial performance gaps.

Evidence from the city of Pittsburgh (Briars, 2000, 2001; Briars & Resnick, 2000; Schoenfeld, 2002), which worked with researchers at the University of Pittsburgh leading the New Standards project, documents what can happen when the conditions are right for consistent improvement:

- A well-designed, mathematically rich set of standards for instruction
- A well-designed curriculum aligned with the standards
- Well-designed assessments aligned with the standards
- Well-designed professional development aligned with the standards
- Enough time and stability in the system for all of the above to take hold

In this particular case, all of the conditions except the presence of well-designed curriculum and assessments linked to the standards had been in place for some time. Pittsburgh had a stable context in the late 1980s and the 1990s, including extensive professional development, which was (in broad-brush terms) consistent with the process and content goals of the *Standards*. However, it did not have a readily accessible curriculum to support curricular goals; *Standards*-based materials did not become available until the

MEETING THE NEEDS OF STUDENTS AT DIFFERENT PERFORMANCE LEVELS

A challenge all teachers face is how to develop activities that are mathematically rich yet appropriate for the range of students in their classrooms. Here is one such activity, developed by a second-grade teacher for a class whose students ranged comparably in ability, from those who could barely count to those who had a sophisticated sense of proportional reasoning.

The activity has four sets of materials:

A bag of lentil beans

A bag of popcorn kernels

Unifix cubes, which are about 1 centimeter on a side, with one open side (like a cubical box without a top)

35mm film canisters

Here is the worksheet for the activity:

1. Fill a unifix cube with popcorn kernels. How many kernels fit into the cube? _____

2. Fill a film canister with popcorn kernels. How many kernels fit into the film canister? _____

3. You are going to fill the unifix cube with lentils. Do you think the unifix cube will hold more lentils than popcorn kernels, or more popcorn kernels than lentils? _____ Why? _____

4. Now fill the unifix cube with lentils. How many lentils fit into the cube? _____

5. You are going to fill the film canister with lentils. How many do you think the canister will hold? _____ Why? _____

6. Now fill the film canister with lentils. Check your guess. How many lentils are there? _____

This task is very engaging for the students, and it opens up multiple avenues for conversation at a number of levels. The students work in groups of four on tasks 1 through 5, but then individually on task 6. In one group that worked on the problem, 15 popcorn kernels fit into the unifix cube and 150 into the film canister. Subsequent discussions ranged widely. For example, consider how many popcorn kernels will fit into one unifix cube. One second grader said that popcorn kernels are larger than lentils, so more of them will fit into any container. Another argued that fewer kernels will fit: "There isn't enough space because each popcorn kernel uses up more space than a lentil and you run out of space." The issue was resolved amicably and confirmed when the students found that 40 lentils fit into the cube. When it came time to guess how many lentils would fill a film canister, most of the students simply guessed large numbers, but one student said, "There will be 400. There are ten times as many popcorn kernels in the film container, so there will be ten times as many lentils in the film container." She, like the rest, set about counting the canisterful of lentils.

Keeping track of about 400 lentils is not easy! Some students counted by ones, but after losing track a few times they started making piles—of twos, of fives, of tens, or (in the case of the girl who reasoned proportionally) twenties. Most discovered on their own, or by looking at their friends' desks, that it was good to order the piles. They made lists on lined paper corresponding to their piles (that is, a student counting by fives drew lines on a sheet of paper, labeled them 5, 10, 15, 20, and so on, and put piles of five lentils on each line). The students were actively engaged each at his or her own level; the challenge of counting such a big set was not easy, but it was within reach, and they really wanted to see whether their guesses were right. Because of this engagement, the teacher and a classroom assistant could circulate around the room, providing assistance or suggestions to the students who needed help. Thus a mathematically rich task created a way for all the students to become engaged.

mid-1990s. New elementary materials (from *Everyday Mathematics*) were adopted in Pittsburgh in 1998. They were adopted into a supportive context. Figures 1 and 2 (adapted from Briars, 2001) show fourth-grade performance data for the city as a whole on a test that had separate components for skills, concepts, and problem solving.

As Figure 1 shows, student scores jumped with introduction of the new materials and kept rising as teachers grew more familiar with the texts. Figure 2 shows that there was a significant impact on low-performing students; the fraction of students scoring "well below standard" decreased significantly. Additional data indicate that racial performance gaps diminished as well.

FIGURE 1

Percentage of Students Who Met or Exceeded the Standard, New Standards 4th-Grade Math Exam

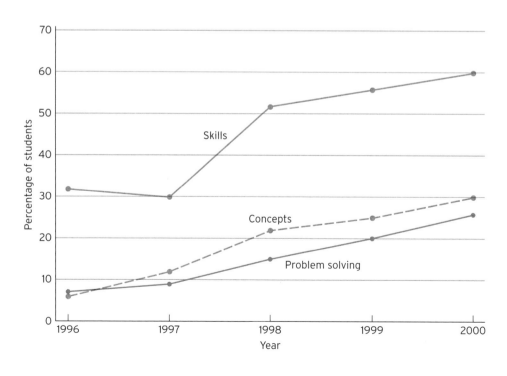

FIGURE 2

Percentage of Students Who Scored Well Below the Standard

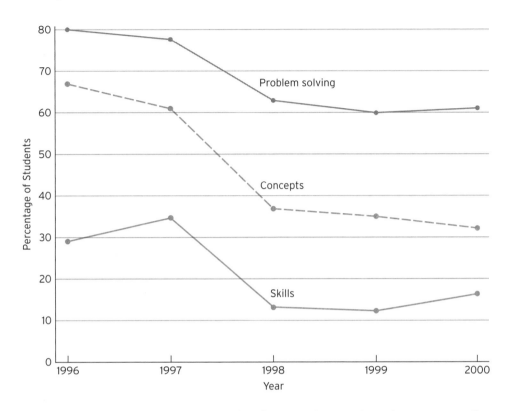

Unfortunately, contexts where the five conditions listed on p. 125 all operate in synch are rare. However, there is converging evidence about the impact of instruction aimed at mathematical sense making. One of the first comprehensive studies was conducted by Boaler (2002). As we discussed in Chapter One, Boaler conducted an extensive analysis (including classroom observations; teacher, administration, and student interviews; standard high-stakes tests; and nonstandard tests) of mathematics teaching and learning at two demographically matched secondary schools in England. "Amber Hill" school exemplified traditional instruction well done. Its teachers were dedicated and competent, its curriculum well-defined, its pedagogy coherent. Typically teachers followed the exposition, practice, feedback model of instruction, where teachers worked example problems at the board, had students work a collection of similar problems at their seats, and then discussed the student solutions. "Time on task" was high, as students worked through units on well-recognizable topics such as factoring polynomials ("factor $x^2 + x - 12$") and solving equations ("solve $x^2 + x - 12 = 0$").

"Phoenix Park" school had similar student demographics to those at Amber Hill, but a radically different curriculum and teaching philosophy. Its curriculum was project-based; students were given complex tasks and a good deal of time to sort through them, sometimes individually and sometimes in small groups. For example, in a task called Volume 216, students were told that the volume of a shape was 216. They were asked to indicate what the shape might be. It might be a cube (in which case the students needed to find its dimensions); but it might be one of a *lot* of shapes. Students were told to explore. There was plenty of student conversation, much of which focused on the relevant mathematics but some of which did not; the school was "progressive" and, from a traditional perspective, lax about discipline. The Phoenix Park curriculum was iconoclastic. However, in acknowledgment of the high-stakes examinations its students faced, the students did do a month of "just in time" test prep before the examinations.

In brief, the story is this. Amber Hill students did somewhat better than Phoenix Park students on the purely procedural aspects of the high-stakes exam, but Phoenix Park students did much better on the conceptual parts. Overall performance on that exam (which was largely procedural) was equivalent. More broadly, Amber Hill students did very poorly on tests of applications and problem solving, while Phoenix Park students did well. Such competency was mirrored in affect: the Phoenix Park students enjoyed mathematics and thought of themselves as being good problem solvers, while Amber Hill students did not like mathematics and recognized that their knowledge was fragile; they were only capable of answering problems that were nearly identical to those they had been taught to solve, and they knew it. The standard gender differences in mathematics were reproduced at Amber Hill, but they vanished at Phoenix Park. Boaler's work (1997, 2002) offers clear evidence that teaching for understanding can pay off, with students still mastering the skills they need while grappling effectively with concepts and problem solving and enjoying the subject matter.

These findings have been replicated in many other studies in the United States. As has been noted, the first comprehensive summary evaluation of the NSF-supported *Standards*-based curricula was published in 2003. Many of the studies reported were early evaluations of curricula. Because commercial assessments often focused on factual and procedural knowledge, the assessors used locally developed measures. This is a point of some concern; it would be better to have access to comparison studies using nationally accessible, validated measures. Nonetheless, the evaluations of the *Standards*-based curricula are remarkably consistent.

In a summary chapter evaluating four elementary curricula (*Math Trailblazers, Everyday Mathematics, Investigations,* and *Number Power*), Putnam (2003) writes: "The first striking thing to note about [them] is the overall similarity in their findings. Students in these new curricula generally perform as well as other students on traditional measures of mathematical achievement, including computational skill, and generally do better on formal and informal assessments of conceptual understanding and ability to use mathematics to solve problems. These chapters demonstrate that 'reform-based' mathematics curricula can work" (Putnam, 2003, p. 161).

Similarly, Chappell (2003) summarizes the evaluations of three middle school curricula (*Connected Mathematics, Mathematics in Context,* and *Middle Grades MATH Thematics: The STEM Project*) as follows: "Collectively, the evaluation results provide converging evidence that *Standards*-based curricula may positively affect middle-school students' mathematical achievement, both in conceptual and procedural understanding. . . . They reveal that the curricula can indeed push students beyond the 'basics' to more in-depth problem-oriented mathematical thinking without jeopardizing their thinking in either area" (Chappell, 2003, pp. 290–291).

Finally, Swafford (2003) summarizes the evaluations of the five high school curricula (*Core-Plus Mathematics Project, Math Connections, Interactive Mathematics Program (IMP), SIMMS Integrated Mathematics Project,* and *UCSMP Secondary School Mathematics Program*) in these words: "Taken as a group, these studies offer overwhelming evidence that the reform curricula can have a positive impact on high school mathematics achievement. It is not that students in these curricul[a] learn traditional content better but that they develop other skills and understandings while not falling behind on traditional content" (Swafford, 2003, p. 468).

All of the curricula examined, though differing substantially in style and content, emphasized conceptual understanding, problem solving, and deep engagement with mathematical concepts. Cumulatively, the weight of evidence shows clearly that such curricula produce greater learning gains than the more traditional, procedurally oriented texts and the rote instruction that typifies their use in classrooms. These individual comparative studies were backed up by a large-scale study conducted by the ARC Center (2003), which examined performance data on matched samples of students spread widely across Illinois, Massachusetts, and Washington State.

The principal finding of the study is that the students in the NSF-funded reform curricula consistently outperformed the comparison students; all significant differences favored the reform students, and no significant difference favored the comparison students. This result held across all tests, all grade levels, and all strands, regardless of SES and racial or ethnic identity. The data from this study show that these curricula improve student

Virtually all of the available scholarly evidence indicates that teaching for understanding in mathematics—devoting significant amounts of class time to conceptual understanding and problem solving, and reasoning; having students communicate mathematical ideas orally and in writing; having students seek and make connections, and reflect on their work—pays significant dividends, at little or no cost.

performance in all areas of elementary mathematics, including both basic skills and higher-level processes. Use of these curricula results in higher test scores.

In sum, virtually all of the available scholarly evidence indicates that teaching for understanding in mathematics—devoting significant amounts of class time to conceptual understanding and problem solving, and reasoning; having students communicate mathematical ideas orally and in writing; having students seek and make connections, and reflect on their work—pays significant dividends, at little or no cost. Another way to frame this is that if one teaches for skills, skills will come— but little else. If one teaches for skills, conceptual understanding, and problem solving, all three will come—and there will be little or no difference along the skills dimensions when you compare performance with instruction on skills alone.

> If one teaches for skills, skills will come—but little else. If one teaches for skills, conceptual understanding, and problem solving, all three will come— and there will be little or no difference along the skills dimensions when you compare performance with instruction on skills alone.

ISSUES IN IMPLEMENTING MATHEMATICS FOR UNDERSTANDING

Although the impact of *Standards*-based curricula in mathematics is clear, it should by no means be assumed that teaching such curricula is easy or straightforward, or that results are guaranteed. Here we identify some issues that will be confronted by anyone trying to ensure that students experience mathematics in ways that do justice to them and to the discipline.

Systemic Coherence, or Lack Thereof

As discussed earlier, the greatest chance for students to emerge from their classrooms with a rich understanding of mathematics, and the ability to use it

Math Immersion at the Elementary School Level

At Fullerton IV Elementary School, in Roseburg, Oregon, students can't help but think about math. It is embedded throughout the curriculum and throughout the school day: in the computer labs students participate in before-school; in first-period "Calendar Math" (daily math problems based on the day of the month); in art classes, where the concepts of symmetry and pattern drive creativity; and in music class during the last period of the day, where thirty minutes of pedagogical alchemy can turn a study of M. C. Escher images and the concept of positive and negative numbers into quarter notes and quarter rests—the sound and silence of music.

The immersion approach to teaching math has led to dramatically improved test scores and national recognition for Fullerton as one of twenty Intel Schools of Distinction. The accomplishments are remarkable, considering challenges such as large class size (one fifth-grade class holds thirty-five students) and moderate income (60 percent of students qualify for free or reduced-cost lunch).

TEACHING TEACHERS

This integrated, immersion approach to mathematics did not come about by chance. Fullerton principal Mickey Garrison championed the math curriculum and an emphasis on cross-disciplinary teacher training. "To me, math is not just a subject," Garrison said. "It really allows kids to learn how to reason and problem solve and learn how to effectively communicate. And if they can think conceptually, it opens up not just math; it makes connections for them in the real world. It allows them to explore music and art. It's all about rhythm and pattern. And if you can get kids to make that association, they have a new way of thinking about what it is they're thinking about."

The first requirement was teachers who could learn new ways of framing math problems, what Garrison terms "teaching mathematics in a real-world context, [presenting] real-world problems or mathematical applications in ways that focus students' attention on the mathematical ideas the problems are intended to develop."

As a result, professional development for teachers was made a priority. "Our district started with small groups of teachers who demonstrated willingness," Garrison said. "These teachers became school leaders who disseminated skill instruction and learning strategies by modeling and engaging everyone, such as small-group dialogue, cooperative-learning strategies, problem solving, gallery walks, and protocols (effective methods of communication)."

Next, she said, "All-school improvement days were allocated for mathematical staff development. [Annual] three-week summer sessions were then implemented to include learning opportunities that emphasized experimentation to increase teachers' ability to help students learn mathematics by increasing teachers' abilities to connect knowledge they were learning to what they already knew, to construct a coherent structure for the knowledge they were acquiring rather than learning a collection of isolated bits of information and disconnected skills; to engage teachers, who would then engage students, in inquiry and problem solving; and to take responsibility for validating their ideas and procedures to help teachers learn how to have mathematical discourse in their instruction."

Linda Dwight, a fifth-grade math teacher, described the shift this training has brought about: "Before, we taught the algorithms: 'You do this first; you do this next.' Kids had no understanding of what they were doing. Today, we tear these problems apart, into pieces. The kids really understand and have a number sense of why the problem works the way it does."

MATH FOR EVERYONE

According to math coach Mike Gould, school staff "value mathematics, and they also value that all people can learn mathematics. They're working very hard at finding ways to bring everybody into the picture. We've come to the realization that everybody can learn mathematics. It's not a question of capacity anymore; it's a question of how you deliver it and how you allow people to think about it. With the leadership of organizations like the National Science Foundation, there's been a lot of research put into curriculums and programs that help everybody learn."

"Everybody," in Fullerton's case, includes the handful of students in Steph Neyhart's Alternative Learning Center, a special class for students with emotional problems and other medical or behavior issues that can be barriers to learning in a regular classroom. One class project, a study of the RMS *Titanic,* began as a reading assignment. "But in the process, we came up with all this math," noted Neyhart. "We discovered that the *Titanic* was 882-1/2 feet long. We knew that was big, but we had no way to put that into context."

Together, the class decided to pace off the distance on a street adjoining the school. Dragging hundred-foot lengths of string behind them, ignoring barking dogs, and moving garbage cans out of their path, Neyhart's students measured out the ship's length. Then, standing at the top of a knoll, the students peered down several blocks at the small sign marking their starting point. "Wow, that's a long way," said one. "Gee," Neyhart mused, "how do you think a ship that big can float? Maybe that's our next investigation."

"They like the problem solving and learning to look at things in different ways, because these kids do look at things in different ways," said Neyhart. "These are also hands-on learners, and they prefer to be doing things when they're learning, and so it gets them very excited about it. They love math."

Whether one is teaching challenged students or training talented teachers, Fullerton principal Garrison believes that unleashing the power of math can work wonders. "My personal belief is, if you can problem solve in life, you can do anything you want."

MORE INFORMATION

- A video on the Fullerton IV integrated math curricula can be viewed at www.edutopia.org/magic-of-math.

Adapted from Edutopia article "The Magic of Math: Integrating Integers Across Disciplines," by Ken Ellis. Originally published Nov. 8, 2005.

Math lessons can be taught in music class . . . like turning positive and negative numbers into quarter notes and rests

effectively, occurs when all the major factors affecting instruction are lined up in the same direction:

- A well-designed, mathematically rich set of standards for instruction
- A well-designed curriculum aligned with the standards
- Well-designed assessments aligned with the standards
- Well-designed professional development aligned with the standards
- Enough time and stability in the system for all of the above to take hold

As indicated by Borko and colleagues (1992), inconsistencies can cause chaos and decrease the effectiveness of instruction. Incoherent standards or curricular goals, inferior curriculum or curricula misaligned with standards, testing that misdirects instructional efforts, problematic teacher knowledge, or the always changing "plan of the year" mentality can undermine progress in serious ways.

Issues of Standards and Linked Assessment

State-level mathematics standards and the assessments that correspond to them vary tremendously across the United States. Some are procedurally oriented, some more focused on generating and assessing more complex thinking and understanding. For teachers and administrators, these are facts of life that must be lived with.

It must be understood that different tests capture different information and support different kinds of conclusions; one can only report on what has been tested, and testing on a subset of skills limits what can be said. A study by Ridgway and colleagues (2000) makes this point clearly. The authors compared more than sixteen thousand students' performance at grades three, five, and seven on a standardized high-stakes, skills-oriented test (the California STAR test) with their performance on a much broader standards-based test (the Balanced Assessment test).

In the most straightforward comparison of test scores, each student was assigned a rating of "proficient" or "not proficient" on each examination. Between 70 and 75 percent of the students at each grade level were rated the same (either proficient or not proficient) on both tests. Fewer than 5 percent of the students were rated proficient on the standards-based test and not proficient on the skills-oriented test, demonstrating once again that procedural competency tends to come as a concomitant of conceptual understanding. However, 22 percent of the students were rated proficient on the skills-oriented test but not proficient on the standards-based test. This group, nearly one-fourth of the students tested, were declared proficient by the state on the basis of their STAR scores, but the Balanced Assessment test revealed that they tended to be below standard on conceptual understanding and problem solving. They can be seen as "false positives," in that they have been certified as being proficient but have significant gaps in their understanding. Procedural skills-oriented tests do not reveal deeper understanding. At the level of individual students, they fail to distinguish between the student who has mastered the relevant skills but has little conceptual understanding and weak problem-solving skills and the student who is strong across the board; at the collective level, they fail to distinguish between curricula that focus on skills and those that develop a broader range of understanding. Here, for example, is an assessment item that typifies testing on use of statistics:

Compute the mean and standard deviation of the following data set:

$-3.5, +.75, +1.5, +4.5, -.75, -2.5, +4.75, +2.75, +.5, -1.5, +2.25,$
$+9.25, +3.5, +1.25, -.5, +2.5, +.5, +7.25, +5.5, +3$

ORDERING A CAB

Sunshine Cabs and Bluebird Cabs are rival companies. Each claims that their company is better than the other.

Sarah takes a cab to work each day. She wants to compare the two companies.

Over several months Sarah orders each taxi twenty times. She records how early or late they are when arriving to pick her up from her home. Her results are shown below.

Sunshine Cabs		Bluebird Cabs	
3 mins 30 secs	Early	3 mins 45 secs	Late
45 secs	Late	4 mins 30 secs	Late
1 min 30 secs	Late	3 mins	Late
4 mins 30 secs	Late	5 mins	Late
45 secs	Early	2 mins 15 secs	Late
2 mins 30 secs	Early	2 mins 30 secs	Late
4 mins 45 secs	Late	1 min 15 secs	Late
2 mins 45 secs	Late	45 secs	Late
30 secs	Late	3 mins	Late
1 min 30 secs	Early	30 secs	Early
2 mins 15 secs	Late	1 min 30 secs	Late
9 mins 15 secs	Late	3 mins 30 secs	Late
3 mins 30 secs	Late	6 mins	Late
1 mins 15 secs	Late	4 mins 30 secs	Late
30 secs	Early	5 mins 30 secs	Late
2 mins 30 secs	Late	2 mins 30 secs	Late
30 secs	Late	4 mins 15 secs	Late
7 mins 15 secs	Late	2 mins 45 secs	Late
5 mins 30 secs	Late	3 mins 45 secs	Late
3 mins	Late	4 mins 45 secs	Late

1. At the moment, it is hard to see which company is better. Use appropriate calculations, graphs, or diagrams to analyze the data so that comparisons are easier to make. Show all of your work.

2. Present a reasoned case that Sunshine Cabs is the better company. Present your reasoning as fully and clearly as possible.

3. Present a reasoned case that Bluebird Cabs is the better company.

4. Which argument do you think is more convincing? Why?

This task is an opportunity to perform certain calculations (mean and standard deviation) and demonstrate knowledge of the definitions of those terms. In contrast, consider the task "Ordering a Cab" in the box above (Balanced Assessment, 2000, pp. 16–18).

Observant readers may note that the data for Sunshine Cabs are the same as the data given in the previous assessment item. Hence, in solving the taxi-cab problem students perform the computations called for in the standardized assessment problem: computing the mean and standard deviation of a set of twenty given numbers. But they do a lot more as well. Overall, this task gives students the opportunity to

- Make a frequency graph from tables of information
- Make charts from a table
- Use mean, median, mode, and range
- Analyze spread of data
- Use given data to come up with logical arguments for one or another course of action

Making a good recommendation calls for conceptual understanding and compelling reasoning. First, here is a table containing the relevant analytic data for the two companies.

	SUNSHINE CABS	BLUEBIRD CABS
Mean	2 min. 3 sec.	3 min. 14 sec.
Median	1 min. 53 sec.	3 min. 15 sec.
Range	12 min. 45 sec.	6 min. 30 sec.
Standard deviation	3 min. 11 sec.	1 min. 40 sec.

On the basis of the mean and median data, one can see that Sunshine averages an earlier arrival time (an argument in favor of Sunshine), but they are more uneven in their arrival time (range and standard deviation, an argument for Bluebird). This case is made more dramatic when one produces the relevant graphs (Figure 3).

These graphs makes it very clear that Bluebird Cabs is the better bet, assuming that Sarah is concerned about not being late. Moreover, the astute student will note that if she asks Bluebird Cabs to come five minutes before she wants them to come, they will almost always be there when she needs them! The key point to understand here is that the Balanced Assessment task taps into students' abilities to understand and use what they have been taught about mathematics. It is this kind of reasoning that we want students to develop.

One message from this research is that in states where standards and assessments are procedurally oriented, assessment changes may be necessary to document the value-added of work focusing on conceptual understanding and problem solving, at the curricular and individual student levels. A second message is aimed at those who want to teach for understanding but are afraid that they have to focus on procedures, because the high-stakes exams their students face are procedurally oriented. Much of the research suggests that if the teachers maintain their concern for a broad diet of procedures, concepts, and problem solving, their students will still do well on many procedurally oriented high-stakes tests.

A third message, though, is that assessments also need to evolve to support teaching for understanding so that teachers will be encouraged to engage in this kind of practice.

FIGURE 3

Sunshine Cabs

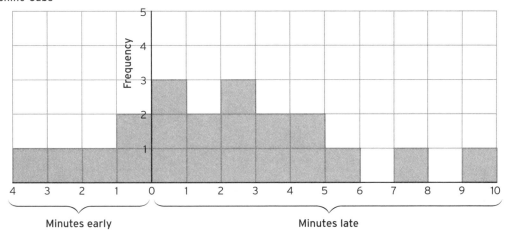

Bluebird Cabs

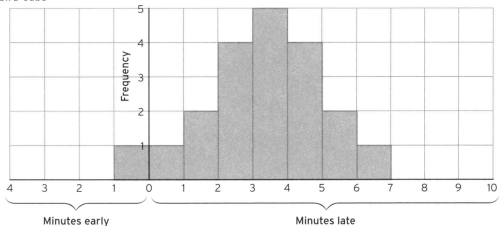

Issues of Curriculum

As the data from Pittsburgh discussed earlier indicate, curricula do make a difference; it is certainly easier to teach for understanding when one has access to a curriculum designed to support that goal. This makes life difficult for teachers in districts in certain textbook adoption states, where such materials are not supported. However, difficult does not mean impossible. First, school storerooms often contain valuable materials. Second, professional development, whether at the district level or through other organizations, can help teachers overcome the limitations of the texts they use. Problems of the week are a standard device; assessment as a tool for professional development and student enrichment is discussed below.

Across the board, there is compelling evidence that the desired goals for mathematics instruction include a range of competencies, at both content and process levels. For example, the National Research Council volume *Adding It Up* (2001, p. 5) describes five interwoven strands of mathematical proficiency:

Conceptual understanding: comprehension of mathematical concepts, operations, and relations

Procedural fluency: skill in carrying out procedures flexibly, accurately, efficiently, and appropriately

Strategic competence: ability to formulate, represent, and solve mathematical problems

Adaptive reasoning: capacity for logical thought, reflection, explanation, and justification

Productive disposition: habitual inclination to see mathematics as sensible, useful, and worthwhile, coupled with a belief in diligence and one's own efficacy

Fine-grained analyses of proficiency tend to be aligned with the content and process delineations found in NCTM's (2000) *Principles and Standards for School Mathematics.* The content dimensions of *Principles and Standards* focus on standard content areas: number and operations, algebra, geometry, measurement, and data analysis and probability. The process sections of the document stress the need for students to become competent at problem solving, reasoning and proof, making connections, oral and written communication, and uses of mathematical representation. The evidence suggests that keeping one's eye on these major ideas pays off for student learning.

HIGH STANDARDS AND ACCOUNTABILITY FOR ALL STUDENTS

This vignette describes a classroom setting in which there were multiple "account-abilities": the students were held accountable to high mathematical standards, to the teacher, and to each other. The combined set of accountabilities resulted in a classroom where the level of mathematical discourse was high, and all students were expected to meet high standards (and did).

The setting is a ninth-grade algebra class in a school with a substantial population of traditionally underrepresented minority students. The students have just been introduced to "algebra tiles," which include unit squares that are one unit on a side and rectangles whose dimensions are 1 and x:

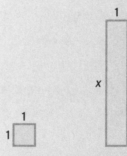

The teacher breaks the class into groups of four and asks each group to determine the perimeter of the following figure made of such tiles.

The "rules of engagement" in this class are well established. Each group is supposed to work together until all group members understand and can explain

(continued)

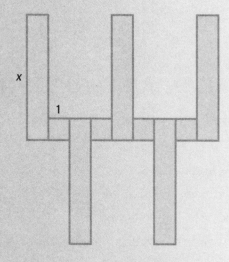

the answer to a problem. The teacher will select one member of the group and ask questions—and will continue to do so until she is satisfied that the student really understands the problem and its solution.

This particular group contains one student who is quick and who arrives at the answer (the perimeter is $10x + 10$) rapidly. There are eighteen segments of length 1 in the object, two of length x, and eight of length $(x − 1)$, so the perimeter is $18 + 2x + 8(x − 1) = 10x + 10$. The student gives a cursory explanation to the rest of the group, at which point the teacher arrives at their table.

The teacher picks another student, who happens to be a second language learner and who is also a bit shaky mathematically. The teacher asks, "Have you figured out the perimeter?" The student says, "It's $10x + 10$." The teacher says, "That's good. Where did the 10 come from?" At this point the student is stymied. The other student's explanation went by much too fast, and the teacher's question really probes for deeper understanding. The teacher sees she can't answer and simply says, "I'll be back."

The student who solved the problem says, "When she comes back, tell her this . . ." and reels off a quick explanation. The student who is on the hot seat responds, "You know that won't work. She's going to keep questioning me and make sure I've got it right. You're supposed to make sure I understand, so I can explain it right."

At this point the students work together as a group and begin to make progress on an explanation. They're getting it, but they are a little bit shaky when the teacher comes by again and asks, "Can you tell me where the 10 came from?" The designated student starts in, talking about how things cancel: "There are 8 pieces that are $(x - 1)$ in length, but these 8 extra ones make up for the missing parts. . . ." But ultimately the student winds up showing that the perimeter includes $10x$. The teacher says, "That's great, that's the $10x$ part; but I asked where the 10 came from. Can you tell me that?" When the student looks confused, the teacher again says simply, "I'll be back."

This time all four students collaborate on both parts of the problem, explaining where the 10x comes from and why the number of units left is 10. This time the student is ready when the teacher comes by, giving a thorough answer in response to all of the teacher's probes. The student is "pumped"; she is excited at doing well and highly motivated for the rest of the lesson. Two of the others at the table have learned the mathematics from the exchanges, and they share in her excitement. The student who got the mathematics from the beginning also profits from his teaching; he has been forced to go beyond his initial clumsy explanation and work on a lucid one that goes more deeply into the underlying mathematics.

In this classroom, the mathematical standards are high and remain so; the teacher demands meaningful explanations and won't settle for anything less. The students understand that they are held accountable for solid mathematics, and that they are accountable to the teacher. But as the verbal exchange shows, they are also accountable to and for each other; it is each student's responsibility to make sure that his or her groupmates really understand the material. Everybody profits from this arrangement.

Issues of Professional Development

Even with the support of good curricular materials and good assessments, teaching for understanding along the lines described earlier in this chapter is extremely difficult. Among other things, the teacher needs a solid grounding in mathematics, to be able to recognize the mathematical potential in what students say and guide instruction so that students engage with and learn fundamentally important mathematics. The need for solid mathematical knowledge should not be underestimated. Nor should the need for the ability to structure group work and conversation so that students are not simply enfranchised into conversation, but that the conversations that take place are centered on meaningful mathematics and are mathematically productive. Early research on group work in the first years of standards-based classroom practices indicated that without specific guidance, conversation was not necessarily *mathematically* rich. As we described earlier, it takes time, and knowledge, to build productive structures for group work (see, for instance, E. G. Cohen, 1994a, 1994b; E. G. Cohen & Lotan, 1997). More generally, it takes time to develop the appropriate knowledge and beliefs, and to act in ways consistent with one's rhetoric (see D. Cohen, 1990).

There are varied models of successful professional development, but some commonalities across them. Some of the things that are clearly necessary are establishing clear goals, setting aside time for teachers to reflect on their work, and maintaining continuity of focus rather than having a series of divergent workshops. Furthermore, a number of studies suggest that when teachers learn content-specific strategies and tools that they are able to try immediately and continue to refine with a group of colleagues in a learning community, they are more able to enact new practices effectively (D. K. Cohen & Hill, 2000; Lieberman & Wood, 2002).

There have also been a series of studies that suggest professional development focused on specific content within subject-matter areas, and how students learn that content is particularly helpful for teachers, even more so if the instruction is focused on assisting students toward deeper conceptual understandings (D. K. Cohen & Hill, 2000; Desimone et al., 2002; Fennema & Romberg, 1996; Ma, 1999). For instance, a study of 595 California elementary school teachers seeking to implement the state's mathematics reforms found that teachers who had opportunities to learn about particular mathematics curriculum treating specific topic areas, and who worked together on teaching strategies for implementing this content, reported more changes in their practice. These changes were associated with stronger student achievement (D. K. Cohen & Hill, 2000). Emerging research suggests that opportunities to engage in "lesson study," where groups of teachers partake of joint construction, observation, analysis, and evaluation of specific lessons, may have particular promise as they help teachers focus on how students learn particular content and work through strategies together for teaching that content (Fernandez, 2002; Lewis & Tsuchida, 1998; Stigler & Hiebert, 1999).

Professional communities, in which teachers share understandings about the nature of good teaching and work together to enact them, amount to a particularly conducive setting for learning to teach. For example, in a three-year longitudinal study of teachers' learning, Desimone and colleagues (2002) found that a number of elements in teachers' learning experiences had a cumulative effect on changing teachers' practices. Not only did a focus on particular teaching practices—in this case, technology use, application of higher-order instructional methods, and alternative student assessments—increase teachers' use of those practices in their classrooms, but active learning strategies for teachers during professional development also increased their use. The effects on practice were stronger when teachers from a school, grade level, or department participated as a group and when the strategy was consistent with other practices in the teachers' classroom or school, thus suggesting the importance of a coherent approach to learning to teach and the potential power of communities of practice.

"Real-Life" Experience in the Classroom

Every spring at Mountlake Terrace High School near Seattle, Washington, students in Eeva Reeder's geometry classes work feverishly to complete an architectural challenge: designing a two-thousand-student high school that will meet learning needs in the year 2050 and fit on a given site. Over a period of six weeks, students must develop a site plan, scale model, floor plans, perspective drawing, cost estimate, and written proposal—all of which make use of geometric and mathematical concepts. They must then make an oral presentation to local school architects who judge the projects and "award" the contract.

COLLABORATION AND CONSENSUS

Students also maintain a design file, which contains their working drawings, notes, and group contracts, such as the Team Operating Agreement (adapted from a similar form at Boeing), in which team members come to consensus on items such as expectations of themselves and each other, how decisions will be made, how misunderstandings will be prevented, and how conflicts will be resolved.

The students work in teams of two to four, constructing models, researching solar panels and other special features, and talking with visiting architects. Reeder is passionate about the importance of hands-on, real-life applications of abstract mathematical concepts, as well as the value of experience in working as a team to produce a product. "The ability to work collaboratively is a learned skill. Students need repeated opportunities to practice it within a complex, high-stakes context—similar to what they'll encounter in the community and workplace as adults," Reeder said.

"It may be fairly easy for teachers to create work for groups of students, and it may also be fairly easy for one member of the group to do all the work. That's why the teamwork rubric that students talk about, refine, and sign is key. They define what is expected of each member and what will happen if a team member is not participating." The results of Reeder's approach are evident: only those who don't attend fail her class, and she consistently scores the highest retention rate in geometry classes in the math department.

Anecdotally, the story is the same. One girl reported being so excited by her team's ideas on the first day of the assignment that she couldn't sleep. A boy found his thinking and design skills so valued by his peers that he became a team leader, which was quite different from his experience in other classes. "This project has been my salvation," he told Reeder.

MULTIPLE FORMS OF ASSESSMENT

Assessment of the design projects occurs in several ways. At the beginning of the project, students are given the scoring rubric by which their work will be measured. Each part of the project is evaluated on the basis of quality and accuracy, clarity and presentation, and concept. Reeder also evaluates teamwork (participation, level of involvement, quality of work as a team member) during the course of the project and at the end.

Throughout the term, she offers feedback and suggestions. She also meets with the class and each team after completion of the project. During this final session, the students reflect on their work and what they would do differently to improve. "The longer I teach, the more I understand the need for reflection," says Reeder. "We learn by doing *and* by thinking about what we've done. It's like learning twice when you reflect. It unquestionably deepens understanding, which is always the goal. I want them to keep their learning, after all."

Sometimes a team will write down their reflections, as with one group that never quite came together as a team and didn't score well—an atypical situation for the individuals involved. The team members honestly assessed their individual contributions and what they would do differently next time. "The best part was the next day, when each team member approached me at different times," recalls Reeder. "They actually expressed gratitude to have had the chance to learn these things now, rather than later, when the stakes might be much higher."

Many forms of assessment determine the grade each student receives. However, Reeder emphasizes the utility of using scoring rubrics as feedback and reflection tools rather than simply a way to assign a grade. "Students are more readily able to separate their personal worth from the quality of their work, and they're able to separate the particular aspects of their work that need improvement from those that don't," she explained. "It demystifies grades, and most importantly, helps students see that the whole object of schoolwork is attainment and refinement of problem-solving and life skills."

PROFESSIONAL INVOLVEMENT

Architects visit the class several times during the work phase, offering suggestions and answering questions. At the culmination of the project, each group makes a short oral presentation to the panel of architects, who view the students' work and fill out a scoring sheet. The next day, they review their evaluations with the students at their downtown offices. They identify the projects' strengths in terms of concept, site planning, educational vision, technology use, environmental impact, and teamwork during the presentation. Students also have the opportunity to ask specific questions about their designs and presentation.

During this visit one year, Reeder recounted, "We heard comments from the architects telling the kids that their work was on par with first-year architecture students at the university. That means a lot to these kids, and it's not something I can say with the same amount of credibility." For herself, Reeder said she felt the same sense of pride, similar to what parents feel when they let their kids go "and they realize they can make it on their own out there in the real world."

MORE INFORMATION

- A video presentation on Eeva Reeder's class can beviewedatwww.edutopia.org/mountlake-terrace -high-school.

Adapted from Edutopia article, "Geometry in the Real World: Students as Architects," by Sara Armstrong. Originally published Feb. 11, 2002.

Issues of Stability

The worst enemies of professional growth on the part of teachers are conflicting mandates and frequent changes in direction, goals, and materials. Professional growth requires time, energy, and consistency. To the greatest degree possible, districts and school administrators need to foster a stable climate, where goals and expectations are made clear and teachers are given the time to develop their understandings and skills. The closer a district comes to achieving the five conditions we have outlined (high-quality standards, well-designed curriculum linked to the standards, well-designed assessments linked to the standards, thoughtful professional development, and continuity of direction), the more likely it is that teachers will develop the skills they need—and the more likely it is that their students will learn well.

> The closer a district comes to achieving the five conditions we have outlined (high-quality standards, well-designed curriculum linked to the standards, well-designed assessments linked to the standards, thoughtful professional development, and continuity of direction), the more likely it is that teachers will develop the skills they need—and the more likely it is that their students will learn well.

CONCLUSION

The evidence is clear. Students who encounter mathematics as just a body of facts and procedures to be mastered will learn just that—facts and procedures—and they will develop little by way of conceptual understandings or problem-solving skills. In contrast, students who encounter a "balanced diet" of facts and procedures, concepts, and problem solving will learn all three, doing as well on skills and procedures as the students who studied just those. Creating rich mathematics environments in classrooms is a difficult but doable task. It requires alignment of the type discussed above, where powerful mathematical concepts and processes are highlighted in standards and exemplified in textbooks and assessments, and where teachers are given the time and assistance needed to craft such environments. The examples in this chapter show that it can be done, and we owe our students no less.

TEACHING SCIENCE FOR UNDERSTANDING

4

Timothy D. Zimmerman and Elizabeth K. Stage

As in the other fields we've discussed, notions of learning and teaching science have undergone a transformation in the last two decades. A key touchstone for these changes, *Science for All Americans* (Rutherford & Ahlgren, 1991), articulated the dreams of many science educators, the assurance that *all* learners have access to, and opportunities for, learning science—and that they *understand* science well enough to apply scientific ideas and concepts to everyday, real-world problems. But are we achieving that dream? Are students, our future citizens, policy makers, and decision makers, becoming science-literate? To examine these questions, we turn to research in the learning sciences, a field of research focused on increasing our knowledge of both how the brain comes to know a concept or idea (learning) and techniques for educating learners about particular concepts or ideas (instruction). In this chapter, we discuss research on how people come to understand science as well as how to teach science so that this occurs, with the hope that acting on this knowledge will move us toward realizing the dreams of scientific literacy for all Americans. But before we investigate what the research says about learning and instruction in science, we briefly examine current measures of scientific literacy and what they reveal about students' understanding in the United States and other countries.

UNDERSTANDING SCIENCE: WHERE THINGS STAND NOW

Three large-scale assessments lend insight into student progress learning science. The National Assessment for Educational Progress (NAEP) measures student progress on many topics, including science, across many grade levels in the United States. The Trends in International Mathematics and Science Study (TIMSS) assesses fourth- and eighth-grade student achievement in mathematics and science on an international level. Finally, the Programme for International Student Assessment (PISA) measures reading, math, and science literacy of fifteen-year-olds in more than forty countries around the world. As Stage (2005) has noted, NAEP, TIMSS, and PISA give us different information about student achievement. In particular, NAEP and TIMSS seek to answer the question, "Did students learn what we taught them?" while PISA asks, "What can students do with what they have learned?" PISA defines scientific literacy as students' ability to *apply* what they know both within science and in a range of contexts. If we compare results from recent NAEP, TIMSS, and PISA assessments, we find differences in science achievement for U.S. students, including critical subgroups, relative to students elsewhere.

Whereas NAEP (NCES, 2005) and TIMSS (NCES, 2003) show some progress in U.S. performance and in closing the historical achievement gaps by gender and race, results from more demanding tests that require higher levels of understanding, such as PISA (2003), paint a more pessimistic picture. Indeed, as shown in Figure 1, the United States ranked nineteenth out of forty countries in science among fifteen-year-olds, performing well below the highest-scoring countries and below the average of countries participating in the Organization for Economic Cooperation and Development (OECD), a

FIGURE 1

Average PISA Science Literacy Scores for Fifteen-Year-Olds, by Country.

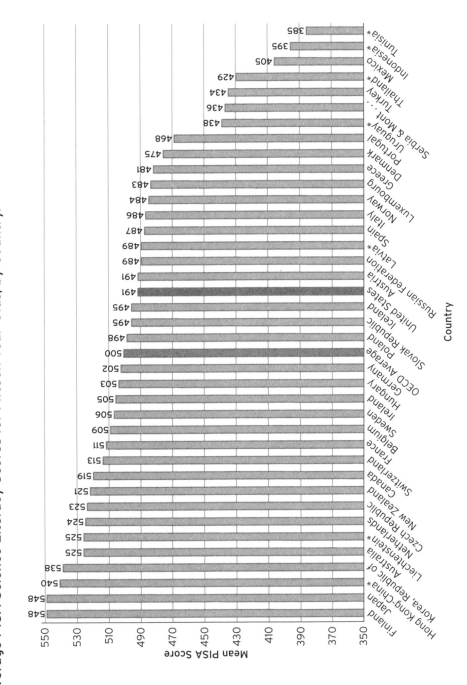

Data from PISA (2003) places the United States nineteenth in scientific literacy among the forty countries tested. *Non-OECD countries voluntarily participating in PISA testing in 2003 (PISA, 2003).

ranking that dropped to 21st by 2006. This result is disconcerting. It implies that U.S. students are not able to *apply* their scientific knowledge on par with most other countries.

Furthermore, the distance between the average scale score for Asian and white students on the one hand and Hispanic and Latino students on the other is equal to the distance between the United States average and the highest-scoring countries (Stage, 2005). (See Figure 2.) Thus, one might conjecture that U.S. students in general, and historically underserved ethnic groups in particular, may be getting access to scientific information, but they are not

FIGURE 2

Average PISA 2003 Scores for Fifteen-Year-Olds, by Ethnicity Subgrouped by Discipline and Problem-Solving Skills.

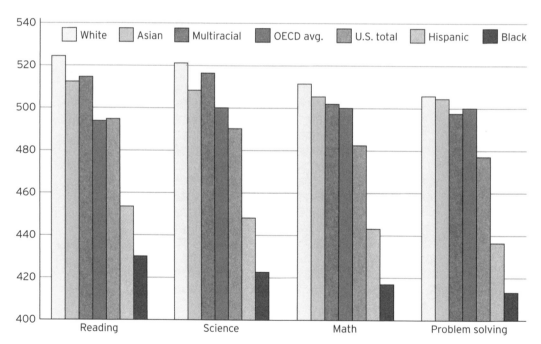

Data from PISA (2003) highlight the continued achievement gap between white/Asian populations and Hispanic/black populations, especially with regard to problem-solving abilities (Stage, 2005).

getting the problem-solving and critical-thinking skills needed to apply this knowledge meaningfully.

Researchers have put forth a variety of explanations for differential test performance (Bybee, Kilpatrick, Lindquist, & Powell, 2005; Stage, 2005) and for differential participation, achievement, and progress through more demanding courses (Clewell & Campbell, 2002), including structural, pedagogical, and psychological explanations. Teachers, however, can only address their own instructional programs and interactions, and it is these that we would like to highlight. To the extent that children's prior knowledge and experiences vary in part with their cultural, linguistic, and economic backgrounds, teachers need to be prepared to make available common experiences and draw multiple connections between these experiences and the phenomena under study.

Furthermore, because scientific discourse varies from ordinary discourse in many important ways—for example, in use of passive voice, abstract nouns derived from verbs ("revolution"), and technical terms with meanings different from those in everyday life (for example, "energy")—the distance in student experiences from such scientific discourse needs to be recognized and negotiated (Duschl, Schweingruber, & Shouse, 2007). These factors and others must be incorporated into science instruction in order to promote an understanding of science.

WHAT DOES IT MEAN TO UNDERSTAND SCIENCE?

Ask most people to recall their science classroom experiences, and you'll likely hear one or more of these caricatures of science:

- Science is memorization of facts, laws, or theories, with an emphasis on identification and recitation, such as "knowing" the kinds of clouds or the three kinds of rocks, complete with the correct spelling of *cirrus* and *metamorphic*.
- Science is the mechanical testing of a contrived hypothesis using "the scientific method" to find out something that everyone already knew,

such as the conclusion that plants that are kept in the closet will not grow as well as those that are placed on a window sill, or implementing a set of preplanned lab procedures.

- Science is making models of the solar system out of Styrofoam and coat hangers and decorating them, or models of volcanoes that use baking soda and vinegar to "erupt," thereby illustrating nothing remotely related to the objects and relationships portrayed.

Reciting interesting facts, especially about dinosaurs, is a passion of young people, and "knowing" a lot is helpful for playing *Trivial Pursuit*. Although memorizing facts to recite or recognize them later is a successful test-preparation strategy in many science classrooms, it hardly constitutes knowing or understanding science where the connections among the facts are more important than the facts themselves. Indeed, research comparing students taught through a "traditional" fashion of memorization and recitation of facts on high-stakes tests to students taught in an inquiry-based fashion emphasizing connections among concepts finds that students in inquiry classrooms outperform those in traditional classrooms (Schneider, Krajcik, Marx & Soloway, 2002; Zimmerman, 2005).

One has to make decisions about the features that are essential and nonessential in a model so that the former are represented and the latter do not become distractors. In short, *understanding* science is more complex (and interesting!) than the way science is portrayed or experienced in most science classrooms.

Understanding and conducting investigations is central to science and science literacy, but the challenge for most people is understanding the relationships between the evidence and one's preconceived views of what the outcome is likely to be. Modeling is a fundamental tool for problem solving as well as representing concepts. However, choosing and using models is a challenging task for teachers, and understanding the concept of a model is difficult for teachers and students alike. For example, one has to make decisions about the features that are essential and nonessential in a model so that the former are represented and the latter do not become distractors. In short, *understanding* science is more complex (and interesting!) than the way science is portrayed or experienced in many science classrooms.

If learning science is a complex task, it is nonetheless something we've been doing since birth. We observe objects and their motion, organisms and their behavior, our surroundings and how they do or don't change over time. Thus all learners bring ideas to any learning context. Our everyday experiences with natural phenomena influence how we learn science in the classroom. This "prior knowledge" can enable deeper conceptual understanding of science phenomena if it is activated, recognized, and not ignored or dismissed as naïve or quaint. Recognition of these ideas is a necessary precondition to developing a deeper understanding of science. In addition, promoting connections between the vast array of science and nonscience content can allow learners to meaningfully access and apply scientific knowledge. Thus viewing science as a body of larger concepts to be used and applied flexibly is more productive than thinking of science as a static body of facts or a mechanical set of procedures. Thinking deeply about one's prior ideas about scientific phenomena, about the process and endeavor of science, and the construction of scientific knowledge is one of the most essential science education practices for developing an *understanding* of science.

How does one develop this kind of connected, flexible thinking in science? Some have argued, in a misinterpretation of Piaget, that young people must go through a multiyear developmental stage where, for example, they can grasp only the directly observable, concrete phenomena before they can engage in abstract, hypothetical deductive reasoning (such as "if, then" reasoning; see, for example, California Department of Education, 1990). However, the National Research Council's (NRC) recent review of the research on science learning at the K–8 level concluded: "We are underestimating what young children are capable of as students of science—the bar is almost always

Teachers promote student understanding of science by activating their prior knowledge of science phenomena

set too low. Moreover, the current organization of science curriculum and instruction does not provide the kind of support for science learning that results in deep understanding of scientific ideas and an ability to engage meaningfully in the practices of science. In sum, science education as currently structured does not leverage the knowledge and capabilities students bring to the classroom. For students from diverse backgrounds, this problem is even more profound" (Duschl et al., 2007).

Our review of the learning sciences literature on teaching science for understanding underscores the NRC report findings and draws on its framework for defining a proficient science learner. This framework moves beyond the false dichotomy between content knowledge and process skills and recognizes the inextricable link between content and process. Duschl and colleagues (2007) suggest that students who are proficient in science:

- Know, use, and interpret scientific explanations of the natural world
- Generate and evaluate scientific evidence and explanations
- Understand the nature and development of scientific knowledge
- Participate productively in scientific practices and discourse

These goals for student learning also offer a broad framework for curriculum design. We reiterate this framework here because we believe it maps onto our findings and promotes a view of science learners that is consistent with research on science learning for understanding.

Density is a difficult science concept for learners of all ages, but the example of Sandra Brooks's classroom illustrates how a teacher can guide a group of students toward a deeper understanding of density. The students are

THE SCIENCE CLASSROOM AS A PLACE TO BUILD UNDERSTANDING

It's noisy. Many of the fifth-grade students are talking all at once. There's a buzz in the air. Some students are attempting to lift a two-liter bottle of colored salt water and squealing directions to other students as water spills out. Others are dumping unmeasured amounts of salt into other two-liter bottles. The teacher, Sandra Brooks, approaches a group of students who are still filling out a questionnaire:

T: "Why did you color both bottles blue?"
S1: "I think once we connect the bottle with the dye and salt water to the bottle without the dye and fresh water, they will mix and it will all be blue."
T: "What makes you think that will happen? Have you ever seen something like that happen before? Or heard about it?"
S1: "Well yes, when we make Kool-Aid at home the color mixes and it all is the same color."
T: "OK, write that down and then try it."

Brooks approaches another group that is intently watching two two-liter bottles connected at the top and lying sideways on the table.

T: "What's happening over here?"
S2: "It's turning blue."
S3: "Well, only part of it is turning blue."
S4: "Yeah, all the blue is on the bottom."
T: "Which bottle started out all blue? The salt water bottle or the fresh water bottle?"
S2: "The salt water bottle was blue" [pointing to one of the bottles].

(continued)

T: "Really? What does this bottle [pointing to the nonsalty bottle] look like when you look at it from the side like this?" (The students crouch down with the teacher and look intently at the bottles.)

S3: "Whoa, I can see the blue water coming in at the bottom."

T: "Why do you think that's happening?"

S3: "Because it's the salty water," claims one student excitedly.

S2: "But shouldn't the salt water just be mixing with the fresh water?"

S3: "No, because the salt water sinks."

T: "Why do you say that?" prompts the teacher. "Have you seen that or heard that before?"

S3: "Um, I think that maybe, well I think that it has more stuff, so, uh, it's heavier and sinks."

S4: "But why doesn't it just mix, like chocolate in milk?"

T: "Has anyone ever made salad dressing before?"

S4: "Ooh, ooh, I did, it was yum," a student claims and laughs.

T: "Do you remember what you put in it?"

S4: "Oil, vinegar. . . ."

S3: "Oh wait: 'Oil and water don't mix,'" one student interrupts excitedly.

T: "How do you know that?"

S3: "Isn't that how the saying goes? Besides, once, I saw this show and there was oil leaking from a ship and all the oil was floating on the water, and the sea otters, they were getting all oiled and stuff . . . it was gross."

T: "Does that tell us anything about what's happening here [pointing to the bottles]?"

S2: "Salt water has more stuff in it than fresh water?" a student tentatively proposes.

T: "Why don't you keep watching the bottles and talk about what you think is happening? Remember, you also need to color in the 'after' bottles on the sheet."

not conducting an "experiment"; they are being led through an activity, where the teacher's careful questioning evokes their prior ideas and experiences. It's clear from their answers that they have considerable experience with mixing liquids and solids, combining liquids, and colloquial expressions that have an impact on their understanding of density, but these experiences and the ideas associated with them appear disconnected. Some are contradictory, and the students have not independently reconciled them.

They are not working through an experiment where they will "show" that liquids of different densities separate out on the basis of those density differences. Nor are they being asked to calculate the density of the liquids using the formula $D = M/V$ (where M is mass and V is volume). If they were asked to calculate density, it is likely that many would divide V by M because the formula itself doesn't represent an understanding of density. Moreover, they are not being asked to recite a definition of density; indeed, the word is not even being used or introduced because their understanding does not yet warrant a label. They are being asked to actively consider what they already know (prior knowledge), prompted to think about their own ideas about that knowledge (metacognition), and then asked to start putting these ideas together, either for the first time or to reconstruct or rearrange those ideas, to develop a conceptual model of density instead of memorizing a meaningless definition and formula. The students are making observations, gathering evidence, learning to support claims with evidence while engaging in a highly social activity similar to activities conducted by scientists. This approach to teaching science is consistent with current research on the learning of science.

It is also consistent with an emerging sense that learners develop successively more sophisticated ways of thinking about a topic or concept over time. Descriptions of a path along which this conceptual development occurs are called learning trajectories or learning progressions (Catley, Lehrer, & Reiser, 2005; Duschl et al., 2007; C. Smith, Wiser, Anderson, & Krajcik, in press; Wilson & Bertenthal, 2006). These progressions begin with nascent ideas, often rooted in real-world experience, that shape the learners' knowledge and understanding. Learning progresses along a path linked by "big ideas" within a particular domain of science. These big ideas often cut across the discipline of science. For example, Catley and colleagues (2005) describe a learning trajectory, or progression of ideas, for students learning about evolution, beginning with a basic notion that organisms differ. This idea can be developed by students at the K–2 level and forms a basis for more complex ideas of evolution. In grades three through five, students build on this notion of diversity by recognizing that not only do organisms differ but there are relationships among those differences (for example, some creatures have feathers, some creature have beaks, and most creatures that have feathers also have beaks) leading to an understanding of biological diversity. This promotes early understanding of classification of species and leads to the idea of descendents. Students continue to build concepts over time and eventually develop a connected and applicable understanding of the topic.[1]

Although no learning progression has yet been analyzed for learning about density, we can envision what one might look like. In fact, learning sciences researchers develop these progressions using their own experience and the research literature, and then they test that progression in classrooms to determine its validity. A learning trajectory for understanding density might begin with a learner recognizing that she has seen liquids layer one on top of another, but she has never thought about why that phenomenon occurs. However, the learner might start to recognize that "things layer." Over time, she may begin to recognize that liquids with solids dissolved in them often form the bottom layer. This idea might launch the learner down the path to

---

[1] *Jim Minstrell from FACET Innovations is compiling a list of what he calls "facets" to assist teachers in recognizing student progression from the least sophisticated to the most evolved notions of basic physics concepts (http://www.facetinnovations.com).*

understanding that liquids on the bottom (more dense) have more "stuff" in them (that is, have a greater mass thanks to the properties of their matter).

The learner might next build a more developed understanding of density when she recognizes that the amount of liquid, as compared to the amount of solid dissolved in that liquid, is important to know. As she progresses, she would come to know that there is a relationship between the amount of liquid (volume) and the total mass (the amount of matter contained in an object) of that liquid, and this makes one liquid lie on top or on the bottom, which then allows the learner to use and apply the formula $D = M/V$ correctly. Eventually, the learner will need to incorporate the relationship between temperature and density, but first things first. Learning a formula or the definition of a word, though important, usually does not result in conceptual understanding, especially not in the short run. Understanding any concept requires processing prior knowledge and ideas and incorporating them into a broader knowledge base, all of which takes time and effort, as is illustrated further in this discussion.

DEVELOPMENT OF CONCEPTUAL UNDERSTANDING

T: "OK, finish cleaning up and we'll have a class discussion about this activity."

The students work noisily as they clean up the materials and finish filling in the questionnaire. As students begin to take their seats once more, the teacher leads them through a discussion of what they found and helps them begin to understand

(continued)

density. The teacher uses an overhead with outlines of the bottles used in the density activity and asks the students to contribute their ideas and results.

T: "Who wants to tell us what the bottles looked like when we started this activity?"

S1: "For the first activity, the bottle on top had the blue food coloring and no salt in the water."

T: "Ok, what did you predict [while coloring the top bottle blue on the overhead] would happen when you pulled the card out from between the bottles?"

S2: "I thought the bottom bottle would become all blue, but it didn't."

T: "Well, what did happen?"

S2: "It kinda just stayed there and didn't mix or anything. Well, I mean there was a tiny bit of blue that I saw mixing but the blue basically stayed on top."

T: "Why do you think that happened? Have you ever seen anything like this happen before?"

S3: "I think it's because the salt water has more in it. I mean we put salt in it."

S4: "Yeah so the salt water stayed on the bottom and the fresh water, with less stuff in it, stayed on top."

T: "So why might a liquid with less stuff in it be on the top?"

S3: "Because it's lighter because it doesn't have the salt in it."

T: "Did anyone notice if the amount, the volume, of water changed when you added the salt to your bottles?"

S2: "Ours didn't really change."

T: "OK, so we put salt in the water but it didn't really change the volume very much. Has anyone ever heard the brain teaser 'Which weighs more, a ton of bricks or a ton of feathers?' Can anyone answer that question?"

S1: "Neither. They both weigh a ton so they both weigh the same."

T: "Right. How about the volume or amount of space taken up by that same ton of bricks and the ton of feathers? Does the ton of feathers take up more space, less space, or the same space as the ton of bricks?"

S1: "Well, I think the feathers would have to take up more space."

T: "What makes you say that?"

S1: "Because the feathers are all fluffy and the bricks are all packed together. There's less space between each brick but there's more space between each feather."

T: "Remember how last week we talked about atoms and molecules and we found that some take up more or less space? Has anyone ever heard the term *density* before?"

S3: "Some things are more dense than others."

T: "Can you tell me more about what you mean by more dense?"

S3: "Well, some have more atoms or molecules in the same amount of space because they are packed tighter."

T: "So if we have two liquids that take up the same amount of space, but one liquid has more molecules because they are packed more tightly. . . ."

S3: "Then the more tightly packed one is more dense."

T: "So if our salt water has the same volume as our fresh water but . . . ."

S1: "Oh, but the salt is packed in tightly with the water molecules, then it's more dense and the fresh water is less dense so it stays on top."

T: "This was a good discussion. Next class we'll talk about what happened when you had one bottle with hot water and one bottle with cold water and you tipped them on their sides."

THE CHALLENGE OF UNDERSTANDING SCIENCE
Misconceptions, Conceptual Change, and Learning Science for Understanding

Research on students' prior knowledge about scientific phenomena has revealed how this knowledge can interfere with development of scientifically accepted understandings of the world. These prior ideas are often referred to as "preconceptions," "misconceptions," or "alternate conceptions." They can be robust and resistant to change, even in the face of conflicting evidence. We use the term *misconceptions* when referring to ideas that are not considered scientifically valid. We recognize that many researchers, teachers, and others in the field of education have concerns over the negative connotation of the term *misconceptions.* Many say, and we agree, that it implies a wrong answer and can leave learners turned off by this idea, but due to the common recognition of this term, we have chosen to use it here.

The Source of Prior Ideas and Misconceptions

Research has shown that many misconceptions stem from prior experience-based knowledge about how the world works. Much of the research documenting students' prior knowledge or misconceptions began more than twenty years ago, but researchers continue to discover unique prior ideas and misconceptions even today. Duit (2006) has compiled a bibliography of some seven thousand citations related to research and theory on students' and teachers' prior ideas about science. The journal articles, book chapters, and conference presentations in this bibliography document the vast array of misconceptions related to chemistry, biology, and physics. Some domains of science have been researched more extensively than others. Physics is the domain where the most extensive research has been done (see, for instance, Clement, 1982; diSessa, 1983; McCloskey, Caramazza, & Green, 1980; McCloskey & Kohl, 1983) whereas little is known about students' common misconceptions about ocean science topics (Zimmerman & Brown, 2006). Whether or not researchers have identified prior ideas and misconceptions in a given domain of science, knowing where students begin their learning is an important component of teaching science for understanding.

Let's consider a specific example. Many researchers have documented the difficulties experienced by both students and adults in attempting to understand scientific concepts of evolution. A commonly held misconception about evolution is that use or lack of use of a particular trait determines whether that trait is passed along to the next generation. For example, Bishop and Anderson (1990) collected pretest and posttest data from 110 college students and found that many of these students reasoned that cave newts "lost" their eyes because they do not use their eyes in their dark cave habitat. In a separate study with college students, Ferrari and Chi (1998) found that more than 60 percent of participants held this view of adaptation. Other researchers have documented similar misconceptions in various populations of learners (Jensen & Finley, 1995; Settlage, 1994; Zimmerman, 2005). Although most of these students were likely taught Darwinian evolution and concepts of natural selection previously, the instruction they received probably did not consider their prior ideas.

Researchers in all studies found the misconceptions to be persistent. However, when instructional materials are designed with knowledge of misconceptions and teachers create opportunities to explicitly evoke these ideas, more students develop scientifically supported ideas. For example, after initial pilot-test data revealed that students often use the term *adapt* in a colloquial fashion (for example, "We are moving to Alaska, but I'm sure I can *adapt* to the cold weather"), Zimmerman (2005) created opportunities for students to discuss how this term might be used differently in science class and outside science class, drawing on research demonstrating the positive effects of such opportunities for learners to identify and express their prior ideas.

Creating Conceptual Change

Everyday experiences lead to notions of how the world works. This prior knowledge may not correlate with a scientifically accurate view of how the world works. Recall our density example, where several students drew on prior experience mixing solids, such as Kool-Aid, into liquids and predicted that mixing salt and fresh water would have a similar result. Students did not make up the ideas of mixing from scratch; they had prior real-world experiences that informed their responses to questions about density and mixing and layering of substances. When learners are attempting to understand a science concept, they often have to alter their current understanding in order to construct a scientifically valid understanding of the phenomena at hand. This alteration or restructuring of prior ideas is referred to as "conceptual change."

Research on conceptual change in science education has demonstrated that a simple "confront-and-replace" model of science learning does not allow deep understanding of science content (Strike & Posner, 1982). A confront-and-replace approach to our evolution example would be to help students recognize they hold the misconception and then present them with ideas of natural selection through readings, lectures, or other direct instruction methodologies, expecting that presenting them with the correct idea will be sufficient. Teaching science for understanding, however, involves a model of conceptual change that accounts for the iterative (or sometimes sudden and revolutionary) *restructuring* of knowledge and includes much more than direct instruction. It involves reflecting on one's own knowledge and how it is structured around a given phenomenon. The current perspective on conceptual change is that it is a process of addition and restructuring, not of replacement (Chi, 1992; diSessa, 2006; diSessa, Gillespie, & Esterly, 2004; Gunstone & White, 2000; Slotta & Chi, 2006; Smith, diSessa, & Roschelle, 1993). In fact, diSessa and Sherin (1998) and others (e.g., D. Clark, 2000) have found that students can hold multiple, even contradictory, ideas about a scientific phenomenon at the same time, further demonstrating that we do not simply replace old ideas with new ideas but that we restructure the network of ideas as they relate to that phenomenon.

Chinn and Brewer (1998, 2001) put the confront-and-replace model to the test. They first presented students with an initial theory (or invoked students' own initial theories) of a scientific phenomenon. Next, they presented the students with what they called "anomalous data" (scientifically correct information that did not resonate with the learners' existing knowledge or beliefs) and asked students to state their belief in the anomalous data. Finally, they asked students to explain their reasoning behind their belief or nonbelief in the anomalous data. This empirical test of their earlier work (see Chinn &

Brewer, 1993) proved compelling. They identified eight ways people respond to anomalous data. One of the eight responses was to change from their prior ideas to the scientifically normative view. However, this occurred only 5 percent of the time (8 out of 168 participants; Chinn & Brewer, 2001). More often than not, learners rejected, ignored, or reinterpreted the anomalous data.

In other words, simply presenting a learner with the correct concept does not promote conceptual change. If the students were simply told that less dense liquids "float" on top of more dense liquids, many of the students would still have the experience of Kool-Aid, which would hinder their ability to reach conceptual understanding. From the research in science education, a broader view of conceptual change has emerged. Researchers are beginning to document processes through which learners restructure knowledge: adding, replacing, changing hierarchies, strengthening or weakening relationships, and shifting categories of ideas. We are also just beginning to recognize the importance of time in the process of conceptual change. For example, insights from recent research on visitor and student learning in museums are interesting and unexpected. Falk, Scott, Dierking, Rennie, and Cohen-Jones (2004) interviewed museum visitors before, immediately after, and four to eight months following their visit. They found visitor self-reported outcomes changed from considering knowledge and skills as the dominant outcome immediately after the visit to developing perspectives and awareness four to eight months later. Thus time had changed how the visitors thought about the learning experience of visiting the museum. A study by Bamberger and Tal (in press) involved day-after interviews and sixteen-month interviews with students who visited a museum. These researchers found a significant decrease in students' knowledge of the topic but a significant increase in the connections students made to ideas presented in the museum exhibits.

Clark (2000, 2006) demonstrated how students use prior knowledge as a foundation for adding new ideas about heat and temperature as they gradually transition from nonscientifically grounded ideas replete with misconceptions to an understanding in line with scientific knowledge. Clark used pretests, posttests, and structured interviews to document students' ideas about heat and temperature. Following fifty students over a two-year time period, he found that as they engaged in a computer-mediated inquiry curriculum designed to help them reflect on concepts of heat and temperature, students' ideas gradually evolved from demonstrating a poor understanding to having a strongly scientific understanding of heat and temperature. He documented how they achieve this conceptual change by first adding to and then restructuring their knowledge. Clearly, then, prior knowledge and misconceptions are not strictly an impediment to understanding science but are crucial in building a deep understanding of scientific ideas and concepts.

Teaching Science for Understanding

Given these challenges to learning science, can we design science curricula that promote an understanding of science? Considerable research has gone into the design of science curricula, much of which is aimed at addressing these challenges.

Integration of Knowledge: A Conceptual Change Model

One example of a conceptual change approach to learning and instruction is the Knowledge Integration Perspective of Linn and colleagues (M. C. Linn, 2006; M. C. Linn, Davis, & Bell, 2004). Knowledge Integration describes learning as a process whereby learners incorporate new concepts, ideas, or experiences into their existing "repertoire of ideas" by creating, removing, or realigning connections among knowledge constructs (such as facts, concepts, beliefs, prior experiences, and so on). Affective components, such as motivation, are part of the "repertoire" and are addressed by designing science curricula that have personal relevance to students (M. C. Linn, 2006). Linn and her colleagues have developed a set of principles for curriculum design and classroom instruction. These principles are listed on page 171 and described in greater detail by

M. C. Linn and colleagues in books on the Knowledge Integration Perspective (see Linn, 2006; Linn, Clark, & Slotta, 2003; Linn, Davis, & Bell, 2004; Linn & Hsi, 2000).

The idea that knowledge integration supports science learning has led to development of a curriculum design approach called the Scaffolded Knowledge Integration (SKI) framework, which contains four pedagogical principles to be used in designing science curricula. These design principles are by now familiar, because we have encountered them in other fields:

Make science accessible. Make science learning personally relevant, by incorporating topics and examples that students can understand, and by providing scaffolding and assistance appropriately.

Make thinking visible. Use models, visualizations and representations, and create opportunities for learners to put their ideas into a visible form (in writing, picture form, or graphical representations).

Help students learn from each other. Create opportunities for social interactions, including sharing and reviewing each other's ideas.

Promote lifelong learning through reflection. Promote critical learning practices such as critiquing, thinking about one's own knowledge (that is, metacognition), and revisiting ideas.

Using pretests, posttests, and embedded assessments (that is, analyzing student work during the course of the curriculum), research employing Linn's Knowledge Integration Perspective has demonstrated significant gains in student understanding of science topics ranging from heat and temperature (Clark, 2006) to genetically modified organisms (Seethaler & Linn, 2004) to electrostatics (Casperson & Linn, 2006) to evolution (Zimmerman, 2005). In all cases, known misconceptions often associated with these science topics are a target of the instructional materials.

In the classroom, these principles are enacted through the design of the curriculum and instructional practices of the teacher. Using Internet technology and desktop and handheld computers, teachers and researchers design science curricula using the Web-based Inquiry Science Environment (WISE). WISE technology allows curriculum designers to insert metacognitive prompts (see the section on metacognition later in this chapter) that get students to *make their own thinking visible*, including their prior knowledge, and thus available for reevaluation. The example in Figure 3 shows how students begin by responding to a prompt asking them what they think about a particular species' ability

FIGURE 3

A WISE Reflection Prompt.

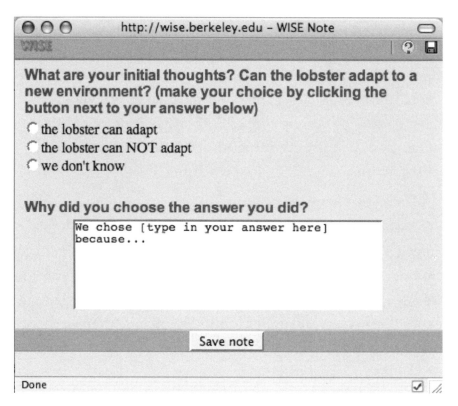

In WISE, reflection notes prompt students to think about their prior ideas while making those ideas, and that thinking, visible to the individual student and to other students.

to adapt before engaging the students in activities designed to teach them about the scientific definition of adaptation (Zimmerman & Slotta, 2003).

Classroom teachers can employ similar strategies, without using technology, such as the Think-Pair-Share techniques often used in inquiry curricula such as GEMS, FOSS, and MARE from the Lawrence Hall of Science. Here, the teacher pairs learners and asks them to think about and discuss topics or answer questions and share their partner's answers with the whole class. For example, "Why is it hotter in the summer than in the winter?" is a good prompt to get learners thinking about the cause of the seasons. In a more complex fashion, concept mapping tools in WISE get students to literally map out relationships between subcomponents of a particular science phenomenon. Students might be asked to show relationships among components of an ecosystem, a chemical reaction, or the path of a projectile. The act of constructing the concept maps, especially when done collaboratively, engages students in activities similar to authentic science (such as model building), promoting reflection and *learning from each other* through the social negotiation of the components of the map.

Similarly, student motivation is activated by choosing examples and using techniques that establish personal relevance to the science topic. For example, Seethaler (2003) helped motivate students by relating the science topic (genetics) to a real-world controversy, consumption of genetically modified foods. The curriculum designers further evoked a sense of personal relevance by having students read an account of a local group against genetically modified food. Finally, allowing students to choose a "side" of a debate in the final stages of the curriculum increased their own personal commitment to doing their best in developing an argument (Seethaler & Linn, 2004).

More than twenty years of classroom-based research has gone into development of the Knowledge Integration Perspective and the pedagogical principles listed on page 171. This approach has been shown to enable conceptual change and deeper understanding of science concepts and principles.

Conceptual Knowledge: Making Connections Promotes Deeper Understanding

Many researchers have successfully addressed student misconceptions and promoted deep understanding of science concepts by presenting students with broad conceptual frameworks of ideas instead of disassociated facts. Much of the research presented in this chapter takes this approach. In one particular example, Passmore and Stewart (2002) used a conceptual modeling approach to teach high school students Darwin's theory of natural selection as a mechanism for biological evolution. They presented students with the conceptual models of Paley, Lamarck, and Darwin successively. Paley believed that organisms appear to be so well suited to their environmental conditions that they must certainly have been designed to fit these conditions. Lamarck generally theorized that organisms obtain traits because their parents "used" existing or acquired traits, so they were passed down to subsequent generations (for example, giraffes used long necks, or stretched shorter necks, and those were passed to the next generation). Finally, Darwin theorized that organisms have slightly different traits and those whose traits allow them to survive within a specific set of environmental conditions live to pass those traits on to their offspring. Students were asked to apply these models to explain evolution of particular traits.

By comparing the underlying assumptions of each conceptual model, students began to understand the strengths and weaknesses of the models. Students were then given an opportunity to apply these models and assumptions to real-world data sets pertaining to trait selection. Over the course of the curriculum, students successively used each theory to first explain how the theory works, then to apply the theory to an example of evolution using a limited data set, and finally apply the theory to a real-world, less-structured example. The curriculum began with efforts to apply Paley's theory, then Lamarck's, then Darwin's. As the students attempted to apply each of these theories in succession, they experienced firsthand how the first two theories break down when used to explain examples of natural selection. The particular theoretical models were chosen because they resemble the misconceptions students often have about the process of evolution and adaptation, as described earlier. As the students experienced the inadequacy of Paley's and Lamarck's theoretical models, they were also likely restructuring their own prior ideas about evolution. The pedagogical approach outlined in this research is exemplary of one way to promote deep scientific understanding through a conceptual knowledge approach.

Another way to help students draw conceptual connections is through use of *analogies* (Brown & Clement, 1989; Gentner & Gentner, 1983; Gick & Holyoak, 1980) that help learners put new science content into context by using ideas or scenarios that are already familiar to the learner. An analogy involves a source idea, something that is known or familiar, and a target idea, something that is unknown and is to be learned. Instruction through analogy reveals the relationship between the two. For example, an analogy often used in ecology is that a wetland is like a sponge, absorbing water when there is a lot of water around (that is, during floods) and slowly releasing water when very little is around (during dry weather events). Here, the source is "what a sponge can do" (a principal function of a sponge) and the target idea is "what a wetland can do" (a principal function of a wetland). Analogies create a context for learning by helping learners see connections and relationships between the source and the target, thus opening a way for learners to reorganize ideas, retrieve information, and apply knowledge in a new way (Mason, 2004).

Pivotal cases can also be used to help learners connect isolated ideas or ideas that are connected to other contexts (Linn & Hsi, 2000; Linn, Clark, & Slotta, 2003; M. C. Linn, 2006). Pivotal cases are new ideas that help learners develop a more normative understanding of a scientific concept by presenting compelling comparisons between two ideas or situations, by accessing relevant information the student already knows, by providing feedback, and by promoting documentation of the students' ideas (Linn, 2006). For example, Clark (2006) used a computer animation of "heat bars" that demonstrated the speed of heat transfer in materials such as wood and metal. This visualization proved to be a pivotal case because it was a compelling comparison that helped students connect ideas about heat transfer. This pivotal case was one instructional component that allowed students to develop more integrated and scientifically normative ideas about heat and temperature.

Contextual Nature of Knowledge and Learning Science for Understanding

For some time now, researchers have known that much of our knowledge is context-bound. For example, in our density scenario, students had several ideas about mixing substances that were clearly related to a kitchen context. Thus many researchers advocate curriculum and pedagogical approaches that contextualize the science content instead of teaching abstract principles and theories (Bransford, Brown, & Cocking, 1999). However, if knowledge is context-bound, how do we promote understanding of science concepts such that they can be applied to real-world, everyday problems, experiences, and decision making across diverse contexts?

This brings us to the problem of transfer. Teaching for understanding inherently implies that learners understand the topic in a way that allows them to apply the knowledge in a new situation. The challenge for science teachers becomes, "How can teachers capitalize on the contextual nature of knowledge to make science concepts salient beyond the test or the classroom?" Researchers have approached this challenge through many routes, prominently the development of instructional tools and pedagogical techniques. The validity of these approaches is often measured through "transfer tasks" that assess students' abilities to apply learned knowledge to a novel problem or context.

Use of Project-Based Learning

The science project is a time-honored approach that seeks to gain the benefits of the contextualized, hands-on learning we have discussed throughout this volume. Investigation using a set of commonly accepted methods for controlling and observing phenomena is the key mode of inquiry and verification in the sciences. Although not all of the work that goes on under the banner of school science projects supports disciplined inquiry linked to central concepts and questions, where these features are in place, learning gains that enable transfer can occur.

Schneider, Krajcik, Marx, and Soloway (2002) define five key elements of project-based science (PBS). In addition to using driving questions to organize students' investigations, they suggest that strong projects:

Programs, like the nationwide nature mapping project, creates new science and incorporates math, science, writing, technology, and art

- Engage students in investigating a real-life question or problem that drives activities and organizes concepts and principles
- Result in students' developing a series of artifacts, or products, that address the question or problem
- Enable students to engage in investigations
- Involve students, teachers, and members of society in a community of inquiry as they collaborate about the problem
- Promote students' use of cognitive tools

In a study implementing a project-based science curriculum with 142 high school students, Schneider and colleagues (2002) found strong effects of this kind of project work on student achievement as measured by the twelfth-grade National Assessment of Educational Progress (NAEP) science test. Comparing students' results with both the national average and a demographically comparable subgroup, the researchers found students in the PBS classrooms significantly outperformed the national sample on 44 percent of the test items.

Creating a Context for Science Through Socially Relevant Topics

Another strategy for contextualizing science concepts is engaging students in research and debate on socially significant scientific issues, such as environmental, public health, or other social issues that are best understood if the science underlying the problem is understood. A review of the empirical research on this approach (Sadler, 2004) suggests its promise for promoting deeper understanding of scientific concepts.

In a form of problem-based learning, for example, Zohar and Nemet (2002) used an experimental design in which one group of students experienced a curriculum on genetics that posed real-world social and moral dilemmas as a means of instruction while another group was taught in a "traditional" manner, without these dilemmas. The students in the experimental classroom, which wrestled with these dilemmas, learned about Huntington's disease and how this genetically dominant trait is detectable at a very young age but does not express itself until adulthood. The students were then asked questions about what a parent should do if a fetus is determined to have a disease such as Huntington's or cystic fibrosis. The researchers found gains both with respect to the arguments students created on pre- and posttests and with respect to factual genetic knowledge assessed on the end-of-unit test. Further, although there was no difference in pretest scores between the classrooms, those students in the classroom that used a socially relevant science context were significantly more likely to correctly consider biological knowledge when asked about a moral dilemma (53.2 percent versus 8.9 percent) during the posttest.

Sadler (2004) concluded his review by stating: "If we want students to think for themselves, then they need opportunities to engage in informal reasoning, including the contemplation of evidence and data, and express themselves through argumentation. As the cited research (Driver et al., 2000; Jimenez-Aleixandre et al., 2000; Kortland, 1996; Patronis et al., 1999; Zohar & Nemet, 2002) suggests, socioscientific issues can provide a context for informal reasoning and argumentation" (p. 533).

Online Investigation of Science Concepts and Problems

The benefits of science inquiry and conceptual integration can now be pursued simultaneously in virtual learning contexts. For example, Zimmerman (2005) used a knowledge integration approach (M. C. Linn et al., 2004) to design a curriculum for teaching about evolutionary concepts of adaptation. This approach posits that, because knowledge is connected in various ways, the more sophisticated the connections, the better one will understand a particular concept. For this Knowledge Integration study, seventy students worked in the computer-mediated Web-based Inquiry Science Environment (WISE), where they viewed Internet resources, answered reflection notes, engaged in online debate, and visited an aquarium, all as tools for developing and integrating their ideas about adaptation. Students learned about variation within populations and how variation arises, how environmental pressures influence the success of individuals with particular traits, and how genetic traits are passed from one generation to the next.

Specific prompting of students' ideas about what they were learning in both the formal and informal learning environments allowed students to make connections among difficult scientific concepts such as individual genetic variation, generational aspects of adaptation, and natural selection. Pretest-posttest results in comparison to a control group revealed that the approach resulted in students' greater ability to *apply* those ideas to a real-world environmental conservation problem posed to the students several weeks after the end of the curriculum. Students who had a more integrated understanding of the concepts of adaptation at the end of the curriculum also demonstrated greater ability to recall and use those ideas in a coherent and scientifically sound manner.

Prompting students to share their ideas leads to rich discussions about science context

Students as Data Collectors

Diane Petersen's fourth-grade students at Waterville Elementary School in central Washington State have spoken at scientific conferences throughout the country. Their subject is the three-inch-long short-horned lizard *(Phrynosoma douglasii)*, also called the horny toad, which is native to the rural area of Waterville. In addition to making a contribution to science, the students improve their reading, writing, arithmetic, and other skills by studying these animals as part of a nationwide project called NatureMapping.

FILLING THE GAPS

Petersen's involvement with NatureMapping began shortly after she began working at Waterville. She said that in looking at the lessons meant to get her started teaching elementary school science, "I quickly realized that the curriculum was boring and shallow. We had to do something different." She signed up for a NatureMapping workshop and then incorporated the program into her curriculum.

The NatureMapping project is designed to fill gaps in existing information about where certain plant and animal species are located. Petersen started with birds, because she knew a lot of bird-watchers. Her students brought in their own sightings and collected other birders' by phone, then wrote up the information and e-mailed it to Karen Dvornich, the NatureMapping coordinator at the University of Washington. Dvornich added it to the growing data about common Washington species.

The change of focus happened one day when Dvornich visited the classroom. The students were talking about the short-horned lizards they often saw, and because the lizards were considered an at-risk species Dvornich was very interested.

At first Petersen thought the students could collect data themselves near their homes over the summer, but they often forgot or would look at the wrong time. Petersen's solution was to ask farmers in the community to make the observations the class needed. Students made a list of every farmer they knew and sent out invitations to participate in the project.

READING AND WRITING

Each year, Petersen's class starts by imagining a day, and then a year, in the life of a horny toad. This leads into work on reading skills. To understand the difficult vocabulary and structure used in scientific field guides, the students use marginal notations, look up new words, and summarize the information in lists and tables. Then they compare their learnings to what they imagined about the lizards. After they collect data, they compare that to what they read.

Later, students use their experience with the horny toads to practice various kinds of writing: instructions for capturing a lizard, a persuasive paragraph on the same topic, a description of horny toads' resemblance to a dirt clod, and an explanation of how this appearance benefits the lizards.

STATISTICAL ANALYSIS

Each student works with one farmer. On a prearranged day, the farmers come to the school with the data they have collected and help students find their fields on maps and arrange the data in tables. With this information—on numbers and location, dates, and times of sightings—the class looks for answers to questions such as, Where are horny toads the most common? When are they most likely to be in the farmers' fields?

Each sighting is plotted on a computer map, and then all the associated information is gathered on a large spreadsheet. From there, students select data to answer their questions and graph the information. They examine their graphs for clarity and then write an analysis of the results (thus fulfilling a state standard). They also decide what information is useful and what isn't and design the data sheet the farmers will use to collect data for the next year's class.

SCIENTIFIC OBSERVATION

The NatureMapping program finds researchers who can help the class plan studies to answer new questions they come up with. One year, students decided to investigate what happened to horny toads during winter. The field guide said they dig down about 2 inches and partially freeze. However, frost levels in the area reach an average of 18 inches below the surface. So how do they stay alive?

To find out, the class made an 18-inch-high pen of chicken wire with a wood floor and set it into the ground. In October, they placed two lizards inside the pen, and they immediately burrowed underground. When spring came, the students carefully dug out the pen. One horny toad had disappeared, but the other was flattened on the floor of the pen, far below the field guide's 2 inches. The following year, students glued radio transmitters onto a few lizards to learn where they burrow for the winter, how deep they go, and how they survive.

INVOLVEMENT WITH THE COMMUNITY AND BEYOND

The project strengthens ties between the school and the community. "I don't really teach my students mapping—the farmers do," Petersen said. Once a year the farmers get to see the results of their efforts, when students present their findings to the farmers. According to Petersen, this relationship makes the students take their work more seriously.

Although they didn't set out to challenge accepted scientific wisdom, Petersen's classes have made several discoveries about where short-horned lizards live and what they eat. Before the students began collecting data in 1997, fewer than 100 lizard sightings had been documented, most from projects in the 1930s and '40s. Those records showed that horny toads inhabited only undeveloped land, but the data were wrong. Waterville fourth graders have quadrupled the number of documented sightings and shown that the lizards thrive on farmland. They have also changed decades-old assumptions about the animals' habitat and diet. For instance, the literature says these lizards eat ants, but the classes' observations show they clearly prefer small grasshoppers.

Petersen's students routinely perform tasks considered beyond the abilities of children at their grade level, such as mapping data to find trends and going to scientific conferences. She said that the latter has become so commonplace "we've developed a system to figure out who gets to go. And in September, students often walk into the classroom asking, 'Where are we going to present this year?' That's not a bad way to begin a school term."

MORE INFORMATION

- For more on the NatureMapping program, visit http://naturemap.blogspot.com and http://depts.washington.edu/natmap.
- Step-by-step nature mapping instructions are available at www.edutopia.org/how-start-counting-critters.
- Waterville Elementary's PowerPoint presentation for the 2003 Nature Mapping regional meeting can be viewed at www.edutopia.org/media/leapinlizards/HornyToad.ppt.
- To watch a video about Diane Petersen's class and their project, go to www.edutopia.org/toad-tracking.

Adapted from Edutopia article "Leapin' Lizards! Students as Data Collectors," by Diane Petersen. Originally published April 2005.

Social and Cultural Nature of Learning Science for Understanding

Many researchers in education emphasize the social and cultural nature of learning. Viewed in this way, learning is something that occurs in social interaction with other learners and is inextricably linked to the cultural practices in which the content is learned. Teaching and learning science must take into account the social dynamics of classrooms (for example, teacher as authority figure, gender interactions), cultural expectations of the individuals and the teachers, religious backgrounds, school district policies, and even national views and expectations. As Lemke (2001) stated, taking a sociocultural view of science education "means viewing science, science education, and research on science education as human social activities conducted within institutional and cultural frameworks." It also means teaching students that science is a highly social endeavor that is embedded in the culture of the time and place in which it is practiced. As Bruno Latour demonstrates in his seminal books *Laboratory Life: The Social Construction of Scientific Facts* and *Science in Action: How to Follow Scientists and Engineers Through Society*, to understand science we must acknowledge that how science is conducted, and what science is, is influenced by the cultural practice of science as it occurs in the laboratory, the field, or wherever it takes place.

Understanding science also involves "identifying" with the culture and practice of science. Recent research on personal identity and science learning demonstrates the importance of creating inclusive environments for promoting scientific literacy. If a student considers himself or herself to be "not good in science" or someone who doesn't like science because "science is for geeks," then he or she may have an even more difficult time learning science. These personal identities are socially derived and often bound to a particular context. Conversely, the process of identifying as a science learner and a scientist triggers greater engagement, attention, and learning.

For example, B. A. Brown (2004) videotaped more than 180 hours of classroom interactions in a large, urban, largely minority-attended high school.

He found that students' talk, as it relates to how students view science and view themselves as science learners, fell into one of four major categories of identity: (1) students who avoided use of science discourse, (2) those who maintained their typical discourse behavior, (3) students who made an attempt to incorporate science discourse, and finally (4) students who were or became proficient in science discourse. Over the yearlong science (biology) course, students revealed different discourse identities and transitioned through them. Brown even documented instances where individual students, though clearly on the verge of scientific understanding, adopted an opposition status (meaning they avoided use of scientific language) because adopting a proficiency status would have significant negative social impact, such as losing credibility with fellow classmates. This avoidance of scientific discourse then interfered with the student's ability to achieve complete conceptual understanding because understanding science involves the ability to engage in scientific discussions. From this work, Brown devised an instructional approach, called the Directed Discourse Approach to Science Instruction, to help students move toward proficiency status where they not only can use scientific language but identify with, and are comfortable engaging in, science discourse.

In the Directed Discourse Approach to Science Instruction, there are four instructional stages that promote proficiency (Brown, 2004). The first stage is a metacognitive approach designed to promote reflection on prior ideas using whatever language the student is comfortable using. Stage two involves introduction of the science content by the teacher but without overloading the content with detailed scientific language. In the third stage, "the teacher must introduce students to the language of the content and require them through classroom talk and written assignments" that open opportunities for students to move toward proficiency (Brown, 2004, p. 832). Finally, in stage four, assessment activities provide opportunities for students to demonstrate their understanding using science discourse. Brown's research (2004, 2006) suggests that scaffolding students through an identity transition can yield greater

Hands-on Science

Every spring for the past several years, third-grade teacher Frances Koontz has involved her class in the activities of Journey North, an Internet project funded by the Annenberg/CPB Project. Journey North traces the migration of butterflies and other species as they head north each spring. Some three hundred thousand students at more than six thousand schools make observations and report their sightings to create digital maps. They also are linked to working scientists who take questions about the different migrations.

In Koontz's class at Rockledge Elementary School in Bowie, Maryland, each child maintains a folder that documents the twenty-five-hundred-mile flight of monarch butterflies from a wildlife preserve in the mountains outside Mexico City to Canada. The students use paper maps and an atlas, as well as the Journey North Web site, to track the monarchs' path and identify the states the butterflies travel across.

Once Journey North officials report sightings in the southeastern United States, the work goes outside the classroom, to incorporate direct observation. Koontz and her students become "scientists," keeping alert for sightings of the butterflies in their own neighborhood. (They are also watchful at other times, in case they see a butterfly that doesn't fit the usual pattern of travel.) As soon as the students spot the monarchs, they report their observations to the Journey North databank.

SCIENTIFIC OBSERVATION

The eight- and nine-year-olds in Koontz's class calculate the time from egg to caterpillar to chrysalis to butterfly. They measure—in centimeters, as scientists do—the growth of milkweed, on which monarch larvae feed. They take daily temperature readings in a garden they have planted outside the classroom. They make charts and graphs of their results. They write in detail about their findings, and they learn about U.S. states, Canada, and Mexico as their curiosity is piqued through monitoring the migration.

Each year brings new discoveries. One year sightings might start in March, another year in April. Students do their own analyses of the differences in weather conditions that cause the changes in migration patterns. Or in response to questions from the Journey North Web site, they might explore milkweed ecology or investigate which birds are monarch predators.

CREATIVE USE OF TECHNOLOGY

The Journey North Web site includes live satellite coverage of the migrations, but the students' use of technology goes beyond just using the Internet. Children in Koontz's class use a digital camera to take pictures of larvae feeding in their milkweed garden and progressing through the life cycle to become butterflies. "We actually were able to watch one of the butterflies emerge from its chrysalis," Koontz said. "That's something they'll never, never forget."

According to Koontz, not only is the science in Journey North extremely rich but the Internet project also crosses disciplines—writing, math, social studies, and geography. Other Journey North projects include growing tulips and noting the bloom times of the flowers across the continent, tracing the migration of birds and whales, and identifying a mystery city.

Koontz uses a remote keyboard to give children an opportunity to work at the computer without leaving their desks. The young technologists take pictures from books with the digital camera, put those photographs on disk, and then include the photos in a PowerPoint presentation that shows their progress in guessing ten mystery cities using geographic clues ("This city is one of the few world capitals not situated on a coast or navigable river") and comparing sunrise and sunset times. Then they use animation and sound effects to write reports about the project.

ENRICHMENT OPPORTUNITIES

As a tie-in to the monarch project, students in Koontz's class participate in Journey North's "Symbolic Migration." Children in the United States and Canada send paper or fabric butterflies, along with letters about their lives and communities, to children in Mexico who live near the monarch sanctuaries. In the spring, the Mexican children send their own butterflies and messages to classes in the north, timed to coincide with the monarch migration.

Koontz sees big dividends in the hands-on approach to learning that Journey North advocates, from better writing to deeper investigation skills. For first-timers, she advises teachers to "start out small" and not try too many Journey North activities at once.

"Start out with one component," Koontz said. "I started with the tulips. That one is wonderful because the children really get to watch that over the school year. And when that garden blooms, it is just wonderful. And then when they realize that there are gardens all over the country blooming with theirs, it's just a real enriching experience for them."

MORE INFORMATION

- A video on Frances Koontz's class and the Journey North program can be seen at www.edutopia.org/journey-north.
- For more on Journey North, visit www.learner.org/jnorth.
- To learn more about the Annenberg/CPB Project and its teacher resources, go to www.learner.org.

Adapted from Edutopia article "March of the Monarchs," by Diane Curtis. Originally published June 6, 2002.

science understanding. The example in the box "Promoting Science Discourse and Investigation to Promote Conceptual Understanding" shows how a fifth-grade teacher began to work through these stages with her students to help them engage in inquiry and acquire scientific language that would promote their understanding.

PROMOTING SCIENCE DISCOURSE AND INVESTIGATION TO PROMOTE CONCEPTUAL UNDERSTANDING

Prompting learners to share their ideas can lead to rich discussions about science content. These social interactions can play a critical role in development of scientific understanding because they often mirror a level of discourse that occurs naturally in science and that reflects culturally appropriate communication. Teachers can act as guides to focus these social interactions toward a science discourse that includes content and conceptual knowledge. Below is a firsthand account of one teacher's successful attempt to guide students' science discourse. Emily Gibson explains:

Near the end of the 2006–07 school year in my fifth-grade classroom, I planned my first hands-on, inquiry-based science investigation: a squid dissection. Although I had led a squid dissection with seventh graders as part of a teaching practicum the previous summer, this would be the first time I would be implementing this type of lesson in my own classroom—with younger children and, most significantly, without the assistance of coaches from the Lawrence Hall of Science.

I had students work with partners that I had selected in advance. Whenever possible, I tried to match students with a partner not at their same skill level. I thought that this would balance the discourse among students in the classroom. Each pair received one squid, which they were expected to observe, discuss, and dissect together.

The challenge of the squid dissection was trying to give students specific instructions about where and how to snip and slice their specimens without standing in the way of their developing observations and investigations. I tried to listen closely to the dialogue between partners and allow their questions and ideas to guide the dissection. For example, when I noticed one pair of children gently touching one of the eyes of their squid, I encouraged them to cut it open with their scissors. "Sam and Miguel are interested in looking inside the eye," I announced to the rest of the class. "What a great idea! Let's use our scissors to snip apart the eyeball. Just make one cut in the middle of the eye with the tip of your scissors."

I gave the students two to three minutes to simply explore and talk freely to each other as they looked at the gooey mess that they'd made of the eyeball.

"Gross! It's like jelly!" said one child.

Another shouted, "Wait—I just touched something with the scissors!" He pulled out the lens of the eye.

"What did you find?" I asked the student, loud enough for the class to hear.

He held up the spherical lens and told the class that it was "something clear and hard."

"Interesting—let's see if we all have that inside the eyes of our squid," I suggested to everyone.

After all pairs of students had found the lens or received some help in finding it, I asked the class what they thought it might be.

"A bone?" said one student.

"Something that helps them see?" said another.

"What do you think?" I asked another student.

"Yeah. Like Simone said. To see."

(continued)

"Interesting ideas," I said. I wanted students to feel their comments were thoughtful insights, but to know that we could find a scientific answer in the books we had in our classroom. I told them I would look in my book on squids to see what we could find out. I then read a paragraph from the book on the parts of the eye.

"So what do you think we found?" I asked the class.

"I think it's the lens," someone shared.

The students' own curiosity directed the next step of the dissection; I merely tried to act as a loudspeaker for their ideas. They worked together to make observations and find answers to their questions; I followed up with probing questions about what they saw. Finally, they offered inferences based on the information they had; I helped them find sources of factual, scientific information that would lead them to a definitive answer.

Source: Emily Gibson, fifth-grade teacher, Moscone Elementary School, San Francisco, CA

Metacognition and Learning Science for Understanding

A critical component of learning for understanding is thinking about one's prior knowledge, connecting that knowledge to other understandings within a conceptual framework, and accessing the knowledge so it can be applied to novel problems. As we have discussed, the process of metacognition, or "thinking about one's own thinking" (Georghiades, 2004) can lead to restructuring of ideas, allowing deeper conceptual understanding of content.

The science education community has incorporated metacognition in science classrooms in a number of ways. For example, Chi (2000; Chi, deLeeuw, Chiu, & LaVancer, 1994) used a metacognitive technique called self-explanations as a tool for promoting understanding of the human circulatory system. In one controlled experiment, a group of eighth-grade students were encouraged to use a "think aloud" protocol while reading about the human circulatory system from an often-used biology textbook (Chi et al., 1994).

More explicitly, these students (the "prompted" group) were asked to read a line of text silently and were then prompted to explain to themselves, out loud, what the text meant. A control group (nonprompted) was asked to read the line of text silently twice to approximate the same amount of time dedicated to learning the material by both groups. Pre- and posttests measured students' knowledge of the circulatory system and their ability to apply complex ideas of the circulatory system to problems related to human health.

Both groups of students improved from pretest to posttest, but the students prompted to use the self-explanation technique improved significantly more overall than those who simply read the text twice. The researchers found that self-explaining raised the posttest score of both high- and low-achieving groups, implying that all students can benefit from this metacognitive technique. Furthermore, the results for the more difficult questions—those that required students to integrate knowledge of what they had just learned about the circulatory system with prior knowledge—indicated even greater gains for the prompted students. In addition, among the prompted students, those who explained a lot when prompted to self-explain the text showed greater gains from pre- to posttest than those who explained less. This result signals that if a learner self-explains more during a learning event, he or she will have a better understanding of the topic and will be able to apply the knowledge to help solve problems.

The researchers sought to understand why this strategy is successful by creating mental models of students' knowledge of the circulatory system both before and after the experiment. Mental models are maps of students' ideas that show the degree to which students' ideas are connected and how they are connected. When they analyzed these maps, they found that the prompted students created the most accurate model of the circulatory system and did so more often than the nonprompted students. Finally, the researchers used the mental models and the pretest-posttests to determine how well this technique helps students link prior knowledge to newly learned knowledge. By analyzing what students said before and after, they found that during self-explanation

Using sophisticated technology, like global positioning systems, engages students and helps them understand science as professional scientists do

students use prior knowledge, that is, knowledge they had at the beginning of the experiment, approximately 30 percent of the time (Chi et al., 1994).

As we saw in examining research on reading, prompting students to be metacognitive and to take the time to verbalize what they have just read promotes a more accurate and more applicable knowledge of the topic than if little "thinking about one's thinking" has occurred. Additionally, prompting students to think about the science content they are learning helps them connect those ideas to what they already know and allows them to achieve a greater understanding of that content.

CONCLUSION

Science is all around us; we experience scientific phenomena from day one and thus arrive at any situation, including the science classroom, with prior knowledge and ideas about how the world works. These notions are highly contextualized and may or may not be representative of how scientists understand the same phenomena. Bringing students to a scientifically grounded understanding thus involves more than rote memorization and recitation of facts, information, algorithms, and so on. *Understanding* science requires attention to prior knowledge, to the contextual nature of knowledge, and to the development of conceptual, integrated knowledge, as well as development of important skills such as metacognition. The research in science education reinforces the principles we have identified in other fields for designing curriculum and instruction:

- Activate, don't ignore, prior ideas.
- Recognize that teaching for understanding requires conceptual knowledge that is organized in a schema, not unconnected knowledge.

- Understand that knowledge is contextual, and inquiry that allows investigation and application of knowledge helps learners understand more deeply.
- Recognize the social, cultural, and personal identity factors influencing how students engage in science in the classroom; therefore giving learners opportunities to learn science within their social and cultural norms can improve learning.
- Incorporate metacognitive tools and approaches, so that learners develop strategies for approaching complex tasks, make thinking visible, and learn to monitor and adjust their own learning.

The authors would like to thank Scott Randol for his comments and Emily Gibson for her contributions to this chapter.

CONCLUSION 5

CREATING SCHOOLS THAT DEVELOP UNDERSTANDING

Linda Darling-Hammond

Today's society has raised expectations for both teachers and students. Teachers are expected to address state standards and assessments in their practice while helping varying kinds of learners meet their individualized needs. They are expected to support the growth and development of diverse learners with a range of learning styles, multiple intelligences, family and cultural backgrounds, and life experiences. Students are expected to learn more challenging material than ever before and demonstrate their learning in ways that illustrate more proficient performance. The rhetoric of our national education agenda is to leave no child behind, "to ensure—for all students in all communities—a genuine right to learn" (Darling-Hammond, 1997, p. 5).

Not only do schools serve more diverse learners than ever before, they are expected to "teach for understanding"—that is, to teach with the goal of helping students develop the ability to use their knowledge in novel ways (Perkins, 1998). Students taught for understanding are expected to evaluate and defend ideas with careful reasoning and evidence, independently inquire into a problem using a productive research strategy, produce a high-quality piece of work, and understand the standards that indicate they have done so. They demonstrate that they understand by using what they've learned to solve novel problems.

Reformers have argued that our twentieth-century educational system was not designed to produce a wide-spread pedagogy for understanding, one that gives students opportunities to test and apply their ideas, look at concepts from many points of view, and develop proficient performances of their own. It is not that students are incapable of doing these things. It is that they have too rarely been taught in a manner that has asked them to do so. The issue was vividly illustrated in side-by-side letters to the editor in the *New York Times* on November 6, 1991. Two students wrote in response to then-President George H. W. Bush's proposed choice plan, arguing that choice was not the issue. The first was from a European student:

> As a student who attended a high school that offered a European education and now attends an American university, I can see the difference between the knowledge acquired by American and European students. American students . . . seem to have been bombarded with facts and figures that they were forced to memorize. European students are taught the same subjects, but instead of memorizing them, they are forced to understand them. This may seem a small detail, but as a result of the difference in teaching, European students have a better understanding of the subjects taught. They are more likely to remember the facts, because what is understood lasts longer than what is memorized. Critical thinking, analysis of subjects in depth and research techniques

Not only do schools serve more diverse learners than ever before, they are expected to "teach for understanding"—that is, to teach with the goal of helping students develop the ability to use their knowledge in novel ways.

are skills that I and other European-educated students learned in our high schools but have to learn again at our American universities.

The second was from a high school student in Madison, Wisconsin:

> I believe that the main reason we rank at the low end in education is that we are primarily taught to memorize text until we reach 10th or 11th grade. As a student in the 11th grade, I am only now being asked to think logically to solve problems. It would have been much easier and a lot more useful if our elementary and middle school teachers had begun to explain why certain equations worked and taught us how to discuss poems or a speech. . . . I cannot remember a teacher ever asking us about our feelings about an event or about the effects of historic decisions. If we do not know how to analyze a problem, how are we ever going to compete in the real world? The problems we are going to face are not all going to be written down in a textbook with the answers in the back.

Guided by more limited conceptions of learning, twentieth-century texts and tests largely presented a view of learning for recognition and recall rather than for analysis and production of ideas.

Fortunately, teaching for understanding is not wholly absent from U.S. schools. Research on how people learn has made the strategies for productive learning clearer, and in some places more common. However, there are a number of system elements that are critically important for the spread of these methods. These include how schools are organized for learning, opportunities for professional learning for teachers, and the broader curriculum and assessment system within which schools operate. In this last chapter, we review what is known about teaching for meaningful learning and about the systems that can support it.

PRINCIPLES OF TEACHING FOR UNDERSTANDING

We have been discussing what kinds of teaching are likely to help students engage in the meaningful learning that will allow them to manage the fast-changing, knowledge-based society of the twenty-first century. Among the key ideas that recur across subject areas:

Active, in-depth learning. Active in-depth learning through well-designed projects, problems, and design tasks focuses student inquiry around central questions in the disciplines and "engages students in *doing* the work of writers, scientists, mathematicians, musicians, sculptors, and critics" (Darling-Hammond, 1997, pp. 107–108). For example, inquiry learning in science includes designing, conducting, evaluating, and representing a scientific investigation or experiment as the core mode of discovery in the discipline. Students use higher-order cognitive skills—analysis, synthesis, and evaluation of alternatives—to develop knowledge and apply it to meaningful questions. Students are actively and meaningfully engaged when they learn strategic approaches to guiding their own reading and writing, and when they apply what they have read in developing arguments and conjectures. They learn actively when they investigate mathematical patterns using a range of materials and share arguments about what they have discovered. Students' learning is designed to enable them to transfer ideas to novel situations and contexts, and to make connections across distinctive situations.

Teachers skillfully design and manage group work for purpose, productivity, and strong problem-solving

Authentic, formative assessment. Curriculum and assessment are integrated around meaningful performances in real-world contexts. Performance tasks are central to the work of the disciplines and are selected to represent the big ideas and modes of inquiry in each subject area. Tasks encourage students to apply what they are learning to real-life situations. Ongoing formative assessments use multiple criteria to determine *how* students are thinking and learning, as well as *what* they know and can do. Formative feedback, through self-, peer-, and teacher-assessment, helps students learn to reflect on their own work, evaluate it against a standard, and improve it. Students are motivated by opportunities to revise their work and succeed in meaningful tasks. Metacognitive skills are developed as students learn to monitor and manage their learning.

Opportunities for collaboration. Classrooms are organized for students' participation in a "learning community," supporting Vygotsky's (1978) notion that learning takes place in a social context and relies on communication and interaction with others. Classrooms are designed to foster communities of discourse that make students' and teachers' thinking visible. Teachers skillfully design and manage group work so that it is purposeful, used to support accomplishment of productive tasks, and generative of both stronger relationships and more insightful problem solving. Individual and collective learning is encouraged as teachers and expert peers assist students in gaining deeper understanding. The classroom environment encourages students' motivation by minimizing comparison, and by fostering opportunities for risk taking and improvement over time. Teachers organize curriculum and teaching to embrace students' differences as opportunities for sharing expertise and learning from one another.

Attention to prior knowledge, experience, and development. Teaching and learning are informed by knowledge about children's development. Teachers observe children carefully and build on students' prior knowledge and progress. They connect the curriculum to learners' experiences and frames of reference, including students' cultural knowledge. They understand developmental progressions of learning in different domains, including common preconceptions or misconceptions that need to be addressed in instruction. They are adept at scaffolding instruction so that it meets students where they are in terms of their knowledge and experiences and helps them systematically expand their abilities, mastering new concepts and proficiencies.

Knowledge organized around core concepts and connections. How teachers organize ideas and learning experiences is another factor that makes a difference in how deeply students understand. Understanding requires drawing connections and seeing how new ideas are related to those already learned—how they are alike and different. Expert teaching in a subject area rests on an understanding of how students are likely to come to this knowledge—what can be done to bridge the distance between what students understand and what counts as expert knowledge in the field—and how it is organized and pursued. Organizing projects and problems around the core concepts and modes of inquiry in the disciplines, and drawing connections among ideas through analogies, contrasting cases, and well-chosen problems, helps students make sense of what otherwise appear to be disconnected or meaningless facts.

Development of metacognitive skills. Teachers help students learn to think about their own thinking, by *reflecting* on their work, gauging what they know and need to know, and learning how to *manage* their own processes of learning by acquiring specific strategies for solving problems. Teachers encourage a reflective stance toward learning that helps students assess and direct their own emerging understandings. Teachers use opportunities for discussion and presentation of ideas, as well as formative assessment tools, to support this reflection. Teachers help students learn how to ask self-monitoring questions as they are learning and teach concrete strategies that enable students to

Powerful learning occurs when student work resembles that of real writers, scientists, mathematicians, and historians

read and write more proficiently, engage in mathematical problem solving, and develop scientific or historical reasoning abilities.

The intersections among these principles can be seen in the *How People Learn* (HPL) framework developed by John Bransford and colleagues (1999). This framework suggests that learning is enhanced when learning environments are *student-centered*, *knowledge-centered*, *assessment-centered*, and *community-centered* (see Figure 1). Each of these lenses on the learning environment influences what is taught, how it is taught, and how it is assessed. Using the framework as an organizer for considering learning principles, teachers can ask from a learner-centered perspective when designing their work, "What do students bring in terms of their experience and knowledge, and what do they need? How am I drawing on students' interests, prior knowledge, and strengths? How can I help learners reflect on and manage their own learning?" From a knowledge-centered vantage point they can ask: "What kind of knowledge am I trying to develop? How does it relate to the core concepts and modes of inquiry of the

FIGURE 1

HPL Framework

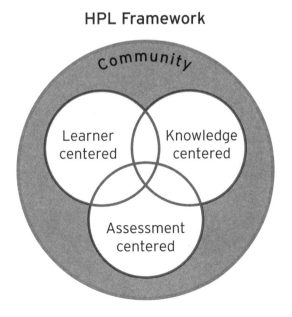

field? How will it be learned so that it can be transferred to other situations?" From an assessment-centered perspective, they can examine: "What kinds of assessments will help me know what students understand and how they learn? How can I use information to help students improve their work? What do I need to know about student learning to guide my own teaching?" From a community-centered framework, they can inquire: "How can I construct a community of learners in the classroom—and beyond—to support students' learning?"

Organizing Schools for Understanding

Some schools have been able to achieve extraordinary results by designing themselves around how students learn (for examples, see Braddock & McPartland, 1993; Darling-Hammond, Ancess, & Ort, 2002; Friedlaender & Darling-Hammond, 2007; Lee, Bryk, & Smith, 1993; Lee, Smith, & Croninger, 1997; Lieberman, 1995; Newmann, Marks, & Gamoran, 1996). Schools organizing the whole curriculum around practices that enhance learning obtain these outcomes because they are working *with* the way people learn rather than against it. They are able to help all students master challenging content and develop critical-thinking skills by organizing teaching so that teachers know their students and the learning process well, build on what students bring, and support their learning with powerful strategies. They organize the curriculum around the core ideas in the disciplines, and then they carefully scaffold students' learning on authentic tasks. Students' work resembles the work that real writers, scientists, mathematicians, and historians do, and it is produced with continuous feedback, reflection, and revision to meet high standards.

The transformation of Keels Elementary School in Columbia, South Carolina, illustrates a whole-school approach. Located near a military base that serves a highly transient group of low-income students of color, the school was nearly slated for closing twenty years ago when its population changed and performance declined. After four years of restructuring its practices, Keels began to produce extraordinary levels of academic success for its students and soon served as a model for many surrounding schools (Berry, 1995). Although fewer than half of the students entering Keels typically meet the state's "readiness" standard in kindergarten, by the end of first grade more than 90 percent meet state standards in reading and mathematics. After the school restructured its work, PTA meetings became standing room only, and a waiting list of families hoping to transfer into the school from outside the attendance zone grew.

Supported by a dynamic principal who engaged teachers in decision making and launched conversations about research and practice, the staff identified and introduced a set of initiatives grounded in what they learned about learning. The initiatives included cooperative learning in heterogeneous classes, integrated instruction in reading and writing and hands-on work in mathematics and science, social studies projects such as studies of the stock market, computer-based learning applied to such programs as Writing to Read, Reading Recovery supports, parent education workshops and home visits, and after-school programs offering tutoring and supervised homework sessions. Students were involved in peer teaching and in decision making about school discipline and extracurricular events. Faculty developed performance assessments and portfolios in science. Teachers began to plan collaboratively and conduct peer observations, helping one another learn new practices.

The Writing to Read classroom is an example of what learning came to look like at Keels:

> A sign proclaimed: "This is a Risk-Free Environment." In one corner of the room, a group of students were working a lab experiment where traits of plants were being investigated and students were classifying, sorting, and measuring. These students were finishing up a 3-week unit on seeds, stems, and leaves. . . . [They] wore visors with the word "scientist" inscribed on top. . . . Other students were writing about what they were learning. Those students wore

visors with the word "author" inscribed on top. [Teacher] Sandra McLain deftly reads and critiques Constance's work and says to her in a resonant voice, "You just about have a science book written." Constance joyously responds with a "YES!" In other corners of the room, a child reads sitting on a bean bag chair and next to him another child "meets an author" on audio-tape. Across the room there are three computers where students brush up on phonemes. Sandra noted "the more they write the more they learn" [Berry, 1995, p. 122].

Because school staff researched and adopted each initiative, they developed a commitment to their work that has driven their ongoing press to improve. The further they stretch and the more they realize about what students can do, the higher the expectations for themselves and their students. These staff comments are typical:

At the first day of school we give them things they can do . . . in fact the first two words we make sure they can read are "I can" and "we can." With every skill we teach, we use the visual, the auditory, and the kinesthetic. We write words, make up sentences, draw pictures. We push them into being complete readers. One way we do this is by cutting the junk and fluff out of reading programs, like all the pages in the workbooks.

Before I thought they just needed to know the basics in science. . . . I do not believe this anymore. . . . We are in the first stages of [restructuring the science curriculum]. We are wedding basic science building blocks with major math principles. Students are learning to sort, graph, weigh, measure, and predict. They are learning about data and constructing hypotheses, all in the first grade. I did not learn this until high school! [Berry, 1995, p. 124].

The same kinds of practices are seen in high schools that have redesigned to become substantially more successful. For example, in a large-scale study of more than eight hundred high schools, students in schools with a high level of what the researchers called "authentic instruction"—instruction focused on active learning calling for disciplined inquiry, higher-order thinking, extended writing, and an audience for student work—were found to experience larger achievement gains on standardized tests than those experiencing more traditional instruction (Lee, Smith, & Croninger, 1995; Newmann & Wehlage, 1995). Another study of twenty-three restructured high schools demonstrated that these benefits transfer to achievement on intellectually challenging performance (Newmann, Marks, & Gamoran, 1996). The restructured schools in this study, identified through a national search, demonstrated "substantial departures from typical organizational features" (p. 293), including shared governance models, teachers working in teams with common planning time, extended instructional periods or block scheduling, heterogeneous grouping of students, and use of cooperative learning and groupwork.

As these examples suggest, when schools are based on what we know about how students develop and learn, every aspect of teachers' work (how their days are organized, how they work with students, how they collaborate with one another) must be reconsidered to support strong relationships as well as challenging intellectual work. However, changing only one aspect of schooling, as many reforms often do, is not enough. All the many dimensions of learning theory have to come together in classrooms and schools to ensure students' learning. For example, if teachers adopt ambitious performance assessments but do not have a curriculum that supports the ongoing revision of student work, that furnishes students with opportunities for assisted performance, and that scaffolds the learning, the assessments will not improve learning. To do those things, teachers also need time in the curriculum and a shared view of learning on throughout the school that supports children's development, sets appropriate expectations, and motivates students to want to learn and succeed.

Redesigning Schools to Support Learning

The process of redesigning schools to support learning, like the process of reflecting on classroom teaching, can be informed by the *How People Learn* framework. Teachers and school leaders can *focus on student learning* and *focus on knowledge* by collectively mapping curriculum and conceptualizing learning experiences. Grant Wiggins and Jay McTighe (1998) suggest a strategy to map curriculum through a "backward design process" by starting with the end, or the "desired results," in mind. Their key design questions are: "What is worthy of understanding? What is evidence of understanding? What learning experiences and teaching promote understanding, interest, and excellence?" (Wiggins & McTighe, 1998, p. 18). Teachers can use this approach to plan instructional activities as well as schoolwide themes and performance assessments.

Teachers can *focus on student learning* and *focus on assessment* by creating assessments together, designing rubrics for exhibitions or projects, observing one another's students, giving feedback to students, and taking time to analyze student work together to examine what has been learned and consider where to go next. Setting schoolwide standards and expectations builds a *community* of teachers and learners who are working together for common goals. When teachers look at student work together, they bring a variety of perspectives about the child and the learning process. Because student work is "the product not only of the child but of the alchemy of teacher, student, and object of study" (Seidel, 1998, p. 88), systematic study of such work can lead teachers to redesign teaching and curriculum and develop more effective supports for individual students. Institutional support for teachers to engage in such study can include exhibitions or portfolio conferences evaluated by panels of faculty, teacher study groups that bring work samples for evaluation and discussion, and workshops for teachers to learn and share ideas about assessments of student learning.

Finally, teachers can *develop a professional community* for themselves by using collaboration as a tool to *reflect on and look at their own teaching*. Institutional support for teachers can include time for peer coaching so that teachers can see each other and get feedback on their practice. It can also include lessons co-designed by teachers and taught by colleagues for teachers to observe, analyze, and reflect on. "Lesson study," for instance, is a technique used in Japan, China, Australia, and New Zealand in which teachers collectively develop and observe the teaching of a model lesson, and then reflect on the lesson and students' responses to it so as to improve on it (Watanabe, 2002).

Teachers learn just as students do: by studying, doing, and reflecting; by collaborating with other teachers; by looking closely at students and their work; and by sharing what they see. This kind of learning cannot occur in college classrooms divorced from engagement in practice or in school classrooms divorced from knowledge about how to interpret practice. Good settings for teacher learning have lots of opportunities for research and inquiry, for trying and testing, for talking about and evaluating the results of learning and teaching. The "rub between theory and practice" (Miller & Silvernail, 1994) occurs most productively when questions arise in the context of real students and real work-in-progress where research and disciplined inquiry are also at hand. Professional development strategies that succeed in improving teaching share several features. They tend to be:

- Experiential, engaging teachers in concrete tasks of teaching, assessment, and observation that illuminate the processes of learning and development
- Grounded in participants' questions, inquiry, and experimentation as well as professionwide research
- Collaborative, involving a sharing of knowledge among educators
- Connected to and derived from teachers' work with their students as well as to examinations of subject matter and teaching methods

- Sustained and intensive, supported by modeling, coaching, and problem-solving around specific problems of practice
- Connected to other aspects of school change [Darling-Hammond & McLaughlin, 1995]

Productive approaches shift from old models of "teacher training" or "inservicing," in which an expert imparts new techniques in drive-by workshops, to a model in which teachers confront research and theory directly, are regularly engaged in evaluating their practice, and use their colleagues for mutual assistance. Growing evidence suggests that investments in this kind of professional development both improve teaching practice and reap learning gains for students, especially at the kind of more challenging learning that new standards demand (D. K. Cohen & Hill, 2001; Desimone et al., 2002; Lampert & Eshelman, 1995; Little, 1993).

Developing School Coherence

Finally, although we have focused primarily on classroom practices, supporting more powerful learning for students also requires creating schools that are more coherent from one classroom to the next and from grade to grade. Research on extraordinarily successful schools has found that, in contrast to the individualistic norms of most, these schools have forged a sense of mission; a shared ethos; common goals for learning; and common strategies for curriculum, instruction, and assessment (Bryk, Camburn, & Louis, 1999; Darling-Hammond, 1997; Lee, Bryk, & Smith, 1993). Although such a strong culture may be easier to forge in the private schools where it was noted early on by researchers, public schools that create a sense of character and strongly shared commitments are equally successful at creating powerful learning for a range of students (Darling-Hammond, 1997; Lieberman, 1995).

Schools that redesign their work around student learning spend a great deal of time thinking through what they value, how they will know if they've achieved it, and what they must do to create connected learning experiences that enable students to achieve these goals. Essential Schools, for example, often engage in a process of "planning backwards" (McDonald, 1993) in developing their graduation requirements, asking first, "What kind of graduate do we want?" then, "How do we get there?" and finally, "How will we know when we have arrived?" This process yields clarity about purpose as well as a shared view of what students ought to know and be able to do as a result of their education.

When common goals and commitments motivate school life, learning becomes more powerful because it is cumulative rather than disjointed. Students and teachers work toward habits that are practiced, reinforced, and supported until they become second nature. Rather than switching mindsets several times each day and many times over the course of a school career, wondering what teachers want or what school is about, students can concentrate on developing their abilities and teachers can collaborate with one another in helping them do so.

THE POLICY CONTEXT

What occurs in classrooms and schools is also shaped by the external policy environment. Since the early 1990s, virtually all states and most districts have created standards for student learning, new curriculum frameworks to guide instruction, and assessments to test students' knowledge. These are often accompanied by accountability schemes that require rewards and sanctions for students, teachers, and schools based on trends in test scores. Standards-based reform is intended to leverage systemwide changes in curriculum, teacher preparation, and school resources. However, in many cases standards have led to mandates for student testing without policy initiatives that directly address the quality of teaching, allocation of resources, or the nature of schooling.

The nature of these standards and assessments matters greatly. In general, studies suggest that in states and districts that have invested in performance-based assessments along with improved teacher quality and school capacity, student achievement has increased on multiple measures, even without high-stakes rewards and sanctions (Darling-Hammond & Rustique-Forrester, 2005). In the 1990s, when performance assessments were launched in a number of states, studies found that teachers assigned more writing and mathematical problem solving of the kinds demanded on the new assessments in states ranging from California (Chapman, 1991; Herman, Klein, Heath, & Wakai, 1995) to Kentucky (Stecher et al., 1998), Maine (Firestone et al., 1998), Maryland (Lane et al., 2000), Vermont (Koretz, Stecher, & Deibert, 1992), and Washington (Stecher et al., 2000).

Benefits for instruction have also depended on how principals and teachers approach the challenge of incorporating new standards—whether they sought to deepen instruction, for example, rather than merely attaching test-like items to lessons—and how much teaching expertise is available in particular schools, along with investment in teacher professional development (Borko et al., 1999; Borko & Stecher, 2001; Wolf, Borko, McIver, & Elliott, 1999). Studies have found that teachers who are involved in scoring performance assessments with other colleagues and discussing their students' work report the experience helped them change their practice to become more problem-oriented and more diagnostic (Darling-Hammond, Ancess, & Falk, 1995; Goldberg & Rosewell, 2000; Murnane & Levy, 1996).

In settings where narrow tests are used, however, especially when high stakes are attached, schools and teachers often reduce the curriculum to what is tested and the way it is tested, undermining the quality of teaching, especially in schools where students struggle to pass the tests. Research identifying negative effects of tests on teaching quality has noted narrowing of the curriculum to subjects and modes of performance that are tested, loss of instructional time to test preparation, and less instruction focused on complex reasoning and performance (Klein et al., 2000; Koretz & Barron, 1998; Koretz, Mitchell, et al., 1996; Koretz, Linn, et al., 1991; R. L. Linn, 2000; Linn, Graue, & Sanders, 1990; Stecher et al., 2000). Studies in high-stakes-testing states using limited multiple-choice measures have found that, under pressure to show improved performance, teachers often prepare students by spending substantial instructional time on exercises that look just like the test items, reducing time on untested subjects or topics and reverting to instructional practices such as recall and recitation that they feel will prepare students for standardized tests. In the process, instructional strategies such as projects, research papers, extended writing, and computer use are deemphasized (Brown, 1992; Haney, 2000; Jones et al., 1999; Jones & Egley, 2004; Popham, 1999; Smith, 1991).

Another side effect of some approaches to standards and tests is more superficial teaching, rather than in-depth investigation. As two teachers remarked in a recent study:

> Before [the state test] I was a better teacher. I was exposing my children to a wide range of science and social studies experiences. I taught using themes that really immersed the children into learning about a topic using their reading, writing, math, and technology skills. Now I'm basically afraid to NOT teach to the test. I know that the way I was teaching was building a better foundation for my kids as well as a love of learning. Now each year I can't wait until March is over so I can spend the last two and a half months of school teaching the way I want to teach, the way I know students will be excited about.

> I believe that the [state test] is pushing students and teachers to rush through curriculum much too quickly. Rather than focusing on getting students to understand a concept fully in math, we must rush through all the subjects so we are prepared to take the test in March. This creates a surface knowledge or many times very little knowledge in a lot of areas. I would rather spend a month on one concept and see my students studying in an in-depth manner.
>
> (Southeast Center for Teaching Quality, 2003, p. 15)

Interestingly, international assessments have shown that higher-scoring countries in mathematics and science teach *fewer* concepts each year but teach them more deeply than tends to be true in the United States, so that students have a stronger foundation to support higher-order learning in the upper grades (McKnight et al., 1987). Many countries also encourage school-based assessments, using projects, research papers, applications of knowledge, and presentations, which are part of their overall assessment systems.

Among the factors that appear to influence the outcomes of testing are the nature of tests (what kinds of things are assessed and how); the uses of tests (what kinds of decisions are made based on test scores); the capacity for improvement represented by teacher knowledge and skills; and the context for school improvement at the state, district, and school levels, including resource levels and professional development opportunities.

Given current pressures to apply higher stakes to student test results, there is a need for more attention to how these increased pressures may influence the practices of schools and teachers, and what the long-term consequences may be for teaching and learning. Reflecting what research has revealed thus far, it seems there are several strategies that could encourage more productive outcomes from standards and testing systems, especially for the most vulnerable students. We would include at least these:

1. Broader *use of performance assessments* that offer "tests worth teaching to" (Resnick, 1987)—assessments that encourage the kinds of higher-order thinking and performance skills students will need to use in the world outside of school. If the goal is stronger education, then investments in more productive assessments are not just testing costs; they are part of the core costs of instruction and professional development. Where teachers are involved in developing and scoring these assessments, their learning is part of the capacity building that is essential if tests are to improve student learning opportunities rather than restrict them.

2. Assessment systems, like those in a number of states and most high-achieving nations, that *combine large-scale and classroom assessments* (using, for example, curriculum-embedded performance tasks), so that teachers are encouraged to engage in formative assessment, strengthen their knowledge about student learning, and increase their capacity to shape instruction to students' needs. As Herman (2002) notes: "To truly understand why student performance is as it is and to get to the root of whatever teaching and learning, issues may exist, schools and teachers really need to move to a more detailed level of assessment and analysis than annual state tests afford. . . . Such local assessments are also necessary to provide teachers with essential, ongoing information to gauge student progress and adjust teaching and learning opportunities accordingly" (p. 22).

3. Systematic *investments in teacher knowledge and school capacity*, including (in addition to standards-based professional development and scoring opportunities associated with performance assessments) systemic investments in teachers' and principals' preservice and inservice education to build a strong foundation of understanding about learning and development, curriculum, effective teaching strategies, and formative assessment.

Ultimately, raising standards for students so that they learn in powerful and productive ways requires raising standards for the *system*, so that it generates the kind of teaching and school settings students need in order to learn, guided by rich information about learning and supported by strong teaching expertise.

APPENDIX

In the following section we've included three tables that summarize various aspects of teaching for understanding, as well as examples of what these look like in practice.

Table 1 presents a summary of design principles that support inquiry-based learning, such as problem design and incorporating authentic audiences into projects.

Table 2 describes the types of assessments that can be used in long-term inquiry approaches, from rubrics to self-assessment.

Table 3 summarizes techniques for fostering productive and meaningful group work, and includes a description of "jigsaw" groups and peer teaching.

TABLE 1

Design Principles for Supporting Inquiry-Based Approaches

TYPE	FEATURES AND FUNCTIONS	EXAMPLES	REFERENCES
Problem design	Projects and problems should be complex, open-ended, and realistic; have multiple solutions and methods for reaching solutions; and resonate with student's experience. They should be designed to maximize the probability that students will encounter the big ideas specified in the learning goal and should lead students to confront and resolve conflicting ideas to prevent "doing for the sake of doing."	(1) Petrosino observed the benefit of asking students to generate causal explanations in a rocket-building exercise. Instead of asking students to simply build rockets to go as high as possible, it is better to require them to identify design features of their rocket that related to performance such as speed or the shape of the rocket. (2) The Jasper series provided broad challenges and problems within a narrative format and embedded the data for solution within the story. This design gave students the opportunity to define the problems and then identify the information that would be relevant for solution.	Barron et. al., 1998; Petrosino, 1998
Cycles of work with ongoing assessment and feedback	Sustained project work needs to be designed so that there are cycles of work and revision and adequate time to complete them. Processes should be set in place such that students frequently encounter feedback on their work to date; both peer and teacher feedback can be useful. Feedback that includes explicit suggestions for revision and time for students to implement the revision supports learning.	(1) Small group critiques, or "crit" sessions, can be organized throughout a cycle in architecture or design projects. (2) A peer review cycle was included in the ThinkQuest competition (2005–06), where teams submit a beta version of their educational Web site and have two weeks to review three sites created by other teams using the evaluation rubric, and then three weeks to revise their own site on the basis of reviews they receive.	Schwartz, Lin, Brophy, & Bransford, 1999; Puntambekar & Kolodner, 2005; www.thinkquest.org

Authentic audiences and deadlines	Working toward a deadline that includes sharing with an outside audience can be highly motivating for students. These deadlines can serve as a vehicle to elicit feedback and revise work before finalizing products.	As a follow up to a problem-based learning unit focused on concepts of scale and measurements, students are asked to work as a team to design a play structure for a local community center. Teams present their designs on video and submit them to a panel of experts who judge if the designs are accurate and meet the design speci-fications. All successful designs are then entered into a drawing, the winner of which builds their play structure for an actual community center.	Barron et al., 1998
Scaffolds and resources	Informational resources, models of good work, exposure to mature thinking about inquiry, and access to experts can support learning in various ways. Building in redundancy across resources is the key as it keeps the focus on learning concepts and encourages students to connect these concepts with their design work. Time is also an important resource. Students must be given enough time to reason well and pursue a problem in depth.	(1) In a science classroom, a problem is related to coastal erosion, where students have access to activities that require a range of resources including paper-based stream tables, video resources, and relevant Web sites. (2) In problem-based approaches, a common strategy is to use a whiteboard divided into quadrants to track the "Facts," "Ideas," "Learning Issues," and "Action Plan" of a problem in order to focus attention and externalize the problem-solving process.	Barron et al., 1998; Puntambekar & Kolodner, 2005

(Continued)

TABLE 1 (Continued)

TYPE	FEATURES AND FUNCTIONS	EXAMPLES	REFERENCES
Productive classroom norms and activity structures	Norms established in the larger classroom context such as accountability, intellectual authority, and respect support small group interactions. Establishment of these norms is accomplished through teachers modeling a stance toward debate and discussion, positioning students as stakeholders, and publicly encouraging use of multiple resources and cognitive strategies such as looking for convergence among sources. Productive norms are also established through framing the assignment. Students are given authority or agency when they have a hand in defining and addressing the problems.	(1) In the communities of learners model, whole-class discussions create an opportunity for students to engage in debate without the teacher playing the role of ultimate authority. Students are positioned as experts but also are held accountable to disciplinary standards of marshalling evidence and responding to the critique of their peers. (2) In Lampert's mathematics classroom, she uses routine ways of questioning and dialoguing that push for student's sense making and intellectual authority. For example, she asks for multiple solutions and justifications. (3) In a middle school pair programming intervention, students identified pair rules for working together, for example, "partners physically get up and move positions when switching roles" and "partners share ownership over the project."	Cobb, 1995; Engle & Conant, 2002; Lampert, 1989; Leinhart & Greeno, 1986; Leinhart & Smith, 1985; Polman, 2004; Werner, Denner, & Bean, 2004; www.pair programming.com/
New roles for teachers and students	Teacher helps to facilitate the progress through the cycle of work and asks questions to make thinking visible, giving students authority to define and address problems and encouraging them to be authors and producers of knowledge.	In a medical school context, the instructor shaped student progress through questioning that helped focus their attention and supported their generation of causal explanations. The continued questioning helped students create accurate mental models of the patient's condition and pushed them to link their hypotheses to patient's symptom profiles.	Hmelo-Silver & Barrows, 2006; Engle & Conant, 2002
Opportunities for ongoing reflection	Time should be built into projects or problems for students to reflect deeply on the work they are doing and how it relates to larger concepts specified in the learning goal, including deep questioning about process and understanding.	Structured diary prompts are used in a project where teams designed a playground for a specific community that asked students to give a rationale and explanation for their decisions at the stages of the design process.	Puntambekar & Kolodner, 2005; Barron et al., 1998

TABLE 2

Forms and Functions of Assessment for Inquiry-Based Approaches

TYPE	FORM OF FEEDBACK	EXAMPLES	REFERENCES
Rubrics	Dimensions of products specified with levels of progress defined. Criteria for excellence should be understandable to students; students should comprehend the assessment criteria before doing work and should revisit it while doing work. Ideally, the rubric is designed by students and teachers. It can be used for formative assessment midproject or a more summative assessment at the end. Rubrics are generally applied to group product rather than to individual work.	(1) The international ThinkQuest competition leads teams of students to create Web sites about an educational topic. Entries are submitted to a panel of judges who weigh the project according to a rubric of assessment criteria with dimensions broken into three sections: educational content, educational perspective, and Web design. (2) FIRST Lego League is a competition for middle school students to build a robot according to a set of criteria and a specific challenge. Three rubrics are given to teams to be used from the beginning to evaluate their own work and guide judging at the competition. Rubrics are included for robot design, project presentation, and teamwork.	Barron et al., 1998; Penuel, Means, & Simkins, 2000; www.thinkquest.org; www.usfirst.org
Solution reviews	Public opportunity to show work in progress and obtain feedback from peers, teachers, or other community members. Work is generally displayed in a way that permits easy review. Intent is to share information that can be used for revision.	In the community of learners model, students created posters based on their research that were reviewed by peers and their teachers. This presentation opportunity sparked debate in the group about what to include. Feedback led to additional research, and this was incorporated into their final reports.	Williams & Black, 1998; Engle & Conant, 2002

(Continued)

TABLE 2 (Continued)

TYPE	FORM OF FEEDBACK	EXAMPLES	REFERENCES
Whole-class discussion	Ideas and explanations are vetted through whole-class structured discussions. Routines can be used to structure conversation. Classroom discourse can yield information for teachers and students about the new ideas and misconceptions. Teachers can observe how students interact with one another around content and use conversation as a way to establish norms and provide informal feedback.	At three times during a month-long "egg drop" project (where teams designed and built a container for a raw egg that could be dropped from a second-story balcony without breaking), the entire class comes together to discuss their progress. Discussion is guided by the teacher to elicit student understanding about key concepts (force, motion, gravity, acceleration), confusion, misunderstanding, progress, and experiences, encouraging the group to use concrete examples from their work.	Cobb & Bauersfield, 1995
Performance assessments	New projects are given, usually of short duration, in order to assess students' ability to apply knowledge in a new context that requires some of same complex processes developed during a longer instructional unit. These can be done individually or in small groups.	In the Multimedia Challenge 2000, project students worked through a long-term multimedia project focused on media literacy. After they completed their projects, they were given a sixty-minute performance task that asked teams of students to develop a brochure to inform school officials about problems faced by homeless students. The brochure was then assessed according to criteria similar to those of the long-term project.	Penuel, Means, & Simkins, 2000
Preparation for future learning problems	Students approach learning new material by cycles of (1) working with a group to invent possible solutions to a given problem, (2) presenting possible solutions to the classroom, and (3) participating in classroom discussion. Following the cycles of group work, the teacher offers a more traditional direct instruction approach to the new material. Success at learning from the new materials is associated with inventing rather than hearing solutions; students are prepared to learn from the direct instruction as a result of their invention work.	In a middle school classroom studying statistics, students are broken into groups of four to complete invention activity number one: they are asked to create a model of probability using a problem about drawing marbles from a jar. After thirty minutes, groups post a representation of their solution on the board. The classroom comes together and students are chosen to explain the work of another team and the implied conclusions about the new material. After each explanation the classroom discusses the solution. Students again break into small groups and the cycle of work is repeated, but with another problem. A teacher-led lecture follows and then students work individually on similar problems.	Bransford & Schwartz, 1999; Schwartz & Martin, 2004

	Description	Example	References
Written journals	Students are asked to keep an ongoing record of experiences and reflections, including working through problems, throughout a project. Journals can take a range of approaches in the classroom, from a pure free-form space for students to explore on their own to a comprehensive record of specific topics and ideas required by the instructor.	In a high school visual design class structured around four major paper and Web-based design projects, students are asked to keep a design journal for the semester. Students are encouraged to record new ideas and attach interesting designs they come across in their daily life. In addition to the free-form journal style, they are also periodically asked to use their journal to answer more formal questions about specific design rationale or ideas for their future. Journals are collected three times during the semester for teacher review.	Kember, 2004; Phelps, 2005
Portfolios	Students create a structure to show a collection of work over time, usually highlighting progress and including some reflection on their work and process.	After working through a number of separate design projects over the course of a semester, high school seniors are asked to design a structure to present all of their projects using the medium they think best suits their objectives. The portfolio is part of the course grade but is created with an authentic audience in mind (e.g., postsecondary school admissions or potential employers).	Barton & Collins, 1997; Danielson & Abrutyn, 1997; www2.edc.org/asap/class_subtheme.asp?pkTheme=35
Weekly reports	Students create weekly written responses to a set of simple questions throughout the duration of a project. Responses to these questions can be used as a source of formative assessment for the classroom teacher.	Every week throughout a ten-week project, students submit answers to three questions: "What did you learn this week?" "What questions do you have about the work you did this week?" and "If you were the teacher, what question would you ask students to find out what they understand?"	Etkina, 2000; Etkina & Harper, 2002
Self-assessment	Students evaluate their own work according to predefined criteria, often using self-assessment tools such as a rubric or focused questions.	In a middle school unit on narrative writing, students are aware of five important goals for their writing as they work through the unit. The day their final narrative is due, they fill out their self-assessment form. They are asked to (1) rank their work in relation to each of the five goals, from 1 (not accomplished) to 5 (went above and beyond what was required) and (2) describe, for each score, their rationale in detail and give examples.	Boud, 1995; www2.edc.org/asap/class_subtheme.asp?pkTheme=14

TABLE 3

Forms and Functions of Group Work for Inquiry-Based Approaches

TYPE	FORM	EXAMPLES	REFERENCES
Learning circles	Learning circles are multimonth project-based partnerships composed of students in several classrooms and often different countries. There is a six-stage process that groups go through to engage in cooperative inquiry: get ready, open circle, plan project, share work, publish, and close circle.	Through the iEARN network, a classroom can choose to be part of a fourteen-week online learning circle project and be linked with six to eight other classrooms around the world. Each learning circle group concentrates on a specific topic area, and each classroom creates a related project using the other classrooms as their audience for feedback, ideas, and communication. The group as a whole creates a final publication or product including all of the classroom pieces.	Riel (1995); www.iearn.org/ circles/lcguide/
Jigsaw	Small groups work on a subtopic together with the goal of each individual becoming an "expert." Making sure everyone understands is critical. Then group members change groups such that there is one expert on each subtopic in each new group. These new groups are then asked to complete a challenge that requires the input of each expert.	In a middle school science classroom doing a unit on sea life, four teams of five students worked for one week conducting research using books and the Internet to become expert on one ocean animal. At the end of the week, new groups formed, each with one member from an expert animal group. At this point, every group member has unique expertise. The new groups are given a series of compelling problems about ocean life to work through for the next two weeks of class, culminating with a final presentation of their findings.	Brown & Campione, 1990; www.jigsaw.org/; www.wcer.wisc.edu/ archive/cl1/cl/doingcl/jigsaw.htm; Aronson et al. (1978)

Pair programming	Pairs of students work on programming challenges together. One student is given the role of driver and the other the role of navigator. The driver types code and the other gives directions, but both discuss the code as they go. This approach can be extended to any technologically mediated design project that involves building products.	In an after-school and summer research intervention program, middle school girls used pair programming to design and develop computer games in Flash using an object-oriented language based on Java. The intervention used specific instructional strategies, including role modeling effective and ineffective pair programming, having girls identify pair programming rules (for example, "partners physically get up and move positions when switching roles" and "partners share ownership over the project").	www.pairprogramming .com/; Werner, Denner, & Bean, 2004
Complex instruction	Complex instruction (CI) is a teaching model that uses collaborative groups, drawing on theories of multiple intelligences and positive group experiences to counter power dynamics related to gender, SES, ethnicity, and social status. In teaching how to use collaborative groups to take advantage of diverse talents, CI addresses the issues of the nature of group tasks, new roles for persons working in groups, problems of unequal participation in group work, integration of group work and other modes of instruction (such as labs and whole-class discussion), and performance assessment in groups.	In the human biology middle grades life science curriculum, students are placed in specific roles within groups to work through units in science class. Each unit is built around a central concept or scientific question, and over the course of a unit the groups rotate through a number of activities that require students to use multiple abilities such as research, analysis, and visual representation. The classroom teacher makes explicit references to the diversity of talents she observes as students work.	Bianchini, 1999; Cohen, 1994a, 1994b; Cohen, Lotan, Scarloss, & Arellano, 1999; cgi.stanford.edu/group/ pci/cgi-bin/site.cgi
Scripted cooperation	Pairs engage in tasks together and share work by taking turns engaging in specific cognitive activities. Both work to elaborate and discuss material. Roles alternate. Scripts may involve very general or very specific prompts for activity.	A male and female student sitting next to each other are responsible for reading a poem and writing a short report. The female student reads the first stanza and her partner summarizes what was read. The female student takes notes and elaborates. Then the male student reads the second stanza and his partner summarizes what was read while he takes notes. Together they write up their final report from their readings and notes.	O'Donnell & Dansereau, 1992

(Continued)

TABLE 3 (Continued)

TYPE	FORM	EXAMPLES	REFERENCES
Team accelerated instruction	Children help one another complete assignments and learn in math classes. Group scores are based on how well individuals learn content. Note that this approach was designed for developing basic skills rather than completion of complex projects or inquiries. Groups are formed on the basis of diverse levels of prior achievement; students work through their own materials individually, check each other's work against answer sheets, and earn points as a group.	Every day in a high school algebra classroom, the students work in groups that have been predetermined at the beginning of the month. Groups include students who are struggling with the material and those who grasp the concepts easily. For the first half of class, the students work independently on problems that are posted on the board from the prior day's instruction. They ask other members of their group for help as they work. Students then swap papers and correct each other's work.	Devires & Edwards, 1973; Slavin, 1986, 1991
Learning together	The focus is on prosocial interaction and interdependence in the context of complex projects. Reflection on interaction is the key and builds social skill development as well as a caring classroom climate. Groups are diverse with respect to prior achievement, and grades are given to the group as a whole on the basis of their joint work.	During a three-week project in a middle school physics classroom, groups of students work together to build a bridge of wooden beams that will withstand pressure. Prior to the project, the classroom is arranged to foster collaboration including tables for face-to-face work. The teacher spends the first week focusing on the ability of all students to learn to work cooperatively; topics include communication, solving disagreements, project management, etc. The teacher is very clear about both the task and the collaborative goal and during the project monitors the groups as they work.	Johnson & Johnson, 1981, 1989

| Reciprocal teaching | This approach was generated to support student acquisition of strategies that support reading comprehension. Students and teachers take turns leading discussion on a text using strategies of prediction, questioning, clarification, and summarizing. | A high school English class is given a short story to read for homework, and each student is expected to independently annotate the text with examples of all four strategies (prediction, questioning, clarification, and summarizing), which they have covered in class. Small groups form the next day to share their work and construct their own meaning as a group for the particular text. One student is elected to facilitate the group's progress. The teacher circulates among the groups to monitor discussion, asking questions as needed. As closure activity, the whole class holds a discussion built around questions that groups still have. | Palincsar & Brown, 1984; www.itrc.ucf.edu/ FORPD/strategies/ stratreciprocalteaching2 .html |
| Peer teaching | Students are responsible for learning a portion of the material necessary to complete a project or problem and teaching it to the class or to their team members. | During the graphic design phase of an eight-month project where students are working in teams to develop an educational Web site, each student is given a design principle (such as "rhythm" and "balance"). Students research their principles and put together a PowerPoint presentation including explanation and examples and present their principle to the entire class. | Goodlad & Hirst, 1989 |

BIBLIOGRAPHY

Abram, P., Scarloss, B., Holthuis N., Cohen, E., Lotan R., & Schultz, S. E. (2001). The use of evaluation criteria to improve academic discussion in cooperative groups. *Asia Journal of Education, 22*, 16–27.

Achilles, C. M., & Hoover, S. P. (1996). *Transforming administrative praxis: The potential of problem-based learning (PBL) as a school-improvement vehicle for middle & high schools.* Annual Meeting of the American Educational Research Association, New York.

Afflerbach, P., Pearson, P. D., & Paris, S. (in press). Clarifying differences between reading skills and reading strategies. *Reading Teacher.*

Albanese, M. A., & Mitchell, S. A. (1993). "Problem-based learning: A review of literature on its outcomes and implementation issues." *Academic Medicine, 68*(1), 52–81.

Almasi, J. (2003). *Teaching strategic processes in reading.* New York: Guilford Press.

Amaral, O. M., Garrison, L., & Klentschy, M. (2002). Helping English learners increase achievement through inquiry-based science instruction. *Bilingual Research Journal, 26*(2), 213–239.

American Association for the Advancement of Science (AAAS). (1989). *Science for all Americans: Project 2061.* New York: Oxford University Press, 1989.

Amigues, R. (1988). Peer interaction in solving physics problems: Sociocognitive confrontation and metacognitive aspects. *Journal of Experimental Child Psychology, 45*(1), 141–158.

Anderson, R. C., Nguyen-Jahiel, K., McNurlen, B., Archodidou, A., Kim, S., Reznitskaya, A., et al. (2001). The snowball phenomenon: Spread of ways of talking and ways of thinking across groups of children. *Cognition and Instruction, 19*, 1–46.

ARC Center. (2003). *Tri-State Student Achievement Study.* Lexington, MA: Arc Center (http://www.comap.com/elementary/projects/arc/index.htm).

Aronson, E., Blaney, N., Stephan, C., Sikes, J., & Snapp, M. (1978). The jigsaw classroom. Thousand Oaks, CA: Sage.

Aronson, E., & Bridgeman, D. (1979). Jigsaw groups and the desegregated classroom: In pursuit of common goals. *Personality and Social Psychology Bulletin, 5*, 438–446.

Azmitia, M. (1988). Peer interaction and problem solving: When are two heads better than one? *Child Development, 59*(1), 87–96.

Baker, L. (2002). Metacognition in comprehension instruction. In C. Block & M. Pressley (Eds.), *Comprehension instruction: Research-based best practices* (pp. 77–95). New York: Guilford Press.

Ball, A. (2003). Geo-literacy: Using technology to forge new ground. *Edutopia*. Retrieved January 29, 2008 (http://www.edutopia.org/geo-literacy-forging-new-ground).

Ball, D. (1988). *Knowledge and reasoning in mathematical pedagogy: Examining what prospective teachers bring to teacher education.* Unpublished doctoral dissertation, Michigan State University.

Ball, D. L., & Bass, H. (2000). Making believe: The collective construction of public mathematical knowledge in the elementary classroom. In D. C. Phillips (Ed.), *Yearbook of the National Society for the Study of Education, Constructivism in education* (pp. 193–224). Chicago: University of Chicago Press.

Bamberger, Y., & Tal, T. (in press). An experience for the lifelong journey: The long term effects of a class visit to a science center. *Visitor Studies.*

Barron, B. (2000a). Achieving coordination in collaborative problem-solving groups. *Journal of the Learning Sciences, 9*(4), 403–436.

Barron, B. (2000b). Problem solving in video-based microworlds: Collaborative and individual outcomes of high-achieving sixth-grade students. *Journal of Educational Psychology, 92*(2), 391–398.

Barron, B. (2003). When smart groups fail. *Journal of the Learning Sciences, 12*(3), 307–359.

Barron, B. (2006a). Configurations of learning settings and networks: Implications of a learning ecology perspective. *Human Development, 49,* 229–231.

Barron, B. (2006b). Interest and self-sustained learning as catalysts of development: A learning ecologies perspective. *Human Development, 49,* 193–224.

Barron, B.J.S., Schwartz, D. L., Vye, N. J., Moore, A., Petrosino, A., Zech, L., et al. (1998). Doing with understanding: Lessons from research on problem- and project-based learning. *Journal of the Learning Sciences, 7*(3–4), 271–311.

Barrows, H. S. (1996). Problem-based learning in medicine and beyond: A brief overview. In *New directions for teaching and learning,* no. 68 (pp. 3–11). San Francisco: Jossey-Bass.

Barton, J., & Collins, A. (Eds.). (1997). *Portfolio assessment: A handbook for educators.* Menlo Park, CA: Addison-Wesley.

Bartscher, K., Gould, B., & Nutter, S. (1995). Increasing student motivation through project-based learning. Master's Research Project, Saint Xavier and IRI Skylight. (ED 392549).

Beck, I. L., Perfetti, C. A., & McKeown, M. G. (1982). Effects of long-term vocabulary instruction on lexical access and reading comprehension. *Journal of Educational Psychology, 74*(4), 506–521.

Bennett, J., Lubben, F., Hogarth, S., Campbell, B., and Robinson, A. (2004). *A systematic review of the nature of small-groups discussions in science teaching aimed at improving students' understanding of evidence: Review summary.* University of York, UK.

Berry, B. (1995). School restructuring and teacher power: the case of Keels Elementary. In A. Lieberman (Ed.), *The work of restructuring schools: Building from the ground up.* New York: Teachers College Press.

Bianchini, J. A. (1999). From here to equity: The influence of status on student access to and understanding of science. *Science Education, 83*(5), 577–601.

Bishop, B. A., & Anderson, C. W. (1990). Student conceptions of natural selection and its role in evolution. *Journal of Research in Science Teaching, 27,* 415–427.

Black, P. J., & Wiliam, D. (1998a). Assessment and classroom learning. *Assessment in Education: Principles, Policy and Practice, 5*(1), 7–73.

Black, P., & Wiliam, D. (1998b). Inside the black box: Raising standards through classroom assessment. *Phi Delta Kappan, 80*(2), 139–148.

Blumenfeld, P., Soloway, E., Marx, R. W., Krajcik, J. S., Guzdial, M., & Palincsar, A. (1991). Motivating project-based learning: Sustaining the doing, supporting the learning. *Educational Psychologist, 26*(3 & 4), 369–398.

Boaler, J. (1997). *Experiencing school mathematics: Teaching styles, sex, and settings.* Buckingham, UK: Open University Press.

Boaler, J. (1998). Open and closed mathematics: Student experiences and understandings. *Journal for Research in Mathematics Education, 29,* 41–62.

Boaler, J. (2002). *Experiencing school mathematics* (revised and expanded edition). Mahwah, NJ: Erlbaum.

Boaler, J., & Greeno, J. (2000). Identity, agency and knowing in mathematics worlds. In J. Boaler (Ed.), *Multiple perspectives on mathematics teaching and learning.* Westport, CT: Ablex.

Borko, H., Eisenhart, M., Brown, C., Underhill, R., Jones, D., & Agard, P. (1992). Learning to teach hard mathematics: Do novice teachers and their instructors give up too easily? *Journal for Research in Mathematics Education, 23*(3), 194–222.

Borko, H., Elliott, R., & Uchiyama, K. (1999). *Professional development: A key to Kentucky's reform effort.* Los Angeles: UCLA National Center for Research on Evaluation, Standards, and Student Testing.

Borko, H., & Stecher, B. M. (2001, April). Looking at reform through different methodological lenses: Survey and case studies of the Washington State education reform. In J. Manise (Chair), *Testing policy and teaching practice: A multi-method examination of two states.* Symposium conducted at the annual meeting of the American Educational Research Association, Seattle.

Bos, M. C. (1937). Experimental study of productive collaboration. *Acta Psychologica, 3,* 315–426.

Boud, D. (1995). Assessment and learning: Contradictory or complimentary? In P. Knight (Ed.) *Assessment for Learning in Higher Education,* London: Kogan Page/SEDA, 35–48.

Braddock, J. H., & McPartland, J. M. (1993). The education of early adolescents. In L. Darling-Hammond (Ed.), *Review of research in education, 19* (135–170). Washington, DC: American Educational Research Association.

Bransford, J. D., Brown, A. L., & Cocking, R. R. (Eds.). (1999). *How people learn: Brain, mind, experience, and school.* Washington, DC: National Research Council.

Bransford, J. D., Darling-Hammond, L., & LePage, P. (2005). Introduction. In L. Darling-Hammond and J. Bransford (Eds.), *Preparing teachers for a changing world: What teachers should learn and be able to do.* San Francisco: Jossey-Bass.

Bransford, J. D., & Schwartz, D. L. (1999). Rethinking transfer: A simple proposal with multiple implications. *Review of Research in Education, 24,* 61–100.

Bransford, J. D., with Cognition and Technology Group at Vanderbilt (1998) Designing environments to reveal, support, and expand our children's potentials. In S.A. Soraci & W. McIlvane, (Eds.), *Perspectives on Fundamental Processes in Intellectual Functioning, Vol. 1,* Greenwich, CT: Ablex

Bransford, J. D., & Stein, B. S. (1993). *The IDEAL problem solver* (2nd ed.). New York: Freeman.

Briars, D. (2000). *Testimony before the Committee on Education and the Workforce, U.S. House of Representatives, September 21, 2000.* Retrieved September 5, 2004 (http://edworkforce.house.gov/hearings/106th/fc/mathsci92100/briars.htm).

Briars, D. (2001, March). *Mathematics performance in the Pittsburgh public schools.* Presentation at a Mathematics Assessment Resource Service conference on tools for systemic improvement, San Diego.

Briars, D., & Resnick, L. (2000). *Standards, assessments—and what else? The essential elements of standards-based school improvement.* Unpublished manuscript.

Brown, A. L. (1994, November). The advancement of learning. *Educational Researcher, 23*(8), 4–12.

Brown, A. L., & Campione, J. C. (1990). Communities of learning and thinking, or a context by any other name. *Human Development, 21,* 108–126.

Brown, A. L., & Campione, J. C. (1996). Psychological theory and the design of innovative learning environments: On procedures, principles, and systems. In L. Shauble & R. Glaser (Eds.), *Innovations in learning: New environments for education.* Mahwah, NJ: Erlbaum.

Brown, A., Pressley, M., Van Meter, P., & Schuder, T. (1996). A quasi-experimental valida-
tion of transactional strategies instruction with low-achieving second grade readers.
Journal of Educational Psychology, 88, 28–37.

Brown, B. A. (2004). Discursive identity: Assimilation into the culture of science and its implications for minority students. *Journal of Research in Science Teaching, 41*(8), 810–834.

Brown, B. A. (2006). "It isn't no slang that can be said about this stuff": Language, identity, and appropriating science discourse. *Journal of Research in Science Teaching, 43*(1),
96–126.

Brown, D. E., & Clement, J. (1989). Overcoming misconceptions via analogical reasoning: Abstract transfer versus explanatory model construction. *Instructional Science,
18,* 237–261.

Brown, D. F. "Altering curricula through state-mandated testing: Perceptions of teachers
and principals." Paper presented at the annual meeting of the American Educational
Research Association, San Francisco, CA, April 1992.

Bryk, A., Camburn, E., & Louis, K. S. (1999). Professional community in Chicago elementary schools: Facilitating factors and organizational consequences. *Educational
Administration Quarterly, 35*(Supplement [Dec. 1999]), 751–781.

Butler, R. (1988). Enhancing and undermining intrinsic motivation: The effects of task-
involving and ego-involving evaluation of interest and performance. *British Journal
of Educational Psychology, 58*(1), 1–14.

Bybee, R., Kilpatrick, J., Lindquist, M., & Powell, J. (2005, Winter). PISA 2003: An introduction. *Natural Selection: Journal of the BSCS,* 4–7.

California Department of Education. (1990). *Science framework for California public schools:
Kindergarten through grade twelve.* Sacramento: Bureau of Publications.

Carpenter, T. P., Lindquist, M. M., Matthews, W., & Silver, E. A. (1983). Results of the third
NAEP mathematics assessment: Secondary school. *Mathematics Teacher, 76*(9), 652–659.

Casperson, J. M., & Linn, M. C. (2006). Using visualizations to teach electrostatics.
American Journal of Physics, 74(4), 316–323.

Catley, K., Lehrer, R., & Reiser, B. (2005). *Tracing a prospective learning progression for developing understanding of evolution.* Washington, DC: National Academy of Sciences.

Cazden, C. (1988). *Classroom discourse: The language of teaching and learning.* Portsmouth,
NH: Heinemann.

Chapman, C. (1991, June). What have we learned from writing assessment that can
be applied to performance assessment? Presentation at ECS/CDE Alternative
Assessment Conference, Breckenbridge, CO.

Chappell, M. (2003). Keeping mathematics front and center: Reaction to middle-grades
curriculum projects research. In S. Senk & D. Thompson (Eds.), *Standards-based*

school mathematics curricula: What are they? What do students learn? (pp. 285–298). Mahwah, NJ: Erlbaum.

Chi, M.T.H. (1992). Conceptual change within and across ontological categories: Examples from learning and discovery in science. In R. N. Giere (Ed.), *Minnesota studies in the philosophy of science* (pp. 129–186). Minneapolis: University of Minnesota Press.

Chi, M.T.H. (2000). Self-explaining expository tests: The dual process of generating inferences and repairing mental models. In R. Glaser (Ed.), *Advances in instructional psychology* (pp. 161–238). Mahwah, NJ: Erlbaum.

Chi, M.T.H., deLeeuw, N., Chiu, M. H., & LaVancer, C. (1994). Eliciting self-explanations improves understanding. *Cognitive Science, 18,* 439–477.

Ching, C. C., Kafai, Y. B., & Marshall, S. K. (2000). Spaces for change: Gender and technology access in collaborative software design. *Journal of Science Education and Technology, 9*(1), 67–78.

Chinn, C. A., & Brewer, W. (1998). An empirical test of a taxonomy of response to anomalous data in science. *Journal of Research in Science Teaching, 35*(6), 623–654.

Chinn, C. A., & Brewer, W. F. (1993). The role of anomalous data in knowledge acquisition: A theoretical framework and implications for science instruction. *Review of Educational Research, 63*(1), 1–49.

Chinn, C. A., & Brewer, W. F. (2001). Models of data: A theory of how people evaluate data. *Cognition and Instruction, 19*(3), 323–393.

Chinn, C. A., O'Donnell, A. M., & Jinks, T. S. (2000). The structure of discourse in collaborative learning. *Journal of Experimental Education, 69*(1), 77–97.

Cincinnati Public Schools (CPS). (1999). *New American schools designs: An analysis of program results in district schools.* Cincinnati, OH: Author.

Clark, A. M., Anderson, R. C., Archodidou, A., Nguyen-Jahiel, K., Kuo, L. J., and Kim, I. (2003). Collaborative reasoning: Expanding ways for children to talk and think in the classroom. *Educational Psychology Review, 15,* 181–198.

Clark, D. (2000). *Scaffolding knowledge integration through curricular depth.* Unpublished doctoral dissertation, University of California, Berkeley.

Clark, D. (2006). Longitudinal conceptual change in students' understanding of thermal equilibrium: An examination of the process of conceptual restructuring. *Cognition and Instruction, 24*(4), 467–563.

Clement, J. (1982). Students' preconceptions in introductory mechanics. *American Journal of Physics, 50*(1), 66–71.

Clewell, B. C., & Campbell, P. B. (2002). Taking stock: Where we've been, where we are, where we're going. (http://www.urban.org/url.cfm?ID=1000779).

Cobb, P (1995) Mathematical Learning and Small-Group Interaction: Four Case Studies. In P. Cobb, & H. Bauersfeld, (Eds) *The Emergence of Mathematical Meaning: Interaction in Classroom Cultures,* Hillsdale, NJ: Lawrence Erlbaum Associates.

Cobb. P., & Bauersfeld, H. (Eds.), (1995). *The emergence of mathematical meaning: Interaction in classroom cultures.* Hillsdale, NJ: Lawrence Erlbaum

Cognition and Technology Group at Vanderbilt (CTGV). (1997). *The Jasper project: Lessons in curriculum, instruction, assessment, and professional development.* Mahwah, NJ: Erlbaum.

Cohen, D. (1990). A revolution in one classroom: The case of Mrs. Oublier. *Education Evaluation and Policy Analysis, 12*(3), 311–329.

Cohen, D. K., & Hill, H. (2000). Instructional policy and classroom performance: The mathematics reform in California. *Teacher College Record, 102*(2), 294–343.

Cohen, D. K., & Hill, H. C. (2001). *Learning policy.* New Haven, CT: Yale University Press.

Cohen, E. G. (1993). From theory to practice: The development of an applied research program. In J. Berger, & M. J. Zelditch (Eds.), *Theoretical research programs: Studies in the growth of theory; theoretical research programs: Studies in the growth of theory.* (pp. 385–415). Stanford University Press.

Cohen, E. G. (1994a). *Designing groupwork: Strategies for heterogeneous classrooms.* Revised edition. New York: Teachers College Press.

Cohen, E. G. (1994b). Restructuring the classroom: Conditions for productive small groups. *Review of Educational Research, 64*(1), 1–35.

Cohen, E. G., & Lotan, R. A. (1995). Producing equal-status interaction in the heterogeneous classroom. *American Educational Research Journal, 32*(1), 99–120.

Cohen, E. G., & Lotan, R. A. (Eds.). (1997). *Working for equity in heterogeneous classrooms: Sociological theory in practice.* New York: Teachers College Press.

Cohen, E. G., Lotan, R. A., Abram, P. L., Scarloss, B. A., & Schultz, S. E. (2002). Can groups learn? *Teachers College Record, 104*(6), 1045–1068.

Cohen, E. G., Lotan, R. A., Scarloss, B. A., & Arellano, A. R. (1999). Complex instruction: Equity in cooperative learning classrooms. *Theory into Practice, 38*(2), 80–86.

Cohen, P. A., Kulik, J. A., & Kulik, C. C. (1982). Education outcomes of tutoring: A meta-analysis of findings. *American Educational Research Journal, 19,* 237–248.

Coleman, E. B. (1998). Using explanatory knowledge during collaborative problem solving in science. *Journal of the Learning Sciences, 7*(3–4), 387–427.

Collins, A., Brown, J. S., & Newman, S. E. (1989). Cognitive apprenticeship: Teaching the crafts of reading, writing, and mathematics. In L. B. Resnick (Ed.), *Knowing, learning, and instruction: Essays in honor of Robert Glaser* (pp. 453–494). Mahwah, NJ: Erlbaum.

Cook, S. B., Scruggs, T. E., Mastropieri, M. A., & Castro, G. C. (1985). Handicapped students as tutors. *Journal of Special Education, 19,* 483–492.

Cornelius, L. L., & Herrenkohl, L. R. (2004). Power in the classroom: How the classroom environment shapes students' relationships with each other and with concepts. *Cognition and Instruction, 22*(4), 467–498.

Dale, H. (1994). Collaborative writing interactions in one ninth-grade classroom. *Journal of Educational Research, 87*(6), 334–344.

Damico, J., & Riddle, R. L. (2004). From answers to questions: A beginning teacher learns to teach for social justice. *Language Arts, 82*(1), 36–46.

Damon, W. (1984). Peer education: The untapped potential. *Journal of Applied Developmental Psychology, 5*(4), 331–343.

Danielson, C. & Abrutyn, L. (1997). *An Introduction to Using Portfolios in the Classroom.* Alexandria, VA: Association for Supervision and Curriculum Development.

Darling-Hammond, L. (1997). *The right to learn: A blueprint for creating schools that work.* San Francisco: Jossey-Bass.

Darling-Hammond, L., & Ancess, J. (1994). *Graduation by portfolio at Central Park East Secondary School.* New York: National Center for Restructuring Education, Schools, and Teaching, Teachers College, Columbia University.

Darling-Hammond, L., Ancess, J., & Falk, B. (1995). *Authentic assessment in action.* New York: Teachers College Press.

Darling-Hammond, L., Ancess, J., & Ort, S. (2002). Reinventing high school: Outcomes of the Coalition Campus Schools Project. *American Educational Research Journal, 39*(3), 639–673.

Darling-Hammond, L., & McLaughlin, M. W. (1995). Policies that support professional development in an era of reform. *Phi Delta Kappan, 76*(8), 597–604.

Darling-Hammond, L., & Rustique-Forrester, E. (2005). The Consequences of Student Testing for Teaching and Teacher Quality. In J. Herman & E. Haertel (Eds.), *The uses and misuses of data in accountability testing.* 104th Yearbook of the National Society for the Study of Education, Part II, pp. 289–319. Malden, MA: Blackwell.

Davis, E. A. (2003). Prompting middle school science students for productive reflection: Generic and directed prompts. *The Journal of the Learning Sciences, 12*(1), 91–142.

Davis, P. J., & Hersh, R. (1981). *The Mathematical Experience.* Boston: Birkhauser.

Deci, E. L., & Ryan, R. M. (1985). *Intrinsic motivation and self-determination in human behavior.* New York: Plenum.

De La Paz, S. (2005). Effects of historical reasoning instruction and writing strategy mastery in culturally and academically diverse middle school classrooms. *Journal of Educational Psychology, 97*(2), 139–156.

Deshler, D., & Schumaker, J. (1986). Learning strategies: An instructional alternative for low-achieving adolescents. *Exceptional Children, 52,* 583–590.

Desimone, L., Porter, A., Garet, M., Yoon, K., & Birman, B. (2002). Effects of professional development on teachers' instruction: Results from a three-year longitudinal study. *Education Evaluation and Policy Analysis, 24*(2), 81–112.

Deutsch, M. (1949). A theory of cooperation and competition. *Human Relations, 2,* 129–152.

Devries, D., I Edwards, K. (1973). Learning games and student teams: Their effect on classroom process. *American Educational Research Journal, 10,* 307–318.

diSessa, A. (1983). Phenomenology and the evolution of intuition. In D. Gentner & A. L. Stevens (Eds.), *Mental models.* Mahwah, NJ: Erlbaum.

diSessa, A. (2006). A history of conceptual change research: Threads and fault lines. In R. K. Sawyer (Ed.), *The Cambridge handbook of the learning sciences.* New York: Cambridge University Press.

diSessa, A., Elby, A., & Hammer, D. (2002). J's epistemological stance and strategies. In G. M. Sinatra & P. R. Pintrich (Eds.), *Intentional conceptual change* (pp. 237–290). Mahwah, NJ: Erlbaum.

diSessa, A. A., Gillespie, N. M., & Esterly, J. B. (2004). Coherence versus fragmentation in the development of the concept of force. *Cognitive Science, 28*(6), 843–900.

diSessa, A. A., & Sherin, B. L. (1998). What changes in conceptual change? *International Journal of Science Education, 20*(10), 1155–1191.

Dochy, F., Segers, M., Van den Bossche, P., & Gijbels, D. (2003). Effects of problem-based learning: A meta-analysis. *Learning and Instruction, 13,* 533–568.

Dole, J., Duffy, G. G., Roehler, L. R., & Pearson, P. D. (1991). Moving from the old to the new: Research on reading comprehension instruction. *Review of Educational Research, 61*(2), 239–264.

Donovan, M. S., & Bransford, J. D. (Eds.). (2005). *How students learn: Science in the classroom.* Washington, DC: National Academies Press.

Driver, R., Newton, P., & Osborne, J. (2000). Establishing the norms of scientific argumentation in classrooms. *Science Education, 84,* 287–312.

Drucker, P. F. (1994, November). The age of social transformation. *Atlantic Monthly,* pp. 53–80.

Duit, R. (2006). *Bibliography: Students' and teachers' conceptions of science education.* Retrieved Jan. 2006 (www.ipn.uni-kiel.de/aktuell/stcse.html).

Duke, N., & Pearson, P. D. (2002). Effective practices for developing reading comprehension. In A. Farstrup & J. Samuels (Eds.), *What research has to say about reading instruction* (3rd ed., pp. 205–242). Newark, DE: International Reading Association.

Duke, N. K., & Pearson, P. D. (2001). How can I help children improve their comprehension? In *Teaching every child to read: Frequently-asked questions.* Ann Arbor, MI: Center for the Improvement of Early Reading Achievement.

Dunkin, M., & Biddle, B. (1974). *The study of teaching*. New York: Holt, Rinehart, and Winston.

Duschl, R. A., Schweingruber, H. A., & Shouse, A. W. (Eds.). (2007). *Talking science to school: Learning and teaching science in grades K-8*. Washington, DC: National Academies Press.

Edelson, D., Gordon, D., & Pea, R. (1999). Addressing the challenges of inquiry-based learning through technology and curriculum design. *Journal of the Learning Sciences, 8*(3&4), 391–450.

Engle, R. A., & Conant, F. R. (2002). Guiding principles for fostering productive disciplinary engagement: Explaining an emergent argument in a community of learners classroom. *Cognition and Instruction, 20*(4), 399–483.

Englert, C. S., Raphael, T. E., & Anderson, L. M. (1992). Socially mediated instruction: Improving students' knowledge and talk about writing. *Elementary School Journal, 92*(4), 411–449.

Etkina, E. (2000). Weekly reports: a two-way feedback tool. *Science Education 84*, 594–605.

Etkina, E., & Harper, K. A. (2002). Weekly Reports: Student Reflections on Learning. An Assessment Tool Based on Student and Teacher Feedback. *Journal of College Science Teaching, 31*(7), 476–480.

Expeditionary Learning Outward Bound (ELOB). (1997). *Expeditionary learning outward bound: Evidence of success*. Cambridge, MA: Author.

Expeditionary Learning Outward Bound (ELOB). (1999a). *A design for comprehensive school reform*. Cambridge, MA: Author.

Expeditionary Learning Outward Bound (ELOB). (1999b). *Early indicators from schools implementing New American Schools Designs*. Cambridge, MA: Author.

Falk, B., & Ort, S. (1997). *Sitting down to score: Teacher learning through assessment*. Presentation at the annual meeting of the American Educational Research Association, Chicago, IL.

Falk, J. H., Scott, C., Dierking, L. D., Rennie, L., & Cohen-Jones, M. (2004). Interactives and visitor learning. *Curator, 47*, 171–198.

Fennema, E., & Romberg, T. (Eds.) (1999). *Mathematics classrooms that promote understanding*. Mahwah, NJ: Erlbaum.

Fernandez, C. (2002). Learning from Japanese approaches to professional development: The case of lesson study. *Journal of Teacher Education, 53*(5), 393–405.

Fernandez, C., & Yoshida, M. (2004). *Lesson study: A Japanese approach to improving mathematics teaching and learning*. Mahwah, NJ: Erlbaum.

Ferrari, M., & Chi, M.T.H. (1998). The nature of naive explanations of natural selection. *International Journal of Science Education, 20*(10), 1231–1256.

Firestone, W. A., Mayrowetz, D., & Fairman, J. (1998). Performance-based assessment and instructional change: The effects of testing in Maine and Maryland. *Educational Evaluation and Policy Analysis, 20,* 95–113.

Fortus, D., Dershimer, R. C., Marx, R. W., Krajcik, J., & Mamlok-Naaman, R. (2004). Design-based science (DBS) and student learning. *Journal of Research in Science Teaching, 41*(10), 1081–1110.

Fountas, I. C., & Pinnell, G. S. (1996). *Guided reading: Good first teaching for all children.* Portsmouth, NH: Heinemann.

Frederiksen, J. R., & White, B. Y. (1997). *Reflective assessment of students' research within an inquiry-based middle school science curriculum.* Paper presented at the annual meeting of the American Educational Research Association, Chicago.

Freebody, P. (1992). A socio-cultural approach: Resourcing four roles as a literacy learner. In A. Watson & A. Badenhop (Eds.), *Prevention of reading failure* (pp. 48–60). Sydney: Ashton-Scholastic.

Freebody, P., & Luke, A. (1990). Literacies programs: Debates and demands in cultural context. *Prospect: Australian Journal of TESOL, 5*(7), 7–16.

Friedlaender, D., & Darling-Hammond, L. (2007). *High schools for equity: Policy supports for student learning in communities of color.* Palo Alto: School Redesign Network at Stanford University.

Gallagher, S. A., Stepien, W. J., & Rosenthal, H. (1992). The effects of problem-based learning on problem solving. *Gifted Child Quarterly, 36,* 195–200.

Gambrell, L. B. (1996). What research reveals about discussion. In L. B. Gambrell & J. F. Almasi (Eds.), *Lively discussions! Fostering engaged reading.* Newark, DE: International Reading Association.

Gambrell, L. B., & Morrow, L. M. (1996). Creating motivating contexts for literacy learning. In L. Baker, P. Afflerbach, & D. Reinking (Eds.), *Developing engaged readers in home and school communities.* Mahwah, NJ: Erlbaum.

Garcia, E. (1993). Language, culture, and education. In L. Darling-Hammond (Ed.), *Review of research in education, 19,* 51–98. Washington, DC: American Educational Research Association.

Gavelek, J. R., Raphael, T. E., Biondo, S. M., & Danhua, W. (1999). *Integrated literacy instruction: A review of the literature* (CIERA Report 2-001). Ann Arbor, MI: Center for the Improvement of Early Reading Achievement.

Gee, J. (2003). *What video games have to teach us about learning and literacy.* New York: Palgrave Macmillan.

Gentner, D., & Gentner, D. R. (1983). Flowing waters or teeming crowds: Mental models of electricity. In D. Gentner & A. L. Stevens (Eds.), *Mental models* (pp. 99–129). Mahwah, NJ: Erlbaum.

Gentner, D., & Markman, A. B. (1997). Structure mapping in analogy and similarity. *American Psychologist, 52,* 45–56.

Georghiades, P. (2004). From the general to the situated: Three decades of metacognition. *International Journal of Science Education, 26*(3), 365–383.

Gertzman, A., & Kolodner, J. L. (1996, July). A case study of problem-based learning in middle-school science class: Lessons learned. In Proceedings of the Second Annual Conference on the Learning Sciences (pp. 91–98), Evanston/Chicago.

Gick, M. L., & Holyoak, K. J. (1980). Analogical problem solving. *Cognitive Psychology, 12,* 306–355.

Gillies, R. (2004). The effects of cooperative learning on junior high school students during small group learning. *Learning and Instruction, 14,* 197–213.

Ginsburg-Block, M. D., Rohrbeck, C. A., & Fantuzzo, J. W. (2006). A meta-analytic review of social, self-concept, and behavioral outcomes of peer-assisted learning. *Journal of Educational Psychology, 98,* 732–749.

Glass, G. V., Coulter, D., Hartley, S., Hearold, S., Kahl, S., Kalk, J., & Sherretz, L. (1977). *Teacher "indirectness" and pupil achievement: An integration of findings.* Boulder: Laboratory of Educational Research, University of Colorado.

Goldberg, G. L., & Rosewell, B. S. (2000). From perception to practice: The impact of teachers' scoring experience on the performance based instruction and classroom practice. *Educational Assessment, 6,* 257–290.

Goldenberg, C. (1991). *Instructional conversations and their classroom applications.* Center for Research on Education, Diversity & Excellence Paper EPR02. Retrieved December 1, 2006 (http://repositories.cdlib.org/crede/ncrcdslleducational/EPR02).

Goldenberg, C. (1993). Instructional conversations: Promoting comprehension through discussion. *Reading Teacher, 46*(4), 316–326.

Good, T. L., & Brophy, J. E. (1986). *Educational Psychology* (3rd ed.). New York: Longman.

Goodlad, S., & Hirst, B. (1989). *Peer tutoring: A guide to learning by teaching.* London: Kogan Page.

Graham, S., & Harris, K. R. (2005a). Improving the writing performance of young struggling writers: Theoretical and programmatic research from the Center on Accelerating Student Learning. *Journal of Special Education, 39*(1), 19–33.

Graham, S., & Harris, K. (2005b). *Writing better: Effective strategies for teaching students with learning difficulties.* New York: Brookes.

Graham, S., & Perin, D. (2007). *Writing next: Effective strategies to improve writing of adolescents in middle and high schools—A report to Carnegie Corporation of New York.* Washington, DC: Alliance for Excellent Education.

Great Books Foundation. (n.d.). Research on Junior Great Books and shared inquiry. Retrieved September 3, 2006 (http://www.greatbooks.org/programs-for-all-ages/junior/jgbadministrators/jgbresearch/research-on-shared-inquiry.html).

Gresalfi, M., & Cobb, P. (2006). Cultivating students' discipline-specific dispositions as a critical goal for pedagogy and equity. *Pedagogies, 1*, 49–58.

Guensburg, C. (2006). Reading rules: The word of the day is 'literacy.' *Edutopia.* Retrieved January 29, 2008 (http://www.edutopia.org/reading-rules).

Gunderson, S., Jones, R., & Scanland, K. (2004). *The jobs revolution: Changing how America works.* Copywriters, Inc.

Gunstone, R., & White, R. (2000). Goals, methods and achievements of research in science education. In R. Millar, J. Leach, & J. Osborne (Ed.), *Improving science education* (pp. 293–307). Buckingham, UK: Open University Press.

Guthrie, J. T., Anderson, E., Alao, S., & Rinehart, J. (1999). Influences of concept-oriented reading instruction on strategy use and conceptual learning from text. *Elementary School Journal, 99*(4), 343.

Guthrie, J. T., & Ozgungor, S. (2002). Instructional contexts for reading engagement. In C. C. Block & M. Pressley (Eds.), *Comprehension instruction: Research-based best practices.* New York: Guilford Press.

Guthrie, J. T., & Wigfield, A. (2000). Engagement and motivation in reading. In M. L. Kamil, P. B. Mosenthal, P. D. Pearson, & R. Barr (Eds.), *Handbook of reading research, vol. 3* (pp. 403–422). Mahwah, NJ: Erlbaum.

Guthrie, J. T., Wigfield, A., Humenick, N. M., Perencevich, K. C., Taboada, A., & Barbosa, P. (2006). Influences of stimulating tasks on reading motivation and comprehension. *Journal of Educational Research, 99*(4), 232–245.

Haney, W. (2000). The myth of Texas miracle in education. *Education Policy Analysis Archives, 8* (41), Retrieved April 19, 2008, from http://epaa.asu.edu/epaa/v8n41/

Hapgood, S., Magnusson, S. J., & Palincsar, A. S. (2004). Teacher, text, and experience: A case of young children's scientific inquiry. *Journal of the Learning Sciences, 13*(4), 455–505.

Harel, I. (1991). *Children designers.* Westport, CT: Ablex.

Hartley, S. S. (1977). *A meta-analysis of effects of individually paced instruction in mathematics.* Unpublished doctoral dissertation, University of Colorado at Boulder.

Hatano & Iganaki. (1991). Sharing cognition through collective comprehension activity. In L. B. Resnick, J. Levine, & S. Teasley (Eds.), *Perspectives on socially shared cognition* (pp. 331–348). Washington, DC: American Psychological Association.

Herman, J. L. (2002). *Black-white-other test score gap: Academic achievement among mixed race adolescents.* Institute for Policy Research Working Paper. Evanston, IL: Northwestern University Institute for Policy Research.

Herman, J. L., Klein, D.C.D., Heath, T. M., & Wakai, S. T. (1995). *A first look: Are claims for alternative assessment holding up?* CSE Technical Report. Los Angeles: UCLA National Center for Research on Evaluation, Standards, and Student Testing.

Hidi, S., & Renninger, K. A. (2006). The four-phase model of interest development. *Educational Psychologist, 41*(2), 111–127.

Hmelo, C. E. (1995). Development of independent learning and thinking: A study of medical problem-solving and problem-based learning. ProQuest Information & Learning. *Dissertation Abstracts International Section A: Humanities and Social Sciences, 56*(1), 143.

Hmelo, C. E. (1998a). Cognitive consequences of problem-based learning for the early development of medical expertise. *Teaching and Learning in Medicine, 10*(2), 92–100.

Hmelo, C. E. (1998b). Problem-based learning: Effects on the early acquisition of cognitive skill in medicine. *Journal of the Learning Sciences, 7*(2), 173–208.

Hmelo-Silver, C. E. (2004). Problem-based learning: What and how do students learn? *Educational Psychology Review, 16*(3), 235–266.

Hmelo-Silver, C. E. (2006). Design principles for scaffolding technology-based inquiry. In A. M. O'Donnell, C. E. Hmelo-Silver, & G. Erkens (Eds.), *Collaborative learning, reasoning, and technology* (pp. 147–170). Mahwah, NJ: Erlbaum.

Hmelo-Silver, C. E., & Barrows, H. S. (2006). Goals and strategies of a problem-based learning facilitator. *Interdisciplinary Journal of Problem-based Learning, 1*, 21–39.

Hmelo, C. E., Holton, D. L., & Kolodner, J. L. (2000). Designing to learn about complex systems. *Journal of the Learning Sciences, 9*(3), 247–298.

Hmelo-Silver, C. E., Nagarajan, A., & Day, R. S. (2002). "It's harder than we thought it would be": A comparative case study of expert-novice experimentation strategies. *Science Education, 86*(2), 219–243.

Hogarth, S., Bennett, J., Campbell, B., Lubben, F., & Robinson, A. (2005). A systematic review of the use of small-group discussions in science teaching with students aged 11–18, and the effect of different stimuli (print materials, practical work, ICT, video/film) on students' understanding of evidence. In *Research Evidence in Education Library*. London: EPPI-Centre, Social Science Research Unit, Institute of Education, University of London.

Holyoak, K. J., & Thagard, P. (1997). The analogical mind. *American Psychologist, 52*, 35–44.

Horan, C., Lavaroni, C., & Beldon, P. (1996). *Observation of the Tinker Tech Program students for critical thinking and social participation behaviors.* Novato, CA: Buck Institute for Education.

Horwitz, R. A. (1979). Effects of the "open" classroom. In H. J. Walberg (Ed.), *Educational environments and effects: Evaluation, policy and productivity* (pp. 275–292). Berkeley, CA: McCutchan.

Jenkins, James J. (1979). "Four Points to Remember: A Tetrahedral Model of Memory Experiments," in Laird S. Cermak & Fergus I.M. Craik (Eds.), *Levels of Processing and Human Memory*. Hillsdale, NJ: Lawrence Erlbaum Associates

Jensen, M. S., & Finley, F. N. (1995). Teaching evolution using historical arguments in a conceptual change strategy. *Science Education, 79*(2), 147–166.

Jimenez-Aleixandre, M. P., Rodriguez, A. B., & Duschl, R. A. (2000). "Doing the lesson" or "Doing science": Argument in high school genetics. *Science Education, 84*(6), 757–792.

Johnson, D. W., & Johnson, R. T. (1981). Effects of cooperative and individualistic learning experiences on interethnic interaction. *Journal of Educational Psychology, 73*, 444–449.

Johnson, D. W., & Johnson, R. T. (1983). Social interdependence and perceived academic and personal support in the classroom. *Journal of Social Psychology, 120*, 77–82.

Johnson, D. Johnson, R. (1989). *Cooperation and competition: Theory and research.* Interaction Book Company; Edina, MN.

Johnson, D. W., & Johnson, R. T. (1999a). *Cooperative learning and assessment.* Access ERIC. Japan: FullText.

Johnson, D., & Johnson, R. (1999b). Making cooperative learning work. *Theory into Practice, 38*(2), 67–73.

Johnson, D. W., Maruyama, G., Johnson, R., Nelson, D., & Skon, L. (1981). Effects of cooperative, competitive, and individualistic goal structures on achievement: A meta-analysis. *Psychological Bulletin, 89*, 47–62 (http://dx.doi.org/10.1037/0033-2909.89.1.47).

Jones, B. D., & Egley, R. J. (2004). Voices from the frontlines: Teachers' perceptions of high-stakes testing. *Education Policy Analysis Archives, 12*(39). Retrieved April 19, 2008, from http://epaa.asu.edu/epaa/v12n39/

Jones, M.G., Jones, B.D., Hardin, B., Chapman, L., & Yarbrough, T.M. (1999). The impact of high-stakes testing on teachers and students in North Carolina. *Phi Delta Kappan, 81*(3), 199–203.

Juel, C. (1988). Learning to read and write: A longitudinal study of 54 children from first through fourth grades. *Journal of Educational Psychology, 80*(4), 437–447.

Jukes, I., & McCain, T. (2002, June 18). *Living on the future edge.* InfoSavvy Group and Cyster.

Kafai, Y. (1994). *Minds in play: Computer game design as a context for children's learning.* Mahwah, NJ: Erlbaum.

Kafai, Y. B., & Ching, C. C. (2001). Talking science within design: Learning through design as a context. *Journal of the Learning Sciences, 10*, 323–363.

Kerbow, D. (1997). *Preliminary evaluation of Junior Great Books Program, Chicago Elementary Schools: 1995–1996 School Year.* Unpublished manuscript.

Kilpatrick, W. H. (1918). The project method. *Teachers College Record, 19*, 319–335.

King, A. (1990). Enhancing peer interaction and learning in the classroom through reciprocal peer questioning. *American Educational Research Journal, 27*(4), 664–687.

Klahr, D., & Nigam, M. (2004). The equivalence of learning paths in early science instruction. *Psychological Science, 15*(10), 661–667.

Klein, S. P., Hamilton, L. S., McCaffrey, D. F., & Stecher, B. M. (2000). *What do test scores in Texas tell us?* Santa Monica: RAND.

Klenowski, V. (1995). Student self-evaluation process in student-centered teaching and learning contexts of Australia and England. *Assessment in Education, 2*, 145–163.

Knapp, M. S. (Ed.). (1995). *Teaching for meaning in high-poverty classrooms.* New York: Teachers College Press.

Kolodner, J. L. (1997). Educational implications of analogy: A view from case-based reasoning. *American Psychologist, 52*(1), 57–66.

Kolodner, J. L., & Barab, S. (2004). Erratum. *Journal of the Learning Sciences, 13*(3), 453.

Kolodner, J. L., Camp, P. J., Crismond, D., Fasse, B., Gray, J., Holbrook, J., et al. (2003). Problem-based learning meets case-based reasoning in the middle-school science classroom: Putting *Learning by Design™* into practice. *Journal of the Learning Sciences, 12*(4), 495–547.

Kolodner, J. L., & Guzdial, M. (2000). Theory and practice of case-based learning aids. In D. H. Jonassen & S. M. Land (Eds.), *Theoretical foundations of learning environments* (pp. 215–242). Mahwah, NJ: Erlbaum.

Kolodner, J. L., Owensby, J. N., & Guzdial, M. (2004). *Case-based learning aids.* Mahwah, NJ: Erlbaum.

Kong, A., & Pearson, D. (2003). The road to participation: The construction of a literacy practice in a learning community of linguistically diverse learners. *Research in the Teaching of English, 38*(1), 85–124.

Koretz, D., & Barron, S. I. (1998). *The validity of gains on the Kentucky Instructional Results Information System (KIRIS).* Santa Monica: RAND, MR-1014-EDU.

Koretz, D., Linn, R. L., Dunbar, S. B., & Shepard, L. A. (1991, April). The effects of high-stakes testing: Preliminary evidence about generalization across tests. In R. L. Linn (Chair), *The effects of high stakes testing.* Symposium presented at the annual meeting of the American Educational Research Association and the National Council on Measurement in Education, Chicago.

Koretz, D., Mitchell, K. J., Barron, S. I., & Keith, S. (1996). *Final report: Perceived effects of the Maryland school performance assessment program.* CSE Technical Report. Los Angeles: UCLA National Center for Research on Evaluation, Standards, and Student Testing.

Koretz, D., Stecher, B., & Deibert, E. (1992). *The Vermont portfolio program: Interim report on implementation and impact, 1991–92 school year.* Santa Monica: RAND.

Kortland, K. (1996). An STS case study about students' decision making on the waste issue. *Science Education, 80*(6), 673–689.

Krajcik, J. S., Blumenfeld, P. C., Marx, R. W., Bass, K. M., Fredericks, J., & Soloway, E. (1998). Inquiry in project-based science classrooms: Initial attempts by middle school students. *Journal of the Learning Sciences, 7*, 313–350.

Lampert, M. (1986). Teachers' strategies for understanding and managing classroom dilemmas. In M. Ben Peretz, R. Bromme, & R. Halkes (Eds.), *Advances of Research on Teacher Thinking* (pp. 70–83). Lisse, The Netherlands: Svets and Zeitlinger.

Lampert, M. (1989). Research into practice: Arithmetic as problem solving. *Arithmetic Teacher, 36*(7), 34–36.

Lampert, M. (1990). When the problem is not the question and the solution is not the answer: Mathematical knowing and teaching. *American Educational Research Journal, 27*, 29–63.

Lampert, M. (2001). *Teaching problems and the problem of teaching*. New Haven, CT: Yale University Press.

Lampert, M. & Eshelman A. S. (1995, April). *Using technology to support effective and responsible teacher education: The case of interactive multimedia in mathematics methods courses*. Paper presented at the annual meeting of the American Educational Research Association, San Francisco.

Lane, S., Stone, C. A., Parke, C. S., Hansen, M. A., & Cerrillo, T. L. (2000, April). *Consequential evidence for MSPAP from the teacher, principal and student perspective*. Paper presented at the annual meeting of the National Council on Measurement in Education, New Orleans.

Latour, B. (1988). Science in action: How to follow scientists and engineers through society. Cambridge, MA: Harvard University Press.

Latour, B. & Woolgar, S. (1979). Labratory life: The social construction of scientific facts. Thousand Oaks, CA: Sage.

Lee, V. E., Bryk, A. S., & Smith, J. B. (1993). The organization of effective secondary schools. In L. Darling-Hammond (Ed.), *Review of research in education*. Washington, DC: American Educational Research Association.

Lee, V. E., Smith, J. B., & Croninger, R. G. (1995). *Another look at high school restructuring*. *Issues in Restructuring Schools*. Madison: University of Madison-Wisconsin, Center on Organization and Restructuring of Schools.

Lee, V. E., Smith, J. B., & Croninger, R. G. (1997). How high school organization influences the equitable distribution of learning in mathematics and science. *Sociology of Education, 70*(2), 128–150.

Lehrer, R., & Romberg, T. (1996). Exploring children's data modeling. *Cognition and Instruction, 14*, 69–108.

Leinhart, G., & Greeno, J. G. (1986). The cognitive skill of teaching. *Journal of Educational Psychology, 78,* 75–95.

Leinhart, G., & Smith, D. (1985). Expertise in math instruction: Subject matter knowledge. *Journal of Educational Psychology, 77,* 241–271.

Lemke, J. L. (2001). Articulating communities: Sociocultural perspectives on science education. *Journal of Research in Science Teaching, 38*(3), 296–316.

Levy, F., & Murnane, R. (2004). *The new division of labor: How computers are creating the next job market.* Princeton, NJ: Princeton University Press.

Lewis, C., & Tsuchida, I. (1998). The basics in Japan: The three C's (connection, character and content). *Educational Leadership, 55*(6), 32–37.

Lieberman, A. (1995). *The work of restructuring schools: Building from the ground up.* New York: Teachers College Press.

Lieberman, A., & Wood, D. (2002). *Inside the national writing project: Connecting network learning and classroom teaching.* New York: Teachers College Press.

Linde, C. (1988). The quantitative study of communicative success: Politeness and accidents in aviation discourse. *Language and Society, 17,* 375–399.

Linn, M. C. (2006). The knowledge integration perspective on learning and instruction. In R. K. Sawyer (Ed.), *The Cambridge handbook of the learning sciences.* New York: Cambridge University Press.

Linn, M. C., Clark, D., & Slotta, J. D. (2003). WISE design for knowledge integration. *Science Education, 87*(4), 517–538.

Linn, M. C., Davis, E. A., & Bell, P. (Eds.). (2004). *Internet environments for science education.* Mahwah, NJ: Erlbaum.

Linn, M. C., & Hsi, S. (2000). *Computers, teachers, peers: Science learning partners.* Mahwah, NJ: Erlbaum.

Linn, R. L. (2000). Assessments and accountability. *Educational Researcher, 29*(2), 4–16.

Linn, R. L., Graue, M. E., & Sanders, N. M. (1990). Comparing state and district test results to national norms: The validity of claims that "everyone is above average." *Educational Measurement: Issues and Practice, 9,* 5–14.

Little, J. W. (1993). Teacher development in a climate of educational reform. *Educational Evaluation and Policy Analysis, 15*(2) 129–151.

Luke, A., & Freebody, P. (1999). Further notes on the four resources model. *Reading Online.* Retrieved December 10, 2006 (http:www.readingonline.org/research/luke-frebody.html).

Lundeberg, M. A., Levin, B. B., & Harrington, H. L. (Eds.) (1999). *Who learns what from cases and how? The research base for teaching and learning with cases.* New Jersey: Lawrence Erlbaum Associates, Inc.

Ma, L. (1999). *Knowing and teaching elementary mathematics*. Mahwah, NJ: Erlbaum.

Madison, B. L., & Hart, T. A. (1990). *A challenge of numbers: People in the mathematical sciences*. Washington, DC: National Academies Press.

Magnusson, S., & Palincsar, A. S. (2004). Learning from text designed to model scientific thinking in inquiry-based instruction. In W. Saul (Ed.), *Crossing borders: Connecting science and literacy*. Newark, DE: International Reading Association.

Markus, H., & Nurius, P. (1986). Possible selves. *American Psychologist, 41*, 954–969.

Marx, R. W., Blumenfeld, P. C., Krajcik, J., Blunk, M., Crawford, B., Kelly, B., and Meyer, K. (1994). Enacting project-based science: Experiences of four middle grade teachers. *Elementary School Journal, 94*(5), 499–516.

Mason, L. (2004). Fostering understanding by structural alignment as a route to analogical reasoning. *Instructional Science, 32*, 293–318.

Mathematics Learning Study Committee, National Research Council, Jeremy Kilpatrick, Jane Swafford, & Bradford Findell (Eds.) *Adding it Up: Helping Children Learn Mathematics. National Academies Press* (2001).

McCloskey, M., Caramazza, A., & Green, B. (1980). Curvilinear motion in the absence of external forces: Naive beliefs about the motion of objects. *Science, 210*(12), 1139–1141.

McCloskey, M., & Kohl, D. (1983). Naive physics: The curvilinear impetus principle and its role in interactions with moving objects. *Journal of Experimental Psychology, 9*, 146–156.

McDonald, J. (1993). Planning backwards from exhibitions. *Graduation by exhibition: Assessing genuine achievement*. Alexandria, VA: Association for Supervision and Curriculum Development.

McDowell, C., Werner, L., Bullock, H., & Fernald, J. (2006, August). Pair programming improves student retention, confidence, and program quality. *Communications of the ACM Archive, 49*(8), 90–95.

McKeachie, W. J., & Kulik, J. A. (1975). Effective college teaching. In F. N. Kerlinger (Ed.), *Review of research in education* (vol. 3, pp. 165–209). Itasca, IL: Peacock.

McKeown, M. G., Beck, I. L., Sinatra, G. M., & Loxterman, J. A. (1992). The contribution of prior knowledge and coherent text to comprehension. *Reading Research Quarterly, 27*(1), 79–93.

McKnight, C. C., Crosswhite, F. J., Dossey, J. A., Kifer, E., Swafford, J. O., Travers, K. J., & Cooney, T. J. (1987). *The underachieving curriculum: Assessing U.S. school mathematics from an international perspective*. Champaign, IL: Stipes.

Mercier, E., Barron, B., & O'Connor, K. (2006). Images of self and others as computer users: The role of gender and experience. *Journal of Computer Assisted Learning* (Special issue on gender and new digital media), *22*, 1–14.

Meyer, D. K., Turner, J. C., & Spencer, C. A. (1997). Challenge in a mathematics classroom: Students' motivation and strategies in project-based learning. *The Elementary School Journal, 97*(5), 501–521.

Miller, L., & Silvernail, D. L. (1994). Wells Junior High School: Evolution of a professional development school. In L. Darling-Hammond (Ed.), *Professional development schools: Schools for developing a profession* (pp. 28–49). New York: Teachers College Press.

Moore, A., Sherwood, R., Bateman, H., Bransford, J., & Goldman, S. (1996, April). *Using problem-based learning to prepare for project-based learning.* Paper presented at the annual meeting of the American Educational Research Association, New York.

Moore, P. J. (1988). Reciprocal teaching and reading comprehension: A review. *Journal of Research in Reading, 11,* 3–14.

More than robots: An evaluation of the FIRST Robotics Competition participant and institutional impacts. Prepared by A. Melchior, F. Cohen, T. Cutter, & T. Leavitt, Center for Youth and Communities, Heller School for Social Policy and Management, Brandeis University, Waltham, MA (http://www.usfirst.org/uploadedFiles/Who/Impact/Brandeis_Studies/FRC_eval_finalrpt.pdf; accessed Oct. 22, 2007).

Murnane, R., & Levy, F. (1996). *Teaching the new basic skills.* New York: Free Press.

Nasir, N. S. (2005). Individual cognitive structuring and the sociocultural context: Strategy shifts in the game of dominoes. *Journal of the Learning Sciences, 14*(1), 5–34.

Nasir, N., & Kirshner, B. (2003). The cultural construction of moral and civic identities. *Applied Developmental Science, 7,* 138–147.

National Center for Educational Statistics (NCES). (2003). *Trends in international mathematics and science study 2003 results.* Washington, DC: Institute of Education Science, U.S. Department of Education.

National Center for Educational Statistics (NCES). (2005). *National assessment of educational progress, the Nation's Report Card: Science 2005 executive summary.* Washington, DC: Institute of Education Science, U.S. Department of Education.

National Commission on Excellence in Education (1983). *A nation at risk.* Washington, DC: U.S. Government Printing Office.

National Council of Teachers of Mathematics (NCTM). (1989). *Curriculum and evaluation standards for school mathematics.* Reston, VA: Author.

National Council of Teachers of Mathematics (NCTM). (1991). *Professional standards for teaching mathematics.* Reston, VA: Author.

National Council of Teachers of Mathematics (NCTM). (2000). *Principles and standards for school mathematics.* Reston, VA: Author.

National Council of Teachers of Mathematics (NCTM). (2006). *Curriculum focal points for prekindergarten through grade 8 mathematics.* Reston, VA: Author.

National Institute for Science Education. 2003. (www.wcer.wisc.edu/nise/CL1).

National Reading Panel. (2000). *Teaching children to read: An evidence-based assessment of the scientific research literature on reading and its implications for reading instruction.* Washington, DC: National Institute of Child Health and Human Development.

National Research Council. (1989). *Everybody counts: A report to the nation on the future of mathematics education.* Washington, DC: National Academies Press.

National Research Council. (1996). *National science education standards.* Washington, DC: National Academies Press.

New American Schools Development Corporation. (1997). *Working towards excellence: Results from schools implementing New American Schools designs.* Washington, DC: Author.

Newmann, F. M. (1996). *Authentic achievement: Restructuring schools for intellectual quality.* San Francisco: Jossey-Bass.

Newmann, F. M., Marks, H. M., & Gamoran, A. (1995). Authentic pedagogy: Standards that boost student performance. *Issues in Restructuring Schools, 8,* 1–4.

Newmann, F. M., Marks, H. M., & Gamoran, A. (1996). Authentic pedagogy and student performance. *American Journal of Education, 104*(4), 280–312.

Newmann, F. M., & Wehlage, G. G. (1995). *Successful school restructuring.* Madison: University of Wisconsin, Center for Organizational Restructuring of Schools.

Newstetter, W. (2000). Bringing design knowledge and learning together. In C. Eastman, W. Newstetter, & M. McCracken (Eds.), *Design knowing and learning: Cognition in design education.* New York: Elsevier Science Press.

North Central Regional Educational Laboratory (2003). EnGauge 21st century skills: Literacy in the digital age. Report by NCREL funded by the Institute of Education Sciences (IES) and the U.S. Department of Education (http://www.ncrel.org/engauge).

Nystrand, M., Gamoran, A., & Heck, M. (1993). Using small groups for response to and thinking about literature. *English Journal, 82*(1), 14–22.

Nystrand, M., Gamoran, A., Kachur, R., & Prendergast, C. (1997). *Opening dialogue: Understanding the dynamics of language and learning in the English classroom.* New York: Teachers College Press.

O'Donnell, A. M. (1987). Cooperative procedural learning: The effects of planning and prompting activities. ProQuest Information & Learning. *Dissertation Abstracts International, 47*(8), 3561–3562.

O'Donnell, A. M. (2006). The role of peers and group learning. In P. Alexander & P. Winne (Eds.), *Handbook of educational psychology* (2nd ed.). Mahwah, NJ: Erlbaum.

O'Donnell, A. M., & Dansereau, D. F. (1992). Scripted cooperation in student dyads: A method for analyzing and enhancing academic learning and performance.

In R. Hertz-Lazarowitz & N. Miller (Eds.), *Interaction in cooperative groups: The theoretical anatomy of group learning* (pp. 120–141). New York: Cambridge University Press.

O'Donnell, A. M., & Derry, S. J. (2005). Cognitive processes in interdisciplinary groups: Problems and possibilities. In S. J. Derry, C. D. Schunn, & M. A. Gernsbacher (Eds.), *Interdisciplinary collaboration: An emerging cognitive science* (pp. 51–82). Mahwah, NJ: Erlbaum.

O'Donnell, A. M., Hmelo-Silver, C. E., & Erkens, G. (Eds.). (2006). *Collaborative learning, reasoning, and technology.* Mahwah, NJ: Erlbaum.

O'Donnell, A. M., & King, A. (Eds.). (1999). *Cognitive perspectives on peer learning.* Mahwah, NJ: Erlbaum.

O'Donnell, A. M., & O'Kelly, J. (1994). Learning from peers: Beyond the rhetoric of positive results. *Educational Psychology Review, 6*(4), 321–349.

O'Donnell, A. M., Rocklin, T. R., Dansereau, D. F., & Hythecker, V. I. (1987). Amount and accuracy of information recalled by cooperative dyads: The effects of summary type and alternation of roles. *Contemporary Educational Psychology, 12*(4), 386–394.

Palincsar, A. S., & Brown, A. L. (1984). Reciprocal teaching of comprehension-fostering and comprehension-monitoring activities. *Cognition and Instruction, 1*(2), 117–175.

Palincsar, A. S., & Brown, A. L. (1986). Interactive teaching to promote independent learning from text. *Reading Teacher, 39,* 771–777.

Palincsar, A. S., & Duke, N. K. (2004). The role of text and text-reader interactions in young children's reading development and achievement. *Elementary School Journal, 105*(2), 183–197.

Palincsar, A. S., & Herrenkohl, L. (1999). Designing collaborative contexts: Lessons from three research programs. In A. M. O'Donnell & A. King (Eds.), *Cognitive perspectives on peer learning* (pp. 151–177). Mahwah, NJ: Erlbaum.

Palincsar, A. S., & Herrenkohl, L. (2002). Designing collaborative learning contexts. *Reading Teacher, 41*(1), 26–32.

Palincsar, A. S., & Magnusson, S. J. (2001). The interplay of firsthand and text-based investigations to model and support the development of scientific knowledge and reasoning. In S. Carver & D. Klahr (Eds.), *Cognition and instruction: Twenty-five years of progress* (pp. 151–194). Mahwah, NJ: Erlbaum.

Paris, S. G., Cross, D. R., & Lipson, M. Y. (1984). Informed strategies for learning: A program to improve children's reading awareness and comprehension. *Journal of Educational Psychology, 76,* 1239–1252.

Paris, S. G., Lipson, M. Y., & Wixson, K. (1983). Becoming a strategic reader. *Contemporary Educational Psychology, 8,* 293–316.

Paris, S. G., Lipson, M. Y., & Wixson, K. K. (1994). Becoming a strategic reader. In R. B. Ruddell, M. R. Ruddell, & H. Singer (Eds.), *Theoretical models and processes of reading* (4th ed., pp. 788–810). Newark, DE: International Reading Association.

Paris, S. G., Wasik, B. A., & Turner, J. C. (1991). The development of strategic readers. In R. Barr, M. Kamil, P. Mosenthal, & P. D. Pearson (Eds.), *Handbook of reading research* (2nd ed., pp. 609–640). New York: Longman.

Partnership for 21st Century Skills. (2004). Learning for the 21st century (http://www.21stcenturyskills.org).

Passmore, C., & Stewart, J. (2002). A modeling approach to teaching evolutionary biology in high schools. *Journal of Research in Science Teaching, 39*(3), 185–204.

Patronis, T., Potari, D., & Spiliotopoulou, V. (1999). Students' argumentation in decision-making on a socio-scientific issue: Implications for teaching. *International Journal of Science Education, 21*(7), 745–754.

Pearson, P. D., & Gallagher, M. C. (1983). The instruction of reading comprehension. *Contemporary Educational Psychology, 8,* 317–344.

Pearson, P. D., Roehler, L., Dole, J., & Duffy, G. (1992). Developing expertise in reading comprehension. In S. J. Samuels & A. E. Farstrup (Eds.), *What research says to the teacher* (2nd ed., pp. 145–199). Newark, DE: International Reading Association.

Peck, J. K., Peck, W., Sentz, J., & Zasa, R. (1998). Students' perceptions of literacy learning in a project-based curriculum. In E. G. Sturtevant, J. A. Dugan, P. Linder, & W. M. Linek (Eds.), *Literacy and community* (pp. 94–100). Texas A&M University: College Reading Association.

Penner, D. E., Giles, N. D., Lehrer, R., & Schauble, L. (1997). Building functional models: Designing an elbow. *Journal of Research in Science Teaching, 34*(2), 1–20.

Penuel, W. R., Means, B., & Simkins, M. B. (2000). The multimedia challenge. *Educational Leadership, 58,* 34–38.

Perkins, D. (1998) "What is Understanding?" In Wiske (Ed.) *Teaching for Understanding.* San Francisco: Jossey-Bass.

Perkins, D. N. (1986). *Knowledge as design.* Mahwah, NJ: Erlbaum.

Peterson, P. (1979). Direct instruction reconsidered. In P. Peterson & H. Walberg (Eds.), *Research on teaching: Concepts, findings, and implications* (pp. 57–69). Berkeley, CA: McCutchan.

Petrosino, A. J. (1998). *The use of reflection and revision in hands-on experimental activities by at-risk children.* Unpublished doctoral dissertation, Vanderbilt University, Nashville.

Phelps, E., & Damon, W. (1989). Problem solving with equals: Peer collaboration as a context for learning mathematics and spatial concepts. *Journal of Educational Psychology, 81*(4), 639–646.

PISA. (2003). *Programme for International Student Assessment*. Retrieved Jan., 2007, from Organisation for Economic Co-operation and Development (http://www.pisa.oecd.org/).

Polman, J. L. (2004). Dialogic activity structures for project-based learning environments. *Cognition and Instruction, 22*(4), 431–466.

Polman, J. L. (2006a). Mastery and appropriation as means to understand the interplay of history learning and identity trajectories. *Journal of the Learning Sciences, 15*(2), 221–259.

Polman, J. L. (2006b). A starting point for inquiry into inquiry. *PsycCRITIQUES, 51*(4).

Popham, W. J. (1999). Why standardized test scores don't measure educational quality. *Educational Leadership, 56*(6), 8–15.

Pressley, M. (1998). Comprehension strategies instruction. In J. Osborn & F. Lehr (Eds.), *Literacy for all: Issues in teaching and learning* (pp. 113–133). New York: Guilford Press.

Pressley, M. (2000). What should comprehension instruction be the instruction of? In M. L. Kamil, P. B. Mosenthal, P. D. Pearson, & R. Barr (Eds.), *Handbook of reading research* (vol. 3). Mahwah, NJ: Erlbaum.

Pressley, M., Wharton-McDonald, R., Rankin, J., Mistretta, J., Yokoi, L., & Ettenberger, S. (1996). The nature of outstanding primary-grades literacy instruction. In E. McIntyre & M. Pressley (Eds.), *Balanced instruction: Strategies and skills in whole language*. Norwood, MA: Christopher-Gordon.

Programme for International Student Assessment (PISA). (2003). *The PISA 2003 assessment framework: Mathematics, reading, science and problem solving knowledge and skills*. Retrieved Jan., 2007, from Organisation for Economic Co-operation and Development (http://www.pisa.oecd.org/).

Puntambekar, S., & Kolodner, J. L. (2005). Toward implementing distributed scaffolding: Helping students learn science from design. *Journal of Research in Science Teaching, 42*(2), 185–217.

Putnam, R. (2003). Commentary on four elementary mathematics curricula. In S. Senk & D. Thompson (Eds.), *Standards-based school mathematics curricula: What are they? What do students learn?* (pp. 161–178). Mahwah, NJ: Erlbaum.

Quin, Z., Johnson, D., & Johnson, R. (1995). Cooperative versus competitive efforts and problem solving. *Review of Educational Research, 65*(2), 129–143.

Raphael, T. E., Florio-Ruane, S., & George, M. (2001). *Book Club plus: A conceptual framework to organize literacy instruction*. Ann Arbor, MI: Center for the Improvement of Early Reading Achievement Report. Retrieved September 15, 2006 (http://www.ciera.org/library/reports/inquiry-3/3-015/3-015.htm).

Raphael, T. E., & McMahon, S. I. (1994). Book Club: An alternative framework for reading instruction. *Reading Teacher, 48*(2), 102–116.

Resnick, L. (1987). *Education and learning to think*. Washington, DC: National Academies Press.

Reznitskaya, A., Anderson, R. C., McNurlen, B., Nguyen-Jahiel, K., Archodidou, A., & Kim, S. (2001). Influence of oral discussion on written argument. *Discourse Processes* (Special Issue: Argumentation in psychology), *32*(2), 155. Retrieved December 10, 2006, from PsycINFO database.

Ridgway, J., Crust, R., Burkhardt, H., Wilcox, S., Fisher, L., & Foster, D. (2000). *MARS report on the 2000 tests*. San Jose, CA: Mathematics Assessment Collaborative.

Riel, M. (1995). Cross-classroom collaboration in global learning circles. In Susan Leigh Star (Ed.), *The Cultures of Computing* (pp. 219–242). Oxford: Blackwell Publishers/ The Sociological Review Monograph Series.

Rohrbeck, C. A., Ginsburg-Block, M. D., Fantuzzo, J. W., & Miller, T. R. (2003). Peer-assisted learning interventions with elementary school students: A meta-analytic review. *Journal of Educational Psychology, 95*, 240–257 (http://dx.doi.org/10.1037/0022-0663.95.2.240).

Romance, N. R., & Vitale, M. R. (1992). A curriculum strategy that expands time for in-depth elementary science instruction by using science-based reading strategies: Effects of a year-long study in grade four. *Journal of Research in Science Teaching, 29*(6), 545–554.

Romance, N. R., & Vitale, M. R. (2001). Implementing an in-depth expanded science model in elementary schools: Multi-year findings, research issues, and policy implications. *International Journal of Science Education, 23*(4), 272–404.

Rosenfeld, M., & Rosenfeld, S. (1998). *Understanding the "surprises" in PBL: An exploration into the learning styles of teachers and their students*. Paper presented at the European Association for Research in Learning and Instruction (EARLI), Sweden.

Rosenshine, B., & Meister, C. (1994). Reciprocal teaching: A review of research. *Review of Educational Research, 64*, 479–530.

Ross, S. M., et al. (1999). *Two- and three-year achievement results on the Tennessee value-added assessment system for restructuring schools in Memphis*. Memphis: Center for Research in Educational Policy, University of Memphis.

Roth, W. M. (2006). *Knowledge Diffusion in a Grade 4–5 Classroom During a Unit on Civil Engineering: An Analysis of a Classroom Community in Terms of Its Changing Resources and Practices Cognition and Instruction, 14*(2), 179–220.

Rueda, R., Goldenberg, C., & Gallimore, R. (1992). *Rating instructional conversations: A guide*. (Research Report EPR4.) National Center for Research on Cultural Diversity and Second Language Learning. Retrieved December 1, 2006 (http://www.ncela.gwu.edu/pubs/ncrcdsll/epr4.htm).

Rutherford, F. J., & Ahlgren, A. (1991). *Science for all Americans*. New York: Oxford University Press.

Sadler, T. D. (2004). Informal reasoning regarding socioscientific issues: A critical review of research. *Journal of Research in Science Teaching, 41*(5), 513–536.

Salomon, G., & Perkins, D. (1998). Individual and social aspects of learning. *Review of Research in Education, 23,* 1–24 .

Saunders, W. M., & Goldenberg, C. (1999). Effects of instructional conversations and literature logs on limited- and fluent-English-proficient students' story comprehension and thematic understanding. *Elementary School Journal, 99*(4), 277–301.

Savery, J. R., & Duffy, T. M. (1996). Problem based learning: An instructional model and its constructivist framework. In B. G. Wilson (Ed.), *Constructivist learning environments* (pp. 135–148). Englewood, NJ: Educational Technology Publications.

Scardamalia, M., Bereiter, C., & Lamon, M. (1994). The CSILE project: Trying to bring the classroom into world 3. In K. McGilly (Ed.), *Classroom lessons: Integrating cognitive theory & classroom practice* (pp. 201–228). Cambridge: MIT Press.

Schmidt, H. G., et al. (1996). The development of diagnostic competence: A comparison between a problem-based, an integrated, and a conventional medical curriculum. *Academic Medicine, 71,* 658–664.

Schmidt, W., Houang, R., & Cogan, L. (2002, Summer). A coherent curriculum: The case of mathematics. *American Educator, 2002*(1), 1–18.

Schneider, R., Krajcik, J., Marx, R. W., & Soloway, E. (2002). Performance of students in project-based science classrooms on a national measure of science achievement. *Journal of Research in Science Teaching, 39*(5), 410–422.

Schoenfeld, A. (1985). Metacognitive and epistemological issues in mathematical understanding. In A. Silver (Ed.), *Teaching and learning mathematical problem solving: Multiple research perspectives* (pp. 361–380). Mahwah, NJ: Erlbaum.

Schoenfeld, A. H. (1992). Learning to think mathematically: Problem solving, metacognition, and sense-making in mathematics. In D. Grouws (Ed.), *Handbook for Research on Mathematics Teaching and Learning* (pp. 334–370). New York: Macmillan.

Schoenfeld, A. H. (2002, January/February). Making mathematics work for all children: Issues of standards, testing, and equity. *Educational Researcher, 31*(1), 13–25.

Schoenfeld, A. H. (Ed.). (in press). A study of teaching: Multiple lenses, multiple views. *Journal for Research in Mathematics Education* monograph series. Reston, VA: National Council of Teachers of Mathematics.

Schwab, J. (1978). Education and the structure of the disciplines. In J. Westbury & N. Wilkof (Eds.), *Science, curriculum, and liberal education*. Chicago: University of Chicago Press.

Schwartz, D. L. (1995). The emergence of abstract representations in dyad problem solving. *Journal of the Learning Sciences, 4*(3), 321–354.

Schwartz, D. L, Lin, X. D., Brophy, S., & Bransford, J. D. (1999). Toward the development of flexibly adaptive instructional design. In C. Reigeluth (Ed.), *Instructional-design theories and models: New paradigms of instructional theory.* Mahwah, NJ: Erlbaum.

Schwartz, D. L., & Martin, T. (2004). Inventing to prepare for future learning: The hidden efficiency of encouraging original student production in statistics instruction. *Cognition and Instruction, 22*(2), 129–184.

Secretary's Commission on Achieving Necessary Skills (SCANS). (1991). *What work requires of schools.* Report published by the National Technical Information Service (NTIS), U.S. Department of Commerce.

Seethaler, S. L. (2003). *Controversy in the classroom: How eighth-grade and undergraduate students reason about tradeoffs of genetically modified food.* Unpublished doctoral dissertation, University of California, Berkeley.

Seethaler, S., & Linn, M. C. (2004). Genetically modified food in perspective: An inquiry-based curriculum to help middle school students make sense of tradeoffs. *International Journal of Science Education, 26*(14), 1765–1785.

Seidel (1998). Learning from looking. In: N. Lyons, Editor, *With portfolio in hand: Validating the new teacher professionalism,* Teachers College Press, New York, NY, pp. 69–89.

Settlage, J. (1994). Conceptions of natural selection: A snapshot of the sense-making process. *Journal of Research in Science Teaching, 31*(5), 449–457.

Shepherd, H. G. (1998). The probe method: A problem-based learning model's effect on critical thinking skills of fourth- and fifth-grade social studies students. *Dissertation Abstracts International, Section A: Humanities and Social Sciences, September 1988, 59*(3-A).

Shepard, L. A. (2000). The role of assessment in a learning culture. *Educational Researcher, 29*(7), 4–14.

Shirouzu, H., Miyake, N., & Masukawa, H. (2002). Cognitively active externalization for situated reflection. *Cognitive Science, 26*(4), 469–501.

Shulman, L. (1987, February). Knowledge and teaching: Foundations of the new reform. *Harvard Educational Review, 57*(1), 1–22.

Slavin, R. (1986). *Using student team learning* (3rd ed.). Baltimore: Center for Research on Elementary and Middle Schools, Johns Hopkins University.

Slavin, R. (1991, February). Synthesis of research on cooperative learning. *Educational Leadership,* 71–82.

Slavin, R., & Oickle, E. (1981). Effects of cooperative learning teams on student achievement and race relations: Treatment by race interactions. *Sociology of Education, 54*(3), 174–180.

Slavin, R. E. (1996). Research on cooperative learning and achievement: What we know, what we need to know. *Contemporary Educational Psychology, 21*(1), 43–69.

Slotta, J., & Chi, M.T.H. (2006). Helping students understand challenging topics in science through ontology training. *Cognition and Instruction, 24*(2), 261–289.

Smith, C., Wiser, M., Anderson, C. W., & Krakcik, J. (in press). Implications of research on children's learning for standards and assessment: A proposed learning progression for matter and the atomic molecular theory. *Measurement: Interdisciplinary Research and Perspectives.*

Smith, J. P., diSessa, A. A., & Roschelle, J. (1993). Misconceptions reconceived: A constructivist analysis of knowledge in transition. *Journal of the Learning Sciences, 3*(2), 115–163.

Smith, M. L. (1991). Put to the test: The effects of external testing on teachers. *Educational Researcher, 20*(5), 8–11.

Soar, R. S. (1977). An integration of findings from four studies of teacher effectiveness. In G. D. Borich (Ed.), *The appraisal of teaching: Concepts and process,* pp. 96–103. Reading, MA: Addison-Wesley.

Southeast Center for Teaching Quality. (2004). High-stakes accountability in California: A view from the teacher's desk. *Teaching Quality RESEARCH MATTERS, 12,* 1–2. RetrievedSeptember 2, 2004, from http://www.teachingquality.org/research matters/issues/2004/issue12-Aug2004.pdf

Stage, E. K. (2005, Winter). Why do we need these assessments? *Natural Selection: Journal of the BSCS,* 11–13.

Stahl, S. A., Hare, V. C., Sinatra, R., & Gregory, J. F. (1991). Defining the role of prior knowledge and vocabulary in reading comprehension: The retiring of number 41. *Journal of Reading Behavior, 23*(4), 487–508.

Stecher, B., & Barron, S. (1999). *Quadrennial milepost accountability testing in Kentucky*

Stecher, B., Barron, S., Chun, T., & Ross, K. (2000). *The effects of the Washington State education reform on schools and classroom.* CSE Technical Report. Los Angeles: UCLA National Center for Research on Evaluation, Standards, and Student Testing.

Stecher, B. M., Barron, S., Kaganoff, T., & Goodwin, J. (1998). The effects of standards-based assessment on classroom practices: Results of the 1996–97 RAND survey of Kentucky teachers of mathematics and writing. CSE Technical Report. Los Angeles: UCLA National Center for Research on Evaluation, Standards, and Student Testing.

Steen, L. A. (1988, April 29). The science of patterns. *Science, 240,* 611–616.

Stepien, W. J., Gallagher, S. A., & Workman, D. (1993). Problem-based learning for traditional and interdisciplinary classrooms. *Journal for the Education of the Gifted Child, 16,* 338–357.

Stigler, J., & Hiebert, J. (1999). *The teaching gap.* New York: Free Press.

Stodolsky, S. S. (1985). Telling math: Origins of math aversion and anxiety. *Educational Psychologist, 20,* 125–133.

Strike, K. A., & Posner, G. J. (1982). Conceptual change and science teaching. *European Journal of Science Education, 4*(3), 231–240.

Stylianides, A. (2005). *Proof in school mathematics classrooms: Developing a conceptualization of its meaning and investigating what is entailed in its cultivation.* Unpublished dissertation, University of Michigan.

Swafford, J. (2003). Reaction to high school curriculum projects' research. In S. Senk & D. Thompson (Eds.), *Standards-based school mathematics curricula: What are they? What do students learn?* (pp. 457–468). Mahwah, NJ: Erlbaum.

Taylor, B. M., Pearson, P. D., Peterson, D. S., & Rodriguez, M. C. (2003). Reading growth in high-poverty classrooms: The influence of teacher practices that encourage cognitive engagement in literacy learning. *Elementary School Journal, 104*(1), 3–28.

Taylor, B. M., Peterson, D. S., Pearson, P. D., & Rodriguez, M. C. (2002). Looking inside classrooms: Reflecting on the "how" as well as the "what" in effective reading instruction. *Reading Teacher, 56*(3), 270–279.

Tharp, R. G., & Gallimore, R. (1991). *The instructional conversation: Teaching and learning in social activity.* Washington, DC: Center for Applied Linguistics.

Tharp, R. G., & Gallimore, R. (1992). *The instructional conversation: Teaching and learning in social activity.* (Research Report RR2). National Center for Research on Cultural Diversity and Second Language Learning. Retrieved December 1, 2006 (http://www.ncela.gwu.edu/pubs/ncrcdsll/rr2.htm).

Thomas, J. W. (2000). *A review of project based learning.* (Prepared for Autodesk Foundation).

Tretten, R. & Zachariou, P. (1995). *Learning about project-based learning: Self-assessment preliminary report of results.* San Rafael, CA: The Autodesk Foundation.

Udall, D., & Rugen, L. (1996). *Introduction.* In D. Udall & A. Mednick (Eds.), *Journeys through our classrooms* (pp. xi–xxii). Dubuque, IA: Kendall/Hunt.

U.S. Department of Labor. (2006). *Number of jobs held, labor market activity, and earnings growth among the youngest baby boomers: Results from a longitudinal survey.* Washington, DC: Bureau of Labor Statistics. Retrieved September 22, 2007 (http://www.bls.gov/news.release/pdf/nlsoy.pdf).

Varelas, M., & Pappas, C. C. (2006). Intertextuality in read-alouds of integrated science-literacy units in urban primary classrooms: Opportunities for the development of thought and language. *Cognition and Instruction, 24*(2), 211–259.

Varian, H., & Lyman, P. (2003). *How much information?* UC Berkeley School of Information Management & Systems (SIMS). Retrieved September 22, 2007

(www2.sims.berkeley.edu/research/projects/how-much-info-2003/printable
_report.pdf).

Vernon, D. T., & Blake, R. L. (1993). Does problem-based learning work? A meta-analysis of evaluative research. *Academic Medicine, 68*(7), 550–563.

Vygotsky, L. S. (1978). *Mind in society.* Cambridge, MA: Harvard University Press.

Watanabe, T. (2002). Learning from Japanese Lesson Study. *Educational Leadership 36*(39).

Webb, N. M. (1985). Verbal interaction and learning in peer-directed groups. *Theory into Practice, 24*(1), 32–39.

Webb, N. M., Troper, J. D., & Fall, R. (1995). Constructive activity and learning in collaborative small groups. *Journal of Educational Psychology, 87*(3), 406–423.

Werner, L. L., Campe, S., & Denner, J. (2005, October 20–22). Proceedings of the 6th conference on information technology education 2005, Newark, NJ.

Werner, L., Denner, J., and Bean, S. (2004). Proceedings of the Seventh IASTED International Conference Computers and Advanced Technology in Education, August 16–18, 2004, 161–166.

White, B., & Frederiksen, J. (2005). A theoretical framework and approach for fostering metacognitive development. *Educational Psychologist, 40*(4), 211–223.

Wiggins, G. (1989, April). Teaching to the (authentic) test. *Educational Leadership,* 41–47.

Wiggins, G., & McTighe, J. (1998). *Understanding by Design.* Alexandria, VA: ASCD.

Wigner, E. P. (1960). The unreasonable effectiveness of mathematics in the natural sciences. *Communications in Pure and Applied Mathematics, 13,* 1–14.

Wilkinson, I.A.G. (2005, April). *Overview and a conceptual framework for discussions.* Paper presented at the International Reading Association annual conference, San Antonio.

Wilkinson, I.A.G., Murphy, P. K., & Soter, A. O. (2005, August). *Group discussions as learning environments for promoting high-level comprehension of texts.* Paper presented at the 11th biennial meeting of the European Association for Research on Learning and Instruction, Nicosia, Cyprus.

Wilkinson, I.A.G., & Reninger, K. B. (2005, April). What the approaches look like: A conceptual framework for discussions. In M. Nystrand (Chair), *Making sense of group discussions designed to promote high-level comprehension of texts.* Symposium presented at the annual meeting of the American Educational Research Association, Montreal, Canada.

Williams, D. C., Hemstreet, S., Liu, M., & Smith, V. D. (1998). *Examining how middle schools students use problem-based learning software.* Proceedings of ED-MEDIA/ED-Telecom 98 World Conference on Educational Multimedia and Hypermedia, Freiburg, Germany.

Williams, S. M. (1992). Putting case-based instruction into context: Examples from legal and medical education. *Journal of the Learning Sciences, 2*(4), 367–427.

Wilson, M. R., & Bertenthal, M. W. (Eds.). (2006). *Systems for state science assessments.* Washington, DC: National Academies Press.

Wolf, S., Borko, H., McIver, M., & Elliott, R. (1999). *"No excuses": School reform efforts in exemplary schools of Kentucky.* Los Angeles: UCLA National Center for Research on Evaluation, Standards, and Student Testing.

Yager, S., Johnson, D., & Johnson, R. (1985). Oral discussion, group-to-individual transfer, and achievement in cooperative learning groups. *Journal of Educational Psychology, 77*(1), 60–66.

Yager, S., Johnson, R., Johnson, D., & Snider, B. (1995). The impact of group processing on achievement in cooperative learning groups. *Journal of Social Psychology, 126*(3), 389–397.

Yore, L. D., Hand, B., Goldman, S. R., Hildebrand, G. M., Osborne, J. F., Treagust, D. F., & Wallace, C. S. (2004). New directions in language and science education research. *Reading Research Quarterly, 39*(3), 347–352.

Zimmerman, T. (2005). *Promoting knowledge integration of scientific principles and environmental stewardship: Assessing an issue-based approach to teaching evolution and marine conservation.* Unpublished doctoral dissertation, University of California, Berkeley.

Zimmerman, T. D., & Brown, J. (2006, September). *Ocean protection through effective communication: Ocean knowledge, misconceptions and public opinion.* Poster presentation at California and the World Ocean Conference, Long Beach.

Zimmerman, T. D., & Slotta, J. D. (2003, April). *Helping students understand complex biology concepts through knowledge integration activities in the classroom and at an aquarium.* Paper presentation at the Annual Meeting of the American Educational Research Association, Chicago.

Zohar, A., & Nemet, F. (2002). Fostering students' knowledge and argumentation skills through dilemmas in human genetics. *Journal of Research in Science Teaching, 39*(1), 35–62.

SUBJECT INDEX

King Middle School (Maine), 40–41
Knowledge
    "anomalous data" versus, 168–169
    conceptual change model of
        integration of, 170–173
    contextual nature of, 176
    creating conceptual change of, 167–170
    increasing need for, 1–2
    investments in teacher, 211
    organized around core concepts and
        connections, 198
    pace of expanding, 2
    using reading and writing in service
        of, 106
    restructuring of, 168
    student conceptual use of, 4
    studies on connecting context ot, 11–13
    See also Learning; Prior knowledge;
        Understandings
Knowledge Integration Perspective,
    170–171, 173
Knowledge-centered learning environ-
    ment, 199fig

L
*Laboratory Life: The Social Construction of
    Scientific Facts* (Latour), 182
Latino student PISA scores, 154fig
Lawrence Hall of Science, 173, 186
LEARN (Quebec), 62
Learners
    characteristics of, 6fig
    different performance levels of, 126–127
    engagement and self-identity as, 68–69
    See also Students
Learning
    active and in-depth, 196
    adapting strategies to kinds of, 5–8
    consequences of rote mathematical,
        120–123
    engaging in authentic, 12

feedback facilitating, 56, 64, 68, 69,
    149, 197
focusing on student, 204–206
HPL (How People Learn) framework
    for, 199fig–200, 204
increasing need for, 1–2
learning environments to enhance,
    199fig–200
"meaningful," 2
metacognition to manage, 197
problem-based, 43–45
project-based, 15, 35–41, 176–177
redesigning schools to support,
    204–206
redundancy of opportunities for, 56
social and cultural nature of, 182–183,
    186, 191
Vygotsky's theory of, 76, 91, 197
See also Inquiry-based learning;
    Knowledge; Understandings
Learning activities
    "algebra tiles," 143–145
    "Blueprint for Success" design
        projects, 57–61
    Build SF, 50–51
    "collaborative seatwork," 21
    collaborative small group, 23–26
    ELS (Expeditionary Learning Schools)
        model for, 36–37, 40–41
    FIRST Robotics Comp;etition (FRC),
        46–47
    focusing on literacy, 92–93
    geo-literacy integrated, 98–99
    Journey North project, 184–185
    math immersion, 134–135
    mathematical even and odd number
        images, 114–118
    meeting needs of different
        performance levels, 126–127
    NatureMapping project, 180–181
    "Ordering a Cab," 138–141fig

Metacognition
    as learning principle, 4–5, 94–95,
        111, 191
    management of learning through, 197
    self-explanations technique of,
        188–190
    strategy instruction use of, 90–91, 94
    as teaching principle, 198–199
"Metacognitive" instruction, 4–5
Mindful engagement framework
    description of, 74–76, 77
    illustrating value of talk for, 85–87
    rich talk about text and, 83–85
    strategy instruction used with,
        94–97
Minority students. *See* Ethnicity/racial
    differences
Misconceptions
    origins of mathematics, 121–122
    about science, 165–170
    See also Understandings
Mountlake Terrace High School
    (Washington), 148–149
Mutual engagement, 27

N

NASA, 47
A Nation at Risk (1983), 1
National Academy of Sciences, 3
National Assessment of Educational
    Progress (NAEP), 120–121, 152, 177
National Council of Teachers of
    Mathematics (NCTM), 119, 120, 123,
    124, 142
National Reading Panel (NRP), 87–89
National Research Council (NRC), 122,
    123, 142, 157
National Science Foundation (NSF), 124
NatureMapping project, 180–181
New American Schools Development
    Corporation, 38

New Standards project (University of
    Pittsburgh), 125
New York Times, 194
Newstetter, 45
1989 *Curriculum and Evaluation
    Standards for School Mathematics,* 123
No Child Left Behind Act (2002), 36, 123

O

OECD (Organization for Economic
    Cooperation and Development),
    152, 153*fig*
"Ordering a Cab" task, 138–141*fig*

P

PAIR programming, 25–26
Pedagogy
    "authentic," 12, 64
    Book Club/Book Club Plus, 78–80, 85
    Collaborative Reasoning, 82–83
    collaborative small group learning,
        18–35, 197
    Directed Discourse Approach to
        Science Instruction, 183, 186
    Instructional Conversations, 81–82
    integrated instruction, 97–110
    Knowledge Integration Perspective,
        170–171, 173
    learning through design, 45–63
    problem-based, 43–45
    project-based, 15, 35–39
    Scaffolded Knowledge Integration
        (SKI), 171
    Shared Inquiry, 80–81
    strategy instruction, 87–97
    Think-Pair-Share techniques, 173
    See also Teaching
Performance assessment
    criteria used for, 66–67
    of current state of science
        understanding, 152–154

formative, 64, 67, 69–70, 196–197
high-stakes testing, 208–209
issues of mathematics instruction, 136–137, 139–141*fig*
meaningful learning and role of, 14
negative effects on teaching by high-stakes, 208–211
policy context of, 207–211
recommendations on conducting, 210–211
research on effectivenss of, 64–66
three elements of, 63–64
See also Assessment; Students
Performance levels
average PISA science literacy, 152, 153*fig*
meeting needs of different, 126–127
students meeting 4th grade math standards, 128*fig*
students scoring well below math standard, 129*fig*
Personal identity factors, 182–183, 191
"Phoenix Park" school (England), 130
"Pin up sessions," 56
PISA (Programme for International Student Assessment), 152, 153*fig*, 154
Pivotal cases, 175–176
Playground design project, 53, 56
Playhouse design project
description and principles used in, 57–60
LEARN guide for, 62–63
presentation of final designs, 60–62
Policy environment
assessment as part of, 207–211
No Child Left Behind Act (2002) impact on, 36, 123
schools shaped by external, 207–211
standards shaping, 123, 143–145, 207–208, 211
See also Schools
Positioning process, 32

Principles and Standards for School Mathematics (NCTM), 120, 123, 142
Prior knowledge
creating conceptual change and role of, 167–170
importance of assessing student's, 98–99
as learning principle, 3–4, 94
science understanding and role of, 157
as teaching principle, 197–198
See also Knowledge
Problem-based learning
educational applications of, 43–44
effectiveness of, 44–45
Professional communities, 147
Professional development
conflicting mandates/changes as barriers to, 150
mathematics instruction and, 146–147
new models of, 206
professional communities component of, 147
See also Teachers
Progressive movement, 15
Project-based learning
benefits of, 15
Challenge 2000 Multimedial Project as, 42
description of, 35
ELS (Expenditionary Learning Schools) Outward Bound model of, 36–37, 38, 40–41
science projects as, 176–177

R
Race. *See* Ethnicity/racial differences
Reader roles
code breaker, 72
meaning maker, 73
text critic, 73
text user, 73

characteristics of proficiency and, 158
current state of, 155–158
development of conceptual, 163–165
elements and meaning of, 155–158,
    161–163
promoting discourse and investigation
    for, 186–188
promoting students to share ideas
    about, 179
science classroom experiments for,
    159–165
social and cultural nature of,
    182–183, 186
teaching for, 170–179
Secondary School Redesign Initiative
    (SFUSD), 50
Self-assessment, 67–68
Self-explanations technique, 188–190
Shared Inquiry, 80–81
Small group inquiry
    collaborative, 18–35, 197
    research on effectivenss of, 13–18
Social identity, 182–183, 191
Southeast Center for Teaching
    Quality, 209
Standards
    benefits of raising student, 211
    importance of student accountability
        and, 143–145
    incorporating into instruction, 208
    mathematics, 123, 143–145
    See also Curriculum
*Standards (1989 Curriculum and
    Evalaution Standards for School
    Mathematics)*, 123, 124
"Sticky glue" project, 107, 108–110
Strategy instruction
    J.E.B. Stuart High School's focus on
        literacy using, 92–94
    metacognition, 90–91, 94
    mindful engagement and, 94–97

origins and description of, 87
reading instruction application of,
    87–90
Reciprocal Teaching, 89–90, 95–97
Transactional Strategies Instruction
    approaches of, 89–90
Student-centered learning environment,
    199*fig*
Students
    accountability of, 33, 143–145
    "anomalous data" response to,
        168–169
    "cognitive apprenticeship" between
        teachers and, 25
    comparing European and American,
        194–195
    disciplinary engagement by, 27
    focusing on learning bys, 204–206
    identity as learner and engagement by,
        68–69
    mutual engagement by, 27
    origins of mathematics
        misunderstandings by, 121–122
    raised expectations for, 193–195
    self-assessment by, 67–68
    self-explanations technique used by,
        188–190
    See also Ethnicity/racial differences;
        Learners; Performance assessment;
        Readers

T
Teachers
    coach role of, 84
    "cognitive apprenticeship" between
        students and, 25
    collaborative small group learning
        support by, 30–35, 197
    focusing on student learning,
        204–206
    investments in knowledge of, 211

NAME INDEX

Herman, J. L., 64, 208, 211
Herrenkohl, L. R., 24, 25
Hidi, S., 69
Hiebert, J., 122, 147
Hill, H., 206
Hill, H. C., 146, 147
Hmelo, C. E., 45, 49, 52
Hmelo-Silver, C. E., 43, 44
Hogarth, S., 22, 23
Holton, D. L., 49
Holyoak, K. J., 44, 175
Hoover, S. P., 54
Horan, 43
Horwitz, R. A., 15
Houang, R., 122
Hsi, S., 171, 175

I
Iganaki, 27

J
Jenkins, J., 6, 8
Jensen, M. S., 167
Jimenez-Aleixandre, M. P., 178
Johnson, D. W., 18, 19, 20, 21, 23
Johnson, R. T., 18, 19, 20, 21, 23
Jones, 209
Jones, D., 125
Jones, R., 1
Jukes, I., 2

K
Kachur, R., 77
Kafai, Y. B., 48
Kelley, C., 93
Kerbow, D., 80
Kilpatrick, J., 155
Kilpatrick, W. H., 15
Kim, I., 82
Kim, S., 82
King, A., 24, 27

Kirshner, B., 68
Klahr, D., 16
Klein, D.C.D., 64, 208
Klenowski, V., 68
Klentschy, M., 103
Knapp, M. S., 106
Kolodner, J. L., 44, 49, 55, 56
Kong, A., 77
Koontz, F., 184–185
Koretz, D., 208
Kortland, K., 178
Krajcik, J. S., 48, 54, 70, 156, 177
Krakcik, J., 161
Kulik, C. C., 18
Kulik, J. A., 15, 18
Kuo, L.-J., 82

L
La Mar, E., 98–99
Lamarck, 174, 175
Lamon, M., 30
Lampert, 206
Lampert, M., 121–122
Lane, S., 64, 208
Latour, 182
LaVancer, C., 188
Lavaroni, 43
Leavitt, T., 47
Lee, V. E., 200, 203, 206
Lehrer, R., 48, 161
Lemke, J. L., 182
Leon, M., 47
LePage, P., 5
Levin, 44
Levy, F., 11, 64, 208
Lewis, C., 147
Lieberman, A., 146, 200, 206
Linde, C., 29
Lindquist, M. M., 120, 121, 155
Linn, M. C., 170, 171, 173, 175, 179
Linn, R. L., 208

Lipson, M. Y., 67, 88, 91
Little, J. W., 206
Liu, M., 45
Lotan, R. A., 24, 25, 29, 66, 146
Louis, K. S., 206
Loxterman, J. A., 105
Lubben, F., 22, 23
Luke, A., 72, 73
Lundeberg, 44
Lyman, P., 2

M
Ma, L., 147
Madison, B. L., 122
Magnusson, S. J., 67, 100, 103
Mamlok-Naaman, R., 48
Markman, A. B., 44
Marks, H. M., 12, 64, 200
Markus, H., 69
Martin, T., 66
Maruyama, G., 18
Marx, R. W., 48, 54, 70, 156, 177
Mason, L., 175
Mastropieri, M. A., 18
Masukawa, H., 27
Matthews, W., 120, 121
McCain, T., 2
McCarthy, M., 41
McCloskey, M., 166
McDonald, J., 207
McDowell, C., 26
McIver, M., 208
McKeachie, W. J., 15
McKeown, M. G., 105
McKnight, C. C., 122, 210
McLaughlin, M. W., 206
McMahon, S. I., 77, 78, 79
McNurlen, B., 82
McPartland, J. M., 200
McTighe, J., 204
Means, B., 42

Meister, C., 88, 89, 90, 96
Melchior, A., 47
Mercier, E., 69
Meyer, 42
Miller, L., 205
Miller, T. R., 18
Mistretta, J., 100
Mitchell, S. A., 44
Miyake, N., 27
Moore, A., 39
Moore, P. J., 90
Morrow, L. M., 77
Murnane, R., 11, 64, 208
Murphy, P. K., 78

N
Nasir, N. S., 68, 69
Nelson, D., 18
Nemet, F., 178
Newman, S. E., 25
Newmann, F. M., 12, 64, 200, 203
Neyhart, S., 135
Nguyen-Jahiel, K., 82
Nigam, M., 16
Nurius, P., 69
Nutter, 42
Nystrand, M., 21, 22, 77

O
O'Connor, K., 69
O'Donnell, A. M., 19, 24
Oickle, E., 19
Ort, S., 64, 200
Ozgungor, S., 100, 101

P
Paley, 174, 175
Palincsar, A. S., 24, 67, 70, 89, 96, 97, 100, 102, 103
Pappas, C. C., 106
Paris, S. G., 67, 75, 88, 91

Schultz, S. E., 66
Schulze, J., 50
Schwab, J., 25
Schwartz, D. L., 27, 66
Schweingruber, H. A., 155
Scott, C., 169
·Scruggs, T. E., 18
Seethaler, S., 171, 173
Segers, M., 45
Seidel, 204
Sentz, J., 42
Settlage, J., 167
Shepard, L. A., 68
Shepherd, 39
Sherin, B. L., 168
Sherwood, R., 39
Shirouzu, H., 27
Shouse, A. W., 155
Shulman, L., 25
Shumaker, J., 88
Silver, E. A., 120, 121
Silvernail, D. L., 205
Simpkins, M. B., 42
Sinatra, G. M., 105
Sinatra, R., 105
Singer, S., 93
Skon, L., 18
Slavin, R. E., 19, 24
Slotta, J. D., 173
Smith, 209
Smith, C., 161
Smith, J. B., 200, 203, 206
Smith, J. P., 168
Smith, V. D., 45
Snider, B., 21
Soar, R. S., 15
Soloway, E., 70, 156, 177
Soter, A. O., 78
Stage, E. K., 88, 151, 152, 155
Stahl, S. A., 105
Stecher, B. M., 64, 208
Stein, B. S., 8

Stepien, W. J., 39, 45
Stewart, J., 174
Stigler, J., 122, 147
Stodolsky, S. S., 121
Strike, K. A., 168
Stylianides, A., 118
Svendsen, N., 93
Swafford, J., 132

T
Tal, T., 169
Taylor, B. M., 74, 77, 106
Thagard, P., 44
Thomas, J. W., 15, 38
Tilson, J. L., 71
Tretten, 42
Troper, J. D., 27
Truong, T., 93
Tsai, J., 47
Tsuchida, I., 147
Turner, J. C., 42, 91

U
Udall, D., 38
Underhill, R., 125

V
Valdes, 25
Van den Bossche, P., 45
Van Maren, R. J., 36, 37
Van Meter, P., 89
Varelas, M., 106
Varian, H., 2
Vernon, D. T., 44
Vitale, M. R., 103, 104
Vygotsky, L. S., 76, 91, 197

W
Wakai, S. T., 64, 208
Wasik, B. A., 91
Watanabe, 205
Webb, N. M., 27

Credits

The Tetrahedral Model is from *Human Cognition: Learning, Understanding, and Remembering* by John D. Bransford. Copyright © 1979 Wadsworth Publishing Company, a part of Cengage Learning, Inc. Reproduced by permission. www.cengage.com/permissions.

Excerpts from Engle & Conant, 2002 are from "Guiding principles for fostering productive disciplinary engagement: Explaining an emergent argument in a community of learners classroom," R.A. Engle and F.R. Conant in *Cognition and Instruction*, 20 (4), 2002: 399–483. Permission conveyed via the Copyright Clearance Center.

The PBL Project Planner is produced by Juel Chouinard and Linda Poulin. Used with permission from LEARN, www.learnquebec.ca.

The Cognition and Technology Group Description. CTGV, 1997. Reprinted with permission.

The Damico and Riddle vignette is from "From answers to questions: a beginning teacher learns to teach for social justice," by J. Damico and R.L. Riddle. September, 2004. *Language Arts*, 82 (1), 36–46. Reprinted by permission of the National Council of Teachers of English.

The excerpt from Palinscar and Brown, 1984 is from "Reciprocal teaching of comprehension-fostering and comprehension-monitoring activities," A.S. Palincsar and A.L. Brown in *Cognition and Instruction*, 1 (2), 1984: 117–175. Permission conveyed via the Copyright Clearance Center.

The excerpt from Palinscar and Brown, 1986 is "Interactive teaching to promote independent learning from text," A.S. Palinscar, and A.L. Brown in Reading Teacher, 39, 1986: 771–777. Permission conveyed via the Copyright Clearance Center.

The Ordering a Cab exercise is from *Balanced Assessment for the Mathematics Curriculum, High School Assessment Package 2*, 2000. Reprinted with permission.

The WISE Berkeley reflection prompt is reprinted with permission of the National Science Foundation and the University of California, Berkeley.

The HPL Framework is from *How People Learn: Brain, Mind, Experience, and School*, edited by John D. Bransford et al. Copyright © 2000 National Academies Press. Reprinted with permission.

Excerpts from Berry, 1995 are reprinted by permission of the Publisher. From Ann Lieberman, *Work of restructuring schools: Building from the Ground up*. New York: Teachers College Press. Copyright © 1995 by Teachers College, Columbia University. All rights reserved.

Photos of student learning that appear throughout the book are courtesy of *Edutopia*.

The photo on page 53 is courtesy of the Architectural Foundation of San Francisco's Build San Francisco Institute.